TRIBALS AND INDIAN CONSTITUTION

M.K. SINGH

SUMIT ENTERPRISES
Delhi 110 002 (INDIA)

First Published 2010

ISBN 978-81-8420-212-0

Published by:

SUMIT ENTERPRISES
4649B/21, Ansari Road, Darya Ganj
New Delhi-110 002
Phone: 011-23279353, 9810217567
E-mail: sumit_enterprises2007@yahoo.co.in

PRINTED IN INDIA

Published by Sri Lokesh Gupta for Sumit Enterprises, New Delhi-110 002, Typeset by Abhijeet Typesetters, Printed at Sachin Printers.

TRIBALS AND INDIAN CONSTITUTION

Preface

The tribals constitute a share of about eight per cent of the country's population and spread over about 1/5 part of the country's land with more than 500 different tribal groups having special cultural traits and identity. The term development has been used in wider sense, it is a slow process of civilization. The purpose of development is to provide increasing opportunities to all the people for better life.

India harbours multiple ethnic groups who have distinct sociocultural identities. It is one of the nation-states in the world, which has provided elaborate preferential arrangements for the tribals. The tribal communities in India are at different levels of socioeconomic development. In view of the deep-rooted historic reasons, which have caused the backwardness of these communities, the Indian Union as well as states are committed to ensure the implementation of the constitutional provisions for their development.

The non-governmental or the voluntary organisations have been playing a crucial role in all the socioeconomic spheres, including that of the tribal peoples, in India. At one level, they can be termed as the 'means' by which the nation makes optimum use of its human resources. However, the mushrooming of voluntary organisations working in the field of rural development in recent years has generated widespread debate about their role, structure, programmes and performance. A unique feature of voluntary organisations is that they stimulate voluntary action among the target community and involve the progressive elements of that community.

The book primarily deals with the tribal social structure and the changes occurring there in. India has a large concentration of tribal population. Though scattered all over the country their concentration is mainly in the northern and central region

—*Author*

Contents

1

Constitution and Bylaws of Indian Tribe and Indian Reservation

CONSTITUTION OF THE NISQUALLY INDIAN TRIBE

PREAMBLE

We, the members of the Nisqually Reservation in order to establish a community organization and secure certain privileges and powers offered to us by the Indian Reorganization Act, do ordain and establish this Constitution and Bylaws for the Nisqually Indian Tribe.

ARTICLE I – TERRITORY

The jurisdiction of the Nisqually Indian Tribe shall extend to the territory within the confines of the Nisqually Reservation as established by the Treaty of Medicine Creek, December 26, 1854 (10 Stat.1132) and by Executive Order of January 20, 1857, to tracts placed in trust or restricted status for individual Indians or for the Tribe located in the Nisqually River basin, and such other lands as may hereafter be added thereto under any law of the United States, except as otherwise provided by law.

ARTICLE II-MEMBERSHIP

Section 1 The membership of the Nisqually Indian Tribe shall consist of:

(a) All persons of Indian blood whose names appear on the official census roll of the Nisqually Reservation as of July 1, 1945, provided that such roll may be corrected by the Nisqually "General Council with the approval of the Secretary of Interior.

(b) All children who are 1/4 degree of Indian blood or more and are born to any member.

Section 2 The governing body shall have the power to promulgate ordinances subject to review by the Secretary of the Interior, governing future membership and the adoption of new members when the resources of the Tribe make such adoptions feasible.

ARTICLE III-THE GOVERNING BODY

Section 1 The governing body of the Nisqually Indian Tribe shall be the Nisqually General Council, which shall be composed of all qualified voters of the Nisqually Indians. Twenty-five percent of the eligible voters shall constitute a quorum.

Section 2 The General Council shall elect from its own members by secret ballot (a) a Chairman, (b) a Vice Chairman, (c) a Secretary, (d) a Treasurer, (e) a Fifth Council Member, (f) a Sixth Council Member, (g) a Seventh Council Member, and (h) such other officers and committees as may be deemed necessary. Such election shall be conducted in accordance with the provisions of Article IV of this Constitution.

Section 3 The General Council shall meet on the second Saturday in March and August.

Section 4 Within sixty days after the ratification and approval of this Constitution and Bylaws, the Community Council shall be called for the purpose of electing the officers named herein, and it may transact such other business as may be necessary.

The officers elected at this meeting shall serve until the January meeting 1947 at which time their successors shall be chosen. Thereafter, officials shall be chosen every two years at the January meeting, except as otherwise provided by amendments to this Constitution.

Section 5 The Chairman, or 10 percent of the qualified voters, may by written notice, call special meetings of the General Council.

Section 6 The Nisqually Tribal Council shall consist of the Chairman, Vice Chairman, Secretary,

Treasurer, and the Fifth, Sixth and Seventh Council Members of the General Council, and shall perform such duties as may be authorized by that General Council and this Constitution.

ARTICLE IV-ELECTIONS FOR THE NISQUALLY TRIBAL COUNCIL

Section 1 Candidates for the offices of Chairman, Vice Chairman, Secretary, Treasurer, and Fifth Council Member must have reached the age of 21 years on or before the election date. Candidates for the offices of Sixth and Seventh Council Members must have reached the age of 18 years on or before the election date.

Candidates eligible for membership on the Tribal Council shall be voted on at the same time on the single ballot at polls open for voting for at least an eight (8) hour period. All elections shall be held in accordance with this Constitution and Bylaws and with rules adopted by the Tribal Council as provided herein. All elections shall be by secret ballot.

Section 2 Absentee ballots may be allowed for any issue or election before the Tribe in accordance with an election ordinance enacted by the Tribal Council.

Section 3 Incumbent members of the Tribal Council under the 1946 Constitution and Bylaws shall continue to serve in their capacities as members of the Council until replaced by the Tribal Council successors in accordance with the provisions herein.

Section 4 The Tribal Council shall, following adoption of this Constitution and Bylaws and approval by the Secretary of the Interior, hold a meeting in January 1995 for the purpose of electing all the officers named herein.

The Chairman, Secretary and Fifth Member elected at the January 1995 meeting shall serve until the first Saturday in May 1997, at which time their successors shall be chosen. Thereafter, the elections for these officers shall be held every three

(3) years. The Vice Chairman, Treasurer and the Sixth and Seventh Members elected at the January 1995 meeting shall serve until the first Saturday in May 1998, at which time their successors shall be chosen. Thereafter, the elections for these officers shall be held every three (3) years.

Section 5 The election of Tribal Council members, under Section 4 above, shall be conducted in accordance with an election ordinance enacted by the Tribal Council.

ARTICLE V-VACANCIES AND REMOVAL FROM OFFICE

Section 1 If an officer of the General Council shall die, permanently leave the Community, or shall be found guilty of a felony or misdemeanor involving dishonesty in any Indian, State, or Federal Court, the General Council shall declare the position vacant and shall appoint a new member to serve until the next regular election when a successor shall be elected.

Section 2 Upon receipt of a petition signed by one-third (1/3) of the eligible voters demanding the recall of any officer of the General Council, it shall be the duty of the General Council to call an election on such recall petition. No member may be recalled in any such election unless at least 30 percent of the qualified voters shall vote in the election.

Section 3 The General Council may by affirmative vote of two-thirds (2/3) of its members expel any officer for neglect of duty or gross misconduct provided that the accused officer shall be given full and fair opportunity to reply to any and all charges at a designated General Council meeting. It is further stipulated that any such officer shall be given a written statement of the charges against him at least ten (10) days before the meeting at which he is to appear.

ARTICLE VI-POWERS OF THE TRIBAL COUNCIL

Section 1 Enumerated Powers. The Tribal Council of the Nisqually Indian Tribe shall exercise the following powers, subject to General Council oversight and any limitations imposed by the Statutes or the Constitution of the United States:

(a) To negotiate with the federal, State and local governments;

(b) To employ legal counsel, the choice of counsel and fixing of fees to be subject to the approval of the Secretary of the Interior.

(c) To veto any sale, disposition, lease or encumbrance of tribal lands, interests in lands or other tribal assets;

(d) To advise the Secretary of the Interior with regard to all appropriation estimates or Federal projects for the benefit of the Tribe prior to submission of such estimates to the Bureau of the Budget and to Congress;

(e) To manage all economic affairs and enterprises of the Nisqually Indian Tribe in accordance with the terms of a charter that may be issued to the Tribe by the Secretary of the Interior.

(f) To promulgate and enforce all ordinances as a full exercise of its police powers which shall be subject to review by the Secretary of the Interior governing the conduct of members of the Nisqually Indian Tribe; providing for the manner of making, holding, and revoking assignments of tribal land or interests therein; providing for the levying of taxes and the appropriation of available funds of the Tribe for public purposes; providing for the regulation of the use of real property within the jurisdiction of the Tribe; providing for the licensing of non-members coming upon the reservation for purposes of hunting, fishing, trading, or other business, and for the exclusion from the territory of the Tribe of persons not so licensed and establishing proper agencies for the enforcement of such ordinances upon the reservation;

(g) To provide for the appointment of guardians for minors and mental incompetents by ordinance or resolution, subject to review by the Secretary of Interior;

(h) To charter subordinate organizations for economic purposes, and to delegate to such organizations, or to any subordinate boards or officials of the Tribe, any of the foregoing powers, reserving the right to review any action taken by virtue of such delegated power;

(i) To adopt resolutions not inconsistent with this Constitution and attached Bylaws regulating the procedure of the General Council and of other Tribal organizations of the Nisqually Indian Tribe.

Section 2 Future Powers. The Tribal Council may exercise such further powers as may in the future be delegated to it by the Secretary of the Interior, or any other duly authorized official or agency of the State or Federal Government.

Section 3 Reserved Powers. Any rights and powers heretofore vested in the Nisqually Indians but not expressly referred to in this Constitution, shall not be abridged by this Article, but may be exercised by the members of the Nisqually Indian Tribe through the adoption of appropriate bylaws and constitutional amendments.

Section 4 Manner of Review. Any resolution or ordinance, which by the terms of this Constitution shall be subject to review by the Secretary of the Interior, shall be presented to the

Superintendent in charge of the reservation, who shall, within ten days after its enactment, approve or disapprove the same. If the Superintendent shall approve any ordinance or resolution, it shall thereupon become effective, but the Superintendent shall transmit a copy of the same, bearing his endorsement, to the Secretary of the Interior, who may, within ninety days from the date of enactment, rescind the said ordinance or resolution for any cause, by notifying the Tribal Council of such decision. If the Superintendent shall refuse to approve any ordinance or resolution submitted to him within ten days after its enactment, he shall advise the Tribal Council of his reason therefore. If these reasons appear to the Council insufficient, it may, by majority vote, refer the ordinance or resolution to the Secretary of the Interior, who may, within ninety days from the date of its enactment, approve the same in writing, whereupon the said ordinance or resolution shall become effective.

ARTICLE VII-BILL OF RIGHTS

Section I Suffrage. All enrolled members of the Nisqually Indian Tribe who are of the age eighteen (18) years or older as of the date of a tribal election shall be a voting member of the General Council.

Section 2 Economic Rights. All members of the Tribe shall be accorded equal opportunities to participate in the economic resources and activities of the Tribe.

Section 3 Civil Liberties. All members of the Tribe shall enjoy without hindrance, freedom of worship, conscience, speech, press, assembly, and association.

ARTICLE VIII-AMENDMENTS

Section I This Constitution and Bylaws may be amended by a majority vote of the qualified voters of the General Council, voting at an election called for that purpose by the Secretary of the Interior: Provided, That at least 30 percent of those entitled to vote shall vote in such election, but no amendment shall become effective until it shall have been approved by the Secretary of the Interior.

Section 2 At any regular or special General Council meeting, amendments to this Constitution and Bylaws may be proposed to be acted upon at the next semi-annual General Council meeting. If approved by a majority vote at such meeting, the proposed amendment shall be submitted to the Secretary of the Interior, who shall thereupon call an election upon the proposed amendment.

BYLAWS OF THE NISQUALLY INDIAN TRIBE

ARTICLE I

It shall be the duty of the Chairman to preside over all meetings of the Nisqually General Council and carry out all orders of the Council. All members of the Nisqually Tribal Council and all subordinate officers shall assist the Chairman in all proper ways to carry out the orders of the Council.

ARTICLE II

The Tribal Secretary shall keep a full report of all proceedings of each regular and special meeting of the General Council and of the Tribal Council, and shall perform such other duties of like nature as the General Council shall from time to time by resolution provide, and shall transmit copies of the minutes of each meeting to the Superintendent in charge of the reservation and to the Commissioner of Indian Affairs.

ARTICLE III

The Tribal Treasurer shall be the custodian of all moneys which may come under the jurisdiction or into the control of the Nisqually Indian Tribe. He/she shall pay out money in accordance with the orders and resolution of the General Council. He/she shall keep account of all receipts and disbursements, and shall report the same to the General Council at each regular meeting. He/she shall be bonded in such an amount as the General Council may by resolution,-approved by the Commissioner of Indian Affairs, provide.

The books of the Tribal Treasurer shall be subject to audit or inspection at the direction of the General Council or the Commissioner of Indian Affairs. Until the treasurer is bonded, the Tribal Council may make such provision for the custody and disbursement of funds as shall guarantee their safe and proper disbursement and use.

ARTICLE IV

The subordinate officers of the General Council shall perform such duties as the General Council may from time to time provide by resolution.

ARTICLE V

It shall be the duty of the General Council and each member thereof to promote the general welfare of members of the Community, and to carry out the provisions and purposes of this Constitution and Bylaws.

ARTICLE VI

Each officer elected or appointed hereunder shall take an oath of office prior to assuming the duties thereof, by which oath he shall pledge himself to support and defend the Constitution of the United States and this Constitution and Bylaws:

Oath: "I,, do solemnly swear that I will support and defend the Constitution of the United States against all enemies; that I will carry out faithfully and impartially the duties of my office to the best of my ability; that I will cooperate, promote, and protect the best interests of my people, in accordance with this Constitution and Bylaws. "

ARTICLE VII

The order of business at any regular or special meeting of the General Council shall be as follows:

1. Call to order by the chairman
2. Roll call
3. Reading of minutes of previous meeting
4. Reports of committees
5. Report of the treasurer
6. Reading of the communications
7. Unfinished business
8. New business
9. Adjournment

ARTICLE VIII

The Tribal Council shall have the power to appoint delegates and/or sub-committees to represent the Nisqually Indian Tribe.

ARTICLE IX

Ratification of Constitution and Bylaws. This Constitution and Bylaws, when adopted by a majority vote of the voters of the Nisqually Indians voting at a special election called by the Secretary of the Interior in which at least 30 percent of those entitled to vote shall vote, shall be submitted to the Secretary of the Interior for his approval, and shall be in force from the date of such approval.

CERTIFICATION OF ADOPTION

Pursuant to an order approved May 29, 1946 by the Assistant Secretary of the Interior, the attached Constitution and Bylaws was submitted for ratification to the members of the Nisqually Indian Tribe of the Nisqually Reservation, Washington, and was on July 27, 1946, duly adopted by a vote of 17 for, and 0 against, in an election in which over 30 percent of those entitled to vote cast their ballots in accordance with section 16 of the Indian Reorganization act of June 28, 1934 (48 Stat. 984), as amended by the act of June 15, 1935 (49 Stat. 378).

CONSTITUTION AND LAWS OF THE HOOPA VALLEY TRIBE

PREAMBLE

We, the members of the Hoopa Valley Tribe in California, in order to exercise our tribal rights and promote our common welfare do hereby ordain and establish this Constitution and Bylaws.

ARTICLE I – PURPOSE

The purpose of this Constitution and Bylaws shall be to protect and promote the interests of the Hoopa Valley Indians, to develop cooperative relations with the agencies of the Federal Government and to cooperate with State and local governments. Upon its effective date this revised Constitution and Bylaws shall supersede the Tribe's initial governing document, approved September 4, 1952. All existing ordinances, resolutions or any other enactment or policies of the Tribe, which are not in conflict with the provisions of this revised constitution and bylaws shall remain in effect.

ARTICLE II – NAME

The Tribal organization shall be called "The Hoopa Valley Tribe."

ARTICLE III – TERRITORY

The jurisdiction of the Hoopa Valley Tribe shall extend to all lands within the confines of the Hoopa Valley Indian Reservation boundaries as established by Executive Order of June 23, 1876, and to such other lands as may hereafter be acquired by or for the Hoopa Valley Indians.

ARTICLE IV – MEMBERSHIP

Section 1. The membership of the Hoopa Valley Tribe shall consist as follows:

(a) All persons of Hoopa Indian blood whose names appear on the official roll of the Hoopa Valley Tribe as of October 1, 1949; provided that corrections may be made in the said roll by the Tribal Council within five years from the adoption and approval of this Constitution, subject to the approval of the Secretary of Interior or his authorized representative.

(b) All children, born to members of the Hoopa Valley Tribe, who are at least one-quarter (1/4) Indian blood, after the effective date of this statement. Degree or quantum of blood to be determined by adding one-half (1/2) the degree of Indian blood of each parent as shown on the approved Roll Schedules of the Hoopa Valley Tribe.

Section 2. The Tribal Council shall have the power to make rules governing the adoption of new members or the termination of membership in the Tribe.

Section 3. ENROLLMENT ORDINANCE. The Tribal Council shall draft an ordinance setting forth the procedures governing tribal membership in accordance with this article. This ordinance shall be submitted to a referendum within one year from the effective date of this revised constitution and bylaws and shall be in effect only when ratified by the tribal referendum and approved by the Commissioner of Indian Affairs. Changes to such ordinance shall require a further vote by the Tribe's general membership and approval by the Commissioner.

ARTICLE V – GOVERNING BODY

Section 1. Name. The governing body of the Hoopa Valley Tribe shall be a council known as the Hoopa Valley Tribal Council.

Section 2. COMPOSITION. The Council shall consist of a chairman, and seven (7) other members. A vice-chairman shall be elected by the Council from within its own membership. A secretary, treasurer, and such other employees, committees as are deemed necessary shall be either appointed or employed by the Council from the outside the membership of the Council.

Section 3. DISTRICTS. The Tribal Council and (7) other Council members shall be elected at large as hereinafter specified in Article VI. The Chairman shall represent the membership as a whole and one Councilman shall be elected to represent each of the following districts:

1. Hostler – Matilton
2. Soctish – Chenone
3. Agency
4. Norton
5. Campbell
6. Bald Hill
7. Mesket

ARTICLE VI – NOMINATIONS AND ELECTIONS

Section 1. Starting with the June 1972 election the Chairman shall be elected for a term of 2 years. The other Tribal Council members shall be elected for terms of two years which shall be staggered. At the June 1973 election four Council members shall be elected to fill the positions on the present Council which are presently due to expire in June 1973. Three Councilmembers shall be elected in 1974 to fill the Council positions on the Council which expire in June 1974. All Councilmembers including those presently serving shall remain in office until their successors are duly elected and installed in office.

Section 2. ELECTION DAY: An election shall be held on the third Tuesday of June of each year. In the event a holiday falls on that date, or for some other reason it is not advisable to hold the election at the specified time, the election board shall designate an alternate time to conduct the election no later than the last day of June.

Section 3. ELECTION BOARD: The membership shall elect an election board composed of 5 members which shall enact an ordinance as set forth in Section 4. The terms shall expire as follows: one in one year, two in two years, to in three years and their successor shall serve three year terms. The candidates in each instance receiving the second highest vote total serve as alternates for the corresponding terms of election board members.

The election board shall be responsible for screening candidates calling and conducting elections, settling any election disputes, certifying election results and installing successful candidates. The election board chairman shall administer oaths of office. The board shall establish its own rules of procedure. Members of the board shall receive fair payment to be set by the Council for the performance of their duties. The board may levy and collect filing fees from candidates to help defray costs of elections. It may also require that a fee accompany protests of elections for Tribal Council members to help defray any costs of recounts or such actions as the protest may require. Such fee may be refunded if the aggrieved party's protest is sustained. Members of the board shall be subject to the recall provisions of Article VII, Section 3.

Section 4. ELECTION ORDINANCE: The election board shall enact an ordinance governing elections and setting forth the procedures to be followed in conducting each of the various types of elections. Such ordinance shall include provisions for secret ballots, absentee voting, registration of voters, screening of candidates, and settling election disputes. A separate section of the ordinance shall spell out the procedure and format to be used whenever it is necessary to submit petitions for any purpose to the Tribal Council or any office or board of the Tribe. Whenever practical such ordinance shall include provisions of the State or local election regulations. The ordinance shall also include provisions for run-off elections in case of tie votes.

Section 5. NOMINATION PROCEDURES: Candidates shall file for a specific position by submitting to the election board a nominating petition signed by not less than five (5) registered voters. A voter may sign only one petition. Petitions for nomination shall be filed with the clerk of the election board at least forty-five (45) days prior to the election in which the candidate intends to compete.

It shall be the duty of the election board to screen all candidates and post in public places on the reservation the names of all candidates who have met the above qualifications and the position for which they have filed. Such lists shall be posted at least forty (40) days prior to the election. Copies of the sample ballot shall be mailed to all registered voters.

Section 6. QUALIFICATIONS OF CANDIDATES: Any member of the Tribe may announce his or her candidacy for a specific position of the Tribal Council provided the following qualifications are met:

(a) Must be at least twenty-one (21) years of age by the date of the election in which he desires to compete.

(b) Must have physically resided within the area shown by a circle drawn on a map representing a one hundred (100) mile radius from the tribal office building. The election board shall rule on whether any prospective candidate meets residence and any other qualifications specified in this article.

(c) Must not have been convicted of a felony or misdemeanor involving moral turpitude such as, but not limited to, fraud, embezzlement, theft. Provided, that person who have completed their sentence for such conviction at least ten (10) years prior to the date of the election in which the intend to run for office, may file as candidates.

(d) Must be bondable.

(e) Each prospective candidate must disclose to the election board any personal, financial and business interests that may create a conflict if that person is elected. Once elected each Council member shall report to the Tribal Council and election board any situation that may create a conflict while in office.

Section 7. QUALIFICATIONS OF VOTER: Any member of the Tribe who will be at least eighteen (18) years of age on election day shall be eligible to vote, provided he has duly registered.

Section 8. ABSENTEE BALLOTS: Absentee ballots shall be provided upon request to all non-resident registered voters and other registered voters who advise the election board that they will be away from the reservation on election day.

Section 9. OATH OF OFFICE: Each successful candidate elected to the Tribal Council shall take an oath of office prior to assuming the duties of such position, by which oath he shall pledge himself to support and defend the Tribe's constitution and bylaws. The following form of oath of office shall be administered by the chairman of the election board:

I ____________, do solemnly swear (or affirm) that I will carry out faithfully and impartially the duties of my office to the best of my ability, that I will promote and protect the best interest of my Tribe, in accordance with its constitution and bylaws.

Section 10. INSTALLATION: Successful candidate shall be installed in office within ten (10) days after the general election following certification of election results. Installation of any candidate for a particular position may be postponed, however, until such time as there is a determination of any dispute or election for that position.

ARTICLE VII – VACANCIES, REMOVAL, RECALL AND REFERENDUM

Section 1. If any member of the Tribal Council or other elected official shall die, resign, be removed from office or shall be found guilty while in office of a felony or misdemeanor involving moral turpitude in any Indian, State or Federal court, or if he shall miss three (3) consecutive regularly scheduled meetings of the Council without being excused by that body, the Council shall declare that position vacant. If more that six (6) months remains in the term of the position the election board shall conduct a special election of the voting membership for the purpose of filling the vacancy. If less than six (6) months remains in the unexpired term, the Council shall appoint a representative to serve the remainder of the unexpired term.

Section 2. REMOVAL: The Tribal Council may by five (5) affirmative votes, expel any member for neglect of duty or gross misconduct. Before any vote for expulsion is taken on the matter, such member or official shall be provided a written statement of the charges against him at least five (5) days before the meeting of the Tribal Council before which he is to appear, and an opportunity to answer any and all charges at such designated Council meeting. The decision of the Tribal Council shall be final.

Section 3. RECALL: Upon receipt of a petition signed by one-third (1/3) of the number of voters, who were registered to vote in the last election, calling for the recall of any member of the Council or election board, it shall be the duty of the election board to call and conduct within forty-five (45) days an election on such recall. Recall shall be effective only if a majority of the Tribe's registered voters shall vote in favour of such recall. Once a member has faced a recall attempt, no further recall action may be brought against him until at least one (1) year has passed. No member of the Council shall be subject to recall action within the first six (6) months of his term.

Section 4. REFERENDUM: Upon receipt of a petition signed by one-third (1/3) of the voters who participated in the last election or upon receipt of a resolution of the Council, the election board shall call and conduct within forty-five (45) days an election on any enacted or proposed enactment of the Council, or any proposal initiated by the voters. Should that measure fail, it cannot be reconsidered until at least one (1) year has passed. Should it pass, the Council is bound by that decision. Any ordinance submitted to referendum for ratification can only be amended by like action.

ARTICLE VIII – RIGHTS OF MEMBERS

Section 1. The Hoopa Valley Tribe, in exercising its powers of self-government, shall not:

(a) Make or enforce any law prohibiting the free exercise of religion, or abridging the freedom of speech, or of the press, or the right of the people peaceably to assemble and to petition for a redress of grievances;

(b) Violate the right of the people to be secure in their persons, houses, papers and effects against unreasonable search and seizures, nor issue warrants, but upon probable cause supported by oath or affirmation, and particularly describing the place to be searched and the person or thing to be seized;

(c) Subject any person for the same offense to be twice put in jeopardy;

(d) Compel any person in any criminal case to be a witness against himself;

(e) Take any private property for public use without just compensation.

(f) Deny to any person in a criminal proceeding the right to a speedy and public trial, to be informed of the nature and cause of the accusation, to be confronted with the witnesses against him, to have compulsory process for obtaining witnesses in his favour, and at his own expense to have the assistance of counsel for his defense;

(g) Require excessive bail, impose excessive fines, inflict cruel and unusual punishments, and in no event impose for conviction of any one offense any penalty or punishment greater than imprisonment for a term of one (1) year or a fine of five thousand dollars ($5,000) or both unless greater penalty or punishment is permitted by federal law;

(h) Deny to any person within it jurisdiction the equal protection of its laws or deprive any person of liberty or property without due process of law;

(i) Pass any bill of attainder or ex post facto law; or

(j) Deny to any person accused of an offense punishable by imprisonment the right, upon request, to a trial by jury of not less than six (6) persons.

ARTICLE IX – POWERS AND DUTIES OF TRIBAL COUNCIL

Section 1. The Tribal Council shall have the following powers subject to any limitations imposed by the federal statutes or by the Constitution of the United States.

(a) To administer all tribal property. Toward this end a land assignment ordinance shall be submitted for ratification to a referendum vote within one year of the effective date of this revised constitution and bylaws.

(b) To borrow money from the Indian credit fund or from any other federal or state agency, and to pledge or assign future tribal income as security for such loans.

(c) To collect and expend any Hoopa Valley Tribal funds within the exclusive control of the Tribe and to recommend the expenditure of any other Tribal funds.

(d) To purchase in the name of the Hoopa Valley Tribe any land or other property the Council may deem beneficial to said Hoopa Valley Indians.

(e) To enforce the protection of Tribal property, wildlife and natural resources of the Hoopa Valley Tribe in accordance with a conservation ordinance which shall be enacted within one year from the effective date of this revised constitution.

(f)

(1) To provide assessments or license fees upon non-members doing business or obtaining special privileges within the reservation, subject to the approval of the Commissioner of Indian Affairs or his authorized representative.

(2) To promulgate and enforce assessments or license fees upon member exercising special privileges or profiting from the general resources of the reservation.

(g) To negotiate with the federal, state and local governments on behalf of the Tribe.

(h) To employ legal counsel, the choice of counsel and fixing of fees to be subject to the approval of the Commissioner of Indian Affairs.

(i) To prevent the sale, disposition, lease or encumbrance of Tribal lands, interests in lands or other Tribal assets.

(j) To exclude from the restricted land of the Hoopa Valley Indian persons not legally entitled to reside therein, under ordinances which shall be subject to the approval of the Commissioner of Indian Affairs or his authorized representative.

(k) To promulgate and enforce ordinances governing the conduct of members and nonmembers of the Hoopa Valley Indian Tribe.

(l) To safeguard and promote the peace, safety, morals and general welfare of the Hoopa Valley Indians by regulating the conduct of trade and the use and disposition of property upon the reservation, provided that any ordinance directly affecting nonmembers of the Hoopa Valley Tribe shall be subject to the approval of the Commissioner of Indian Affairs or his authorized representative.

(m) To confer with Commissioner of Indian Affairs and heads of other Federal agencies, regarding all appropriation estimates and budgets for the benefit of the Tribe prior to their submission to the Office of Management and Budget and Congress.

(n) To establish a tribal court through the necessary ordinances and resolutions.

(o) To establish a Housing Authority.

(p) To create subordinate bodies for the operation of economic enterprises to benefit the Tribe.

(q) To negotiate and conclude contracts for economic purposes except where Tribal assets are involved outside of the approved annual budget, in excess of $100,000, during any budget and year.

Contracts in excess of such amount shall be submitted to the Tribal membership for approval by referendum vote.

Section 2. Any rights and powers heretofore vested in the Hoopa Valley Tribe but not express referred to in this constitution shall not be abridged, but may be exercised by the members of the Hoopa Valley Tribe through the adoption of appropriate amendments to this Constitution and Bylaws.

ARTICLE X – AMENDMENTS

Amendments to this Constitution and Bylaws may be proposed by either the following documents being submitted to the Tribal Election Board along with the desire modification:

(a) A resolution in which at least six (6) of the Tribal Council members have voted in favour of the proposal.

(b) A petition signed by at least twenty percent (20%) of the Tribe's registered voters.

Upon receipt of the resolution provided for in (a) above or a valid petition referred to in (b) above, the Election Board shall call and conduct a special amendment in accordance with this Article and provisions set forth the Tribal Election Ordinance.

The specific language which will become part of the Constitution and Bylaws, if such amendment is adopted and approved, shall appear on the ballot including language changes of any other parts of the governing document that will be affected by such modification.

If at such election the proposed amendment is adopted by a majority of those voting in the election and if at least thirty percent (30%) of the registered voters shall vote, that amendment shall be submitted to the Commissioner of Indian Affairs and if approved by him, shall thereupon take effect.

BYLAWS OF THE HOOPA VALLEY TRIBE

ARTICLE XI – TRIBAL COUNCIL

Section 1. CHAIRMAN: The Chairman shall preside over all meeting of the Tribal Council and of the Tribe's general membership. He shall perform all duties of the Chairman and exercise any authority delegated to him by the Tribal Council. The specific duties and responsibilities of the Chairman and other members of the Tribal Council shall be spelled out in appropriate ordinance of the Tribal Council. The Chairman shall vote only in case of a tie.

Section 2. VICE-CHAIRMAN: The Vice-Chairman shall assist the Chairman when called upon to do so. In the absence of the Chairman, he shall preside, and when so presiding shall have all the rights, privileges and duties, as well as the responsibilities of the Chairman.

Section 3. SECRETARY: The Secretary shall conduct all correspondence and keep a complete and accurate record of all matters transacted at Council and Committee meetings. It shall be his duty to submit promptly to the Superintendent of the Hoopa Agency, copies of all minutes of regular and special meetings of the Tribal Council and Tribe's general membership. Other duties shall be spelled out in a job description.

Section 4. TREASURER: The Treasurer shall be the custodian of all monies which may come into the control of the Tribal Council. He shall pay out money in accordance with ordinances and resolutions of the Tribal Council. He shall keep an account of all receipts and disbursements, and shall report same to the Tribal Council monthly. He shall be bonded in such an amount as the Tribal Council may by resolution provide, approved by the Commissioner of Indian Affairs. The books of the Council Treasurer shall be subject to audit or inspection at the direction of the Tribal Council or the Commissioner of Indian Affairs.

The Hoopa Agency of the Bureau of Indian Affairs shall be responsible for the custody and disbursement of Tribal funds in the event the Treasurer does not possess an adequate bond. The Treasurer shall perform other duties as assigned in accordance with the ordinance mentioned in Section 1 of this Article.

Section 5. APPOINTIVE OFFICERS: The duties of all committees and officers appointed by the Tribal Council shall be clearly defined by resolution of the Tribal Council at the time of their creation or appointment. Such committees or officers shall report from time to time, as required, to the Tribal Council, and their activities and decision shall be subject to review by the Tribal Council upon the petition of any person aggrieved.

ARTICLE XII – TIME AND PLACE OF MEETINGS AND PROCEDURE

Section 1. Regular meetings of the Tribal Council shall be held on the first and third Thursday of each month in a hall designated by the Tribal Council. Special meetings may be called by written notice signed by the Chairman and shall be called by him upon receipt of a petition signed by at least five (5) Council members, and when so called, the Tribal Council shall have power to transact business as in regular meetings.

General Council meetings shall be called in like manner upon ten (10) days notice.

Section 2. QUORUM: No business shall be transacted unless a quorum is present. A quorum shall consist of any five (5) of the eight (8) Council members.

Section 3. ORDER OF BUSINESS: The following order of business is established for all meetings but may be changed if deemed necessary:

(a) Call to Order by Chairman

(b) Roll call

(c) Ascertainment of a quorum

(d) Reading of minutes of the last meeting

(e) Adoption of minutes by a vote or common consent

(f) Unfinished business

(g) New business

(h) Non-agenda items

(i) Adjournment

Section 4. TRIBAL LEGISLATION: Any enactment of the Tribal Council which is of a temporary nature or for a specific one-time use shall take the form of a RESOLUTION. Enactments of a permanent nature which are to be effective over an extended period of time shall be embodied in ORDINANCES.

Section 5. REPORT OF MEETINGS: It shall be the duty of each member of the Tribal Council to make reports concerning the proceedings of the Tribal Council to the members of his district.

Section 6. SALARIES: The Tribal Council may prescribe by resolution such salaries for officers, committees, Tribal employees, or members of the Council as it deems advisable from such funds as may be available. Provided any changes in the rates of per diem for attending Council or committee meetings shall not be effective until one (1) year from the date of such action.

ARTICLE XIII – RATIFICATION OF CONSTITUTION AND BYLAWS

This Constitution and Bylaws shall become effective upon approval by the Commissioner of Indian Affairs following its adoption by a majority of those who vote in an election called for that purpose. Provided at least thirty percent (30%) of those Hoopa Valley Tribal members entitled to vote shall cast ballots in such election. Upon the effective date of this Constitution and Bylaws, the original constitution and Bylaws adopted on May 13,1950, and approved by the Commissioner of Indian Affairs on September 4, 1952, and any amendments since is hereby expressly revoked.

CONSTITUTION AND BYLAWS OF THE MAKAH INDIAN TRIBE OF THE MAKAH INDIAN RESERVATION

PREAMBLE

We, the members of the Makah Indian Tribe, in order to establish a more perfect tribal organization, promote the general welfare, conserve and develop our land, timber, and other resources, and secure to ourselves and our posterity the power to exercise certain rights of home rule, not inconsistent with the Federal, State, and local laws, do ordain and establish this constitution for the Makah Indian Tribe of the Makah Indian Reservation, of the. State of Washington.

ARTICLE I.-TERRITORY

The jurisdiction of the Makah Indian Tribe shall extend to the territory within the confines of the Makah Indian Reservation boundaries as established in the treaty of January 31, 1855, and by Executive orders made pursuant thereto, and to such other lands as may be hereafter added thereto.

ARTICLE II.-MEMBERSHIP

Section 1. The membership of the Makah Indian Tribe shall consist as follows:

a. All persons of Indian blood whose names appear on the official census roll of the tribe as of April 1, 1935.
b. All children born to any member of the Makah Indian Tribe who is a resident of the reservation at the time of the birth of said child.
c. Persons of Makah Indian blood who may hereafter be adopted as tribal members by order of the tribe.

Section. 2. The tribal council shall have the power to promulgate ordinances, subject to review by the Secretary of the Interior, governing future membership and the adoption of new members. Property rights shall not be changed by any action under this section.

ARTICLE III.-GOVERNING BODY

Section 1. The governing body of the Makah Indian Tribe shall consist of a council known as the Makah Indian tribal council.

Section. 2. This council shall consist of five members, duly elected to serve 3 years, except as provided in section 4, two members being elected each year except that every third year, one shall be elected.

Section 3. The council so organized shall elect from within its own number (1) a chairman; (2) a vice chairman; and from within or without (3) a secretary; and (4) a treasurer; and may appoint or employ such other officers or committees as may be deemed necessary.

Section 4. The present tribal council within 60 days after the ratification and approval of this constitution, shall call a general tribal meeting for the election of officers in accordance with this constitution. The two candidates receiving the highest number of votes shall hold office until December 1938. The two candidates receiving the next highest number of votes shall hold office until December 1937, and the next highest until December 1936.

Thereafter, the term of office for councilmen elected under this constitution shall be 3 years. After the first election elections for the tribal council shall be held on the last Monday in December.

ARTICLE IV.-ELECTIONS FOR THE TRIBAL COUNCIL

Section 1. Any member of the tribe 21 years or over who has maintained a legal residence on the reservation for 1 year immediately preceding any election shall be entitled to vote or be elected to office therein.

Section 2. Any legal voter shall be eligible to serve as a member of the council.

Section 3. All elections shall be by secret ballot and shall be held in accordance with rules and regulations prescribed by the tribal council, or by any election board appointed by the tribal council.

ARTICLE V.-VACANCIES AND REMOVAL FROM OFFICE

Section 1. If a council member shall die, resign, or permanently leave the reservation, or be removed from office for cause, the council shall declare the position vacant and appoint a successor to serve until the annual general tribal meeting in December, at which time the general tribal meeting shall elect a successor for the unexpired term.

Section 2. The tribal council may, by a four fifths vote of its total membership, expel any member for neglect of duty or gross misconduct, provided such charges are in writing, subscribed by competent witnesses and formally served upon the accused at least 5 days prior to the hearing. The accused member shall be given a full and fair opportunity to reply to any and all such charges against himself and also the opportunity to summon witnesses in his behalf.

Section 3. Upon a petition of at least one third of the eligible voters of the Makah Indian Tribe it shall be the duty of the tribal council to call a special election to consider the recall of the member or members of the council named in such petition. In the event that a majority of those voting in such election favour such recall from office, the office shall be declared vacant and the tribal council shall proceed in the usual manner to hold an election to fill the said vacancy.

ARTICLE VI.-POWERS OF THE TRIBAL COUNCIL

Section 1. The tribal council shall exercise the following powers, subject to any limitations imposed by the Federal statutes, the Constitution of the United States, and subject further to all express restrictions upon such powers provided in this constitution and bylaws.

a. To negotiate with the Federal, State, and local Governments on behalf of the tribe, and to advise and consult with the representatives of the Interior Department on all activities of the Department that may affect the tribe and its members.

b. To employ legal council for the protection and advancement of the rights of the tribe and its members, the choice of such counsel and the fixing of fees to be subject to the approval of the Secretary of the Interior.

c. To approve or veto any sale, disposition, lease, or encumbrance of tribal lands, interests in lands, or other tribal assets which may be authorized or executed by the Secretary of the Interior, the Commissioner of Indian Affairs, or any other official or agency of Government, provided that no tribal lands shall ever be sold or encumbered except for governmental purposes, or leased for a period exceeding 5 years, except that leases for mining purposes may be made for such longer periods as may be authorized by law.

d. To advise with the Secretary of the Interior or his representatives on all appropriation estimates, or Federal projects for the benefit of the tribe prior to their submission to the Bureau of the Budget and to Congress.

e. To manage all economic affairs and enterprises of the tribe, in accordance with the terms of a charter that may be issued to the tribe by the Secretary of the Interior.

f. To levy and collect taxes upon members of the tribe, or to require the performance of community labor in lieu thereof, provided that no taxes may be levied, nor community labor required, except when approved at the annual December general tribal meeting or at a special general tribal meeting called for that purpose.

g. To levy and collect taxes or license fees upon nonmembers doing business on the reservation, to exclude from the territory of the tribe persons not legally entitled to reside thereon, or trespassers upon the reservation, under ordinances, all of which shall be subject to review by the Secretary of the Interior.

h. To enact resolutions or ordinances not inconsistent with article II of this constitution, governing adoption and abandonment of membership, and to keep at all times a correct roll of the members of the Makah Indian Tribe.

i. To promulgate and enforce ordinances, which shall be subject to review by the Secretary of the Interior, governing the conduct of members of the Makah Indian Tribe, and providing for the maintenance of law and order, and the administration of justice by establishing a reservation Indian court and defining its duties, powers, and limitations.

j. To safeguard and promote the peace, safety, morals and general welfare of the Makah Indian Tribe by regulating the conduct of trade and the use and disposition of property upon the reservation: *Provided,* That any ordinances directly affecting nonmembers of the tribe shall be subject to review by the Secretary of the Interior.

k. To charter subordinate organizations for economic purposes, and to regulate the activities of cooperative associations of members of the Makah Indian Tribe by ordinance: *Provided,* That any such ordinance shall be subject to review by the Secretary of the Interior.

l. To appropriate for public purposes of the tribe any available tribal funds, provided that any such appropriation made prior to July 1, 1940, shall be subject to review by the the Secretary of the Interior.

m. To provide for the appointment of guardians for minors and mental incompetents by ordinance or resolution subject to review by the Secretary of the Interior.

n. To adopt resolutions regulating the procedure of the council itself and other tribal agencies and tribal officials of the reservation.

o. To delegate to subordinate boards, or to cooperative associations which are open to all members of the tribe, any of the foregoing powers, reserving the right to review any action taken by such body to whom such power has been delegated.

Section 2. *Manner of review.*—Any resolution or ordinance which by the terms of this constitution is subject to review by the Secretary of the Interior, shall be presented to the superintendent of the reservation who shall, within 10 days thereafter, approve or disapprove the same. If the superintendent shall approve said ordinance or resolution it shall thereupon become effective, but the superintendent shall transmit a copy of the same, bearing his endorsement, to the Secretary of the Interior, who may within 90 days from the date of enactment rescind the said ordinance or resolution for any cause by notifying the tribal council of such decision.

If the superintendent shall refuse to approve any resolution or ordinance submitted to him within 10 days after its enactment, he shall advise the Makah tribal council of his reasons therefor. If these reasons appear to the council insufficient, it may by a majority vote refer the ordinance or resolution to the Secretary of the Interior, who may, within 90 days from the date of its enactment, approve the same in writing, whereupon the said ordinance or resolution shall become effective.

Section 3. *Further powers.*—The Makah Indian tribal council may exercise such further powers as may in the future be delegated to it by the Secretary of the Interior, or by any other duly authorized official or agency of government.

Section 4. *Reserved powers.*—Any rights or powers heretofore vested in the Makah Indian Tribe but not expressly referred to in this constitution shall not be abridged by this article, but may be exercised by the people of the Makah Indian Tribe through the adoption of appropriate bylaws and constitutional amendments.

ARTICLE VII.-BILL OF RIGHTS

Section 1. *Suffrage.*—All members of the tribe over the age of 21 shall have the right to vote in all tribal elections. The residence qualifications established by article IV of this constitution shall apply to all elections except elections for the amendment of this constitution and bylaws.

Section 2. *Economic right.*—All members of the tribe shall be accorded equal opportunities to participate in the economic resources and activities of the reservation.

Section 3. *Civil liberties.*—All members of the tribe may enjoy, without hindrance, freedom of worship, conscience, speech, press, assembly, and association.

Section 4. *Rights of accused.*—Any member of the Makah Indian Tribe accused of any offense shall have the right to a prompt, open, and public hearing, with due notice of the offense charged, and shall be permitted to summon witnesses on his own behalf. Trial by jury may be demanded by any prisoner accused of any offense punishable by more than 30 days imprisonment or by more than $45 fine.

Excessive bail shall not be required and cruel punishment shall not be imposed.

ARTICLE VIII.-LAND

Section 1. *Allotted lands.*—Allotted lands, including heirship lands, within the Makah Reservation shall continue to be held as heretofore by their present owners. It is recognized that under existing law such lands may be condemned for public purposes, such as roads, public buildings, or other public improvements, upon payment of adequate compensation, by any agency of the State of Washington or of the Federal Government, or by the tribe itself. It is further recognized that under existing law such lands may be inherited by the heirs of the present owner, whether or not they are members of the Makah Indian Tribe.

Likewise it is recognized that under existing law the Secretary of the Interior may, in his discretion, remove restrictions upon such land, upon application by the Indian owner, whereupon the land will become subject to State taxes and may then be mortgaged or sold. The right of the individual Indian to hold or to part with his land, as under existing law, shall not be abrogated by anything contained in the constitution, but the owner of restricted land may, with the approval of the Secretary of the Interior, voluntarily convey his land to the Makah Indian Tribe either in exchange for a money payment or in exchange for an assignment covering the same land, or other land, as hereinafter provided.

Section 2. *Tribal lands.*—The unallotted lands of the Makah Reservation, and all lands which may hereafter be acquired by the Makah Indian Tribe or by the United States in trust for the Makah Indian Tribe shall be held as tribal lands, and no part of such land shall be mortgaged or sold. Tribal lands shall not be allotted to individual Indians but may be assigned to members of the Makah Indian Tribe, or leased, or otherwise used by the tribe, as hereinafter provided.

Section. 3. *Leasing of tribal lands.*—Tribal lands may be leased by the tribal council, with the approval of the Secretary of the Interior, for such periods of time as are permitted by law.

In the leasing of tribal lands preference shall be given, first, to Indian cooperative associations of members of the tribe; and secondly, to individual Indians who are members of the Makah Indian Tribe.

Section. 4. *Grant of standard assignments.*—In any assignment of tribal lands which now are owned by the tribe or which hereafter may be acquired for the tribe by the United States or purchased by the tribe out of tribal funds, reference shall be given, first, to heads of families which are entirely landless; and secondly, to heads of families which shall have no allotted lands or interests in allotted lands, but shall have already received assignments consisting of less than an economic unit of agricultural land or other laud or interest in land of equal value.

No allotted member of the Makah Indian Tribe who may hereafter have the restrictions upon his land removed and whose land may thereafter be alienated except to the tribe shall be entitled to receive an assignment of land as a landless Indian.

The tribal council may, if it sees fit, charge a fee of not to exceed $5 on approval of an assignment made under this section.

Assignments made under this section shall be for the primary purpose of establishing homes for landless Indians, and shall be known as standard assignments.

Section 5. *Tenure of standard assignments.*—If any member of the tribe holding a standard assignment of land shall, for a period of years fail to use the land so assigned or use such laid of any unlawful purpose, his assignment may be cancelled by the tribal council after due notice and an opportunity to be heard, and the said land may be reassigned in accordance with the provisions of section 4 of this article.

Upon the death of any Indian holding a standard assignment, his heirs or other individuals designated by him, by will or by written request, shall have a preference in the reassignment of the land, provided such persons are members of the Makah Indian Tribe who would be eligible to receive a standard assignment.

Section 6. *Grant of exchange assignments.*—Any member of the tribe who owns an allotment or any share of heirship land may voluntarily transfer his interests in such land to the tribe in exchange for an assignment to the same land or other land of equal value. If the assignee prefers, he may receive, in lieu of a specific tract of land, a proportionate share in a larger grazing unit.

Assignments made under this section shall be known as "exchange assignments."

Section 7. *Leasing of exchange assignments.*—Exchange assignments may be used by the assignee or leased by him to Indian cooperative associations of members of the tribe to individual members of the tribe, or, if no individual Indian or Indian cooperative association of members is able and willing to rent the land at a reasonable fee, such assignments may be leased to nonmembers in the same manner as allotted lands.

Section 8. *Inheritance of exchange assignments.*—Upon the death of the holder of any exchange assignment, such land shall be reassigned by the tribal council to his heirs or devisees, subject to the following conditions:

a. Such lands may not be reassigned to any heir or devisee who is not a member of the Makah Indian Tribe, except that a life assignment may be made to the surviving widower or widow of the holder of an assignment.
b. Such lands may not be reassigned to any heir or devisee who already holds more than an economic unit of land to be determined from time to time by the tribal council.
c. Such lands may not be subdivided among heirs or devisees into units too small for convenient management. No area of uncleared or timber land shall be subdivided into units smaller than 40 acres, and no area of tillable agricultural

land shall be subdivided into units smaller than 2½ acres, except that land used for buildings or other improvements may be divided to suit the convenience of the parties. Where it is impossible to divide the land properly among the eligible heirs or devisees, the tribal council may issue to the eligible heirs or devisees interests in tribal lands of the same value as the assignment of the decedent.

d. If there are no eligible heirs or devisees of the decedent, the land shall be eligible for reassignment in accordance with the provisions of section 4 of this article.

Section 9. *Inheritance of improvements.*— Improvements of any character made upon assigned land may be bequeathed to and inherited by members of the Makah Indian Tribe or otherwise disposed of under such regulations as the tribal council shall provide: *Provided further,* That sales of improvements on the land of any decedent can be made only to members of the Makah Indian Tribe.

Section 10. *Exchange of assignments.*—Assignments may be exchanged between members of the Makah Indian Tribe by common consent in such manner as the tribal council shall designate

Section 11. *Use of unassigned tribal land.*— Tribal land which is not assigned, including tribal timber reserve, shall be managed by the tribal council for the benefit of the members of the entire tribe, and any cash income derived from such land accrue to the benefit of the tribe as a whole. All action of the tribal council with respect to such lands shall be in conformity with departmental regulations for the protection of Indian range and timber resources authorized by section 6 of the act of June 18, 1934.

Section 12. *Purchase of land by tribe.*—Tribal funds may be used, with the consent of the Secretary of the Interior, to acquire land, under the following conditions:

(a) Land within the Makah Reservation or adjacent to the boundaries thereof which is not now in Indian ownership may be purchased by or for the Makah Indian Tribe.

(b) Restricted land, which is in heirship status at the time of the adoption and approval of this constitution, may be purchased by or for the tribe, with the consent of all the adult heirs, and the legal guardians of minor heirs, payment therefor to be made as may be agreed upon.

(c) Land owned by any member of the tribe who is over the age of 60 years, or who is physically incapacitated, may be transferred by its owner to the tribe in exchange for a pension of not more than twice the annual rental value of the land for the life of the pensioner, to be paid out of available tribal funds.

(d) Land owned by any member of the tribe in excess of his needs for domestic purposes may be purchased by the tribe with the consent of the owner, payments to be made on such terms as may be agreed upon by the council and the owner.

(e) Land owned by any members of the tribe who desire to leave the reservation permanently may be purchased by the tribe under such terms as may be agreed upon.

Section 13. *Method of making assignments.*—Applications for assignment shall be filed with the secretary of the council and shall be in writing, setting forth the name of the person or persons applying for the land and as accurate a description of the land desired as the circumstances will permit.

Notices of all applications received by the secretary shall be posted by him in the agency office and in at least three other conspicuous places on the reservation for not less than 20 days before action is taken by the council. Any member of the tribe wishing to oppose the granting of an assignment shall do so in writing, setting forth his objections, to be filed with the secretary of the council, and may if he so desires, appear before the council to present evidence.

The secretary of the council shall furnish the superintendent or other officers in charge of the agency a complete record of all action taken by the council on applications for assignment of land, and a complete record of assignments shall be kept in the agency office and shall be open for inspection by members of the tribe.

The council shall draw up one or more forms for standard and exchange assignments, which shall be subject to the approval of the Secretary of the Interior.

ARTICLE IX.-REFERENDUM

Upon a petition of least one-third of the qualified voters of the Makah Indian Tribe, a referendum may be demanded on any enacted or proposed ordinance or resolution of the tribal council, and the vote of the majority of the qualified voters in such referendum shall be conclusive and binding on the tribal council.

ARTICLE X.-AMENDMENTS

This constitution and bylaws may be amended by a majority vote of the qualified voters of the tribe voting at an election called for that purpose by the Secretary of the Interior, provided that at least 30 percent of those entitled to vote shall vote in such election; but no amendment shall become effective until it shall have been approved by the Secretary of the Interior.

It shall be the duty of the Secretary of the Interior to call an election on any proposed amendment upon receipt of a petition signed by one-third of the qualified voters, members of the tribe.

BYLAWS OF THE MAKAH INDIAN TRIBE

ARTICLE I.-DUTIES OF OFFICERS

Section 1. *Chairman of the council.*—The chairman of the council shall preside over all meetings of the council; shall perform all duties of the chairman, and exercise any authority delegated to him by the council. The chairman shall also preside at all regular and special meetings of a general tribal nature. He shall vote only in case of a tie.

Section 2. *Vice chairman of the council.*—The vice chairman shall assist the chairman when called upon so to do. In the absence of the chairman he shall preside; when so presiding he shall have all the rights, privileges, duties, and responsibilities, of the chairman.

Section 3. *Secretary of the council.*—The secretary of the tribal council shall conduct all tribal correspondence and shall keep an accurate record of all business transacted at council meetings. It shall be his duty to keep minutes of regular and special tribal meetings and to submit copies of such minutes to the superintendent of the jurisdiction and also to the Commissioner of Indian Affairs.

Section 4. *Treasurer of the council.*—The treasurer of the tribal council shall account for, receive, receipt for, preserve, and safeguard all funds in the custody of the council whether same be tribal or other funds for which the council is acting as trustee or custodian. Deposits of such funds shall be made in a bank or elsewhere, as designated by the council, and he shall make and preserve a financial record of all such funds and shall report on all receipts and expenditures, and the amount and nature of all funds in his possession or custody such report being made in writing to the council at regular meeting and at such other times as requested by the council. He shall not pay out or otherwise disburse any funds in his possession or custody, or in the possession or custody of the tribal council, until properly authorized so to do by resolution duly passed by the council.

The books and records of the treasurer shall be audited at least once each year by a competent auditor employed by the council and at such other times as the council or the Commissioner of Indian Affairs may direct. The treasurer shall be required to furnish a bond satisfactory to the council and to the Commissioner of Indian Affairs, and the council is hereby authorized to pay the premium on such bond from any available funds. The treasurer shall be present at all special or regular meeting of the council.

Section 5. *Duties of appointive officers and boards.* The duties of all appointive boards or officers of the council shall be clearly defined by resolution of the council at the time of their creation or appointment. Such boards and officers shall report from time to time, as required to the council, and their activities and decisions shall be subject to review by the council upon the complaint of any person aggrieved.

ARTICLE II.-CERTIFICATION OF ELECTION

It shall be the duty of the tribal council, or a board appointed by them, to certify to the election of the newly elected tribal council members within 5 days after the election and thereupon they shall be notified by the secretary of their election.

ARTICLE IV.-COMPENSATION

The tribal council may prescribe such compensation of officers or members of the council as it deems advisable from such funds as may be available, subject to approval of the general tribal meeting.

ARTICLE V.-TIME AND PLACE OF MEETINGS

Section 1. *Meetings.*—Regular meetings of the tribal council shall be held at the agency at Neah Bay on the first Monday of January, April, July, and October, and at such other times as the tribal council may by resolution provide.

Special meetings may be called by a written notice signed by the majority of the tribal council, and, when so called, the tribal council shall have power to transact business as in regular meetings.

Section 2. *Quorum.*—No business shall be transacted unless a quorum is present. A quorum shall consist of four council members.

Section 3. *Order of business.*—The following order of business is established for all meetings:

1. Call to order by chairman.
2. Roll call.
3. Reading the minutes of last meeting.
4. Unfinished business.
5. Reports.
6. New business.
7. Adjournment.

ARTICLE VI.-GENERAL TRIBAL MEETINGS

Section 1. There shall be an annual general tribal meeting open to all members of the tribe held at the agency on the last Monday in December. At this annual meeting, elections shall be held as designated heretofore in this constitution. The bylaws, orders, and resolutions, which are subject to approval at the general tribal meeting, shall be taken up for consideration at this time.

It shall also be the duty of the chairman to make a report at said meeting of the activities of the council throughout the year and to outline proposed plans for economic and social betterment of tribe.

Section 2. Special general tribal meetings may be called by the chairman of the general council: *Provided,* That due notice is posted throughout the reservation at least 15 days prior to such meeting.

Fifty legal voters of the tribe may at any time, by written petition, call a general tribal meeting, provided that at least 15 days' notice is posted throughout the reservation.

ARTICLE VII.-ADOPTION OF CONSTITUTION AND BYLAWS

This constitution and bylaws, when ratified by a majority vote of the qualified voters of the Makah Indian Tribe of the Makah Reservation voting at an election called for the purpose by the Secretary of the Interior, provided that at least 30 percent of those entitled to vote shall vote in such election, shall be submitted to the Secretary of the Interior, and, if approved, shall be effective from the date of approval.

CONSTITUTION OF THE ZUNI TRIBE

PREAMBLE

We, the members of the Zuni Tribe, Zuni Indian Reservation, New Mexico, in order to secure to us and to our posterity the political and civil rights guaranteed to us by treaties and by the Constitution and statutes of the United States; to secure educational advantages; to encourage good citizenship; to exercise the right of self-government; to administer both as a municipal body and as a proprietor of our tribal affairs; to utilize; increase and protect our tribal resources; to encourage and promote all movements and efforts leading to the general welfare of our tribe; to guarantee individual rights and freedom of religion; and to maintain our tribal customs and traditions; do ordain and establish this constitution.

ARTICLE I-JURISDICTION

The jurisdiction of the Zuni Tribe, Zuni Indian Reservation exercised through the Zuni Tribal Council, the Executive Department and the Judicial Department, acting in accordance with this constitution and the ordinances adopted in accordance herewith, shall extend to all tribal lands included within the present boundaries of the Zuni Indian Reservation and to such other lands as may hereafter be added thereto, unless otherwise provided by law. This jurisdiction shall apply to and be for the benefit and protection of all indians who now, or may in the future, reside on the Zuni Reservation. The name of this organization shall be the Zuni Tribe.

ARTICLE II-MEMBERSHIP

Section 1. The membership of the Zuni Tribe, Zuni Indian Reservation, shall consist of the following:

a. All persons enrolled on the Zuni Agency census roll of April 1, 1963; provided that the roll may be corrected at any time by the tribal council, subject to the approval to of the Secretary of the Interior.

b. All descendants of such persons, provided such descendants shall have not less than one-quarter (1/4) Zuni Indian blood.

c. The membership roll of the Zuni Tribe shall be kept current by striking thereform the names of persons who have relinquished in writing their membership in the tribe; and of deceased persons upon receipt of a death certificate or other evidence of death acceptable to the Zuni Tribal Council, and by adding thereto the names of persons who meet the membership requirements and who comply with the procedure for enrollment as members of the tribe. The membership roll will be maintained by the tribal secretary.

Section 2. The Zuni Tribal Council shall determine eligibility for membership in the Zuni Tribe. No decree of any outside court determining paternity or degree of Zuni Indian blood shall be binding on the tribe for membership purposes.

Section 3. The Zuni Tribal Council shall have the authority to enact ordinances, consistent with this constitution, governing future membership, and to establish enrollment procedures, which ordinances shall be subject to approval by the Secretary of the Interior. No person shall be adopted as a member unless he shall have at least one-quarter (1/4) degree Indian blood.

Section 4. Honorary tribal membership may be bestowed by the Governor of the Zuni Tribe. This honorary membership will entitle the individual to the title of "honorary tribal member" only.

Section 5. No person may be at the same time enrolled as a member of the Zuni Tribe and as a member of any other Indian tribe.

ARTICLE III-BILL OF RIGHTS

Section 1. Subject to the limitations prescribed by this constitution, all members of the Zuni Tribe shall have equal political rights and equal opportunities to share in tribal assests, and no member shall be denied freedom of conscience, speech, religion, association or assembly, nor shall he be denied the right to bear arms.

Section 2. The Zuni Tribe, in exercising its powers of self-government, shall not:

a. Make or enforce any law prohibiting the free exercise of religion, or abridging the freedom of speech, or of the press, or the right of the people peaceably to assemble and to petition for a redress of grievances;
b. Violate the right of the people to be secure in their persons, houses, papers, and effects against unreasonable search and seizures, nor issue warrants, but upon probable cause, supported by oath or affirmation, and particularly described the place to be searched and the person or thing to be resized;
c. Subject any person for the same offense to be twice put in jeopardy;
d. Compel any person in any criminal case to be witness against himself;
e. Take any private property for a public use without just compensation;
f. Deny to any person in a criminal proceeding the right to a speedy and public trial, to be informed of the nature and cause of the accusation, to be confronted with the witnesses against him, to have compulsory process for obtaining witnesses in his favour, and, at his own expense, to have the assistance of counsel for his defense;
g. Require excessive bail, impose excessive fines, inflict cruel and unusual punishments, and in no event impose for conviction of any one offence any penalty or punishment greater than imprisonment for a term of six months or a fine of $500, or both;
h. Deny to any person withing its jurisdiction the equal protection of its laws or deprive any person of liberty or property without due process of law;

i. Pass any bill or attainder or ex post facto law; or

j. Deny to any person accused of an offence punishable by imprisonment the right, upon request, to a trial by jury of not less than six persons.

ARTICLE IV-ORGANIZATION OF THE GOVERNMENT OF THE ZUNI TRIBE

Section 1. The government of the Zuni Tribe shall consist of a Legislative, and Executive, and a Judicial department.

ARTICLE V-THE LEGISLATIVE DEPARTMENT: COMPOSITION AND QUALIFICATION

Section 1. The legislative authority of the Zuni Tribe shall rest in the Zuni Tribal Council, hereinafter sometimes called the tribal council, which shall hold its sessions at Zuni, New Mexicso.

Section 2. The tribal council shall consist of eight (8) members, including a governor and lieutenant governor, all elected at large by popular vote as hereinafter provided.

Section 3. No person shall serve as a member of the Zuni Tribal Council while holding any other elective office, or policy making or judicial position with the tribe.

Section 4. Members of the Zuni Tribal Council shall be no less than twenty-five years of age at the time of their election and shall have lived within the reservation for not less than one(1) year immediately preceding the date of the election. Any person who has been convicted of a felony shall be ineligible for membership on the Zuni Tribal Council for a period of not less than three (3) years following release from confinement.

ARTICLE VI-AUTHORITIES OF THE TRIBAL COUNCIL

Section 1. The Zuni Tribal Council, as the Legislative body of the tribe, shall exercise the following authorities subject to any limitations imposed by statues of the United States applicable to Indians or Indian tribes, and subject to all expressed restrictions contained in this constitution.

a. To regulate its own procedures; to appoint subordinate boards, committees, officials and employees not otherwise provided for in this constitution and to prescribe for in this constitution and to prescribe their salaries, tenure and duties, provided that the tribal council shall, by appropriate ordinance, establish the personnel policies and procedures of the tribe, including a requirement that a statement of qualifications and standards be developed and published for all personnel employed by the tribe;

b. To establish tribal corporations, associations and other subordinate organizations for economic and other purposes, and to transfer assets of the tribe thereto for management and control;

c. To borrow money for tribal purposes;

d. To represent the tribe, and to act in all matters that concern the welfare of the tribe;

e. To negotiate with the Federal, State or local governments, and with the governments of other Indian tribes, and to advise and consult with representatives of the Interior Department on all activities that may affect the tribe, and in regard to all appropriation estimates and Federal projects for the benefit of the tribe before such estimates or projects are submitted t the Bureau of the budget and to Congress;

f. To prevent the sale, disposition, lease or encumbrance of tribal land, interests in land, water, minerals or other tribal assets; to approve and provide for the execution of any sale, grant, lease, or relinquishment of any interests in land, water, minerals or other assets of the tribe or the use thereof, subject to the approval of the Secretary of the Interior where required by law;

g. To regulate the use of tribal property; to protect the wildlife and natural resources of the tribe; to foster Indian arts and crafts; to administer charity; to levy and collect taxes and fees on tribal members; and to impose taxes or fees on non-members of the tribe doing business on the Zuni Reservation, provided that the impostition of such taxes and fees on non-members of the tribe shall be in conformity with appropriate ordinances subject to approval by the the Secretary of the Interior. All actions of the tribal council relating to the use and protection of tribal lands shall be in conformity with applicable regulations of the Department of the Interior designed for the protection of Indian range and timber resources;

h. To appropriate and administer any funds or property withing the exclusive control of the tribe and to make expenditures from available funds for public purposes of the tribe, including salaries and remuneration of officers and other employees; limited only by provisions of this constitution;

i. To provide by ordinance, subject to approval by the Secretary of the Interior, for the removal or exclusion from the reservation of non-members, whose presence may be injurious or undesirable to the tribe or the members thereof;

j. To employ legal counsel for the protection and advancement of the rights of the tribe and its members, the choice of counsel and fixing of fees to be subject to the approval of the Secretary of the Interior, so long as such approval is required by Federal law;

k. To enact ordinaces, subject to approval by the Secretary of the Interior, for the maintenance of peace and order on the Zuni Reservation; for the protection of individual rights and property of tribal member; to govern the inheritance of personal property of tribal members; and to provide for the appointment of guardians for minors and mental incompetents;

l. To provide for the enforcement of tribal ordinances;

m. To provide by ordinance for the conduct of tribal elections and the orderly management of tribal affairs;

Section 2. The tribal council shall approve an annual budget to finance the programs and governmental functions of the tribe. No expenditures of tribal funds will be made except in comformity with the approved tribal budget.

ARTICLE VII-MEETINGS OF THE ZUNI TRIBAL COUNCIL: QUORUM

Section 1. At the first meeting of the Zuni Tribal Council after each regular election, the tribal council shall see that the members have a correct and clear understanding of the constitution, and procedures regulating the conduct of the governing body of the tribe.

Section 2. The tribal council shall meet at least once each month.

Section 3. Special meetings may be called by the Governor of the Zuni Tribe, or at the request of not less than four (4) members of the tribal council.

Section 4. A legal quorum of the Zuni Tribal Council for the conduct of official business shall be four (4) or more councilmen and the presiding officer. The presiding officer shall be entitled to vote as a member of the tribal council.

Section 5. No enactment of the tribal council shall have any validity or effect in the absence of a quorum of the membership thereof at a legally called session.

Section 6. Only regularly called meetings, or meetings announced by written notice to each council member and posted on the official tribal bulletin board, shall constitute legally called sessions.

ARTICLE VIII-CONFLICTS OF INTEREST

Section 1. Any councilman who may be personally interested in any matter before the Zuni Tribal Council shall not vote on such matter without the consent on the remaining members. Failure to reveal a personal interest, not similary shared by all members of the council, to the Zuni Tribal Council, in a matter before the council, shall constitute dereliction of official duty, and may be cause for removal from office.

ARTICLE IX-TRIBAL ENACTMENTS

Section 1. All final decisions of the Zuni Tribal Council on matters of general and permanent interest to members of the Zuni Tribe and to the tribal administration shall be embodied in resolutions or ordinances. Such enactments shall be available for inspection by members of the Zuni Tribe at normal office hours.

Section 2. All final decisions of the Zuni Tribal Council on matters of temporary interest or relating to particular individuals, officials, or committees shall be noted in the minutes of the council deliberations and shall be available for inspection by members of the Zuni Tribe during normal office hours.

Section 3. All resolutions and ordiances shall be dated and numbered, and shall include a certification showing the presence of a quorum and the number of tribal council members voting for and against any proposed enactment.

Section 4. Every resolution or ordinance passed by the tribal council shall, within five(5) days of its passage, be presented to the governor for approval.

If he approves, he shall sign it within ten(10) days following its reciept and deposit it with the secretary of the Zuni Tribe for such further action as may be necessary.

If he does not sign an enactment of the tribal council within ten(10) days following its reciept by him, he shall, at the next legally constituted meeting of the tribal council following its submittal to him for signiture, return it to the tribal council with a statement of his objections. It shall thereafter not become effective unless it is again approved by at least five(5) council members voting in favour of the issue.

Section 5. Any enactment of the tribal council which is subject to approval by the Secretary of the Interior shall be presented to the Superintendent of the Zuni Agency who shall, within ten(10) days following receipt thereof, transmit the same to the Secretary of the Interior with his recommendation for or against approval.

ARTICLE X-THE SECRETARY OF THE COUNCIL

Section 1. The secretary of the tribal council shall be appointed by the governor from within or without the membership of the tribal council, with the concurrence of a majority of the members of the tribal council.

Section 2. The secretary shall call the roll, handle all official correspondence of the council, keep the minutes of all regular and special meetings of the tribal council, and it shall be his duty to submit promptly to the tribal governor and the Superintendent of the Zuni Agency copies of minutes of all regular and special meetings of the tribal council.

ARTICLE XI-THE EXECUTIVE DEPARTMENT

Section 1. The governor, lieutenant governor and the treasurer shall comprise the executive department of the tribal government, exercising the authorities set forth in this constitution, and such other authorities as the tribal council may, from time to time, by appropriate ordiance, delegate to the executive officers.

Section 2. The governor and lieutenant governor shall be elected as provided in this constitution.

ARTICLE XII-DUTIES OF EXECUTIVE OFFICERS

Section 1. The Governor of the Zuni Tribe shall exercise the following authorities as the chief executive officer of the tribe; and such other authorities as the tribal council may assign.

a. The governor shall preside over meetings of the Zuni Tribal Council;
b. The governor shall appoint all non-elected officials and employees of the executive department of the tribal government and shall direct them in their work, subject only to applicable restrictions embodied in this constitution or in enacments of the tribal council established personnel policies or governing personnel management;
c. The governor, subject to the approval of the tribal council, may establish such boards, committees or subcommittees as the business of the council may require, and shall serve as an ex-officio member of all such committees and boards;
d. The governor shall serve as contracting officer for the tribe, following approval of all contracts by the tribal council;
e. The governor shall have veto power over enactments of the tribal council, as provided in Article IX, Section 4;
f. The governor shall present a budget for consideration by the tribal council not less than sixty(60) days before the beginning of the fiscal year of the tribe. The proposed budget shall be posted in not less than three(3) public places for at least ten(10) days prior to presentation of the budget to the council. It shal be the responsibility of the governor to operate the tribal government within the approved budget. The annual tribal budget shal be subject to approval by the Secretary of the Interior as may be required under Federal Law;
g. The governor shall direct the tribal police, to assure the enforcement of ordinances of the tribal council;
h. The governor shall hold no other tribal office or engage in private remunerative employment without the consent of the tribal council, during his term as governor.

Section 2. In the absence of the governor, the lieutenant governor or a governor pro tempore, who may be appointed by the governor from within the membership of the tribal council, shall preside and shall have all authorities, privileges and duties of the governor. The lieutenant governor shall perform such other duties as the governor, with the consent of the tribal council, may direct.

Section 3. All checks shall be signed and all vouchers shall be approved for payment by two(2) officers of the Zuni Tribal Council as follows: The governor or, in his absence, the lieutenant governor or the governor pro tempore, together with the treasurer or, in his absence, the secretary.

Section 4. The tribal council will require all tribal officials and employees who handle tribal funds to be placed under surety bond. The premium for the bond shall be paid by the tribe.

ARTICLE XIII-TREASURER

Section 1. The treasurer shall be appointed from within the tribal council by the governor, with the concurrence of a majority of the members of the tribal council.

Section 2. The treasurer may be removed from office by the governor with concurrence of a majority of the members of the tribal council.

Section 3. The treasurer shall supervise the tribal accountant, and shall be responsible to accept, reciept for, keep and safeguard all funds under the exclusive control of the Zuni Tribe by depositing them in a bank insured by an agency of the Federal Government, or in tribal accounts as directed by the governor, and shall keep an accurate record of such funds, in his custody to the tribal council at regular meetings, and at such other times as the governor may direct. He shall not authorize payment or disbursment of any funds in the custody of the tribe except as duly authorized by the approved tribal budget.

Section 4. The books and records of the treasurer shall be audited at least once each year by a competent auditor, and at such other times as the governor or the tribal council may require.

ARTICLE XIV-THE JUDICIAL DEPARTMENT

Section 1. The tribal court shall consist of a chief judge and two associate judges, appointed by the Governor of the Zuni Tribe, with the concurrence of the tribal council. Any one of the judges may hold court as determined by the chief judge.

Section 2. By ordinance, subject to approval by the Secretary of the Interior, the tribal council shall establish a court of appeals.

Section 3. The tenure of trial judges shall be six(6) years. Their salary shall be established by ordinance of the tribal council.

Section 4. No person shall be appointed to the office of trial judge unless he is at least thirty(30) years of age and not more than seventy(70) years of age; nor shall any person be appointed as a trial judge who has ever been convicted of a felony or within one year, of a misdemeanor.

Section 5. The Trial and Appellate Courts of the Zuni Tribe shall have jurisdiction over all criminal offenses and civil causes involving Indians on the Zuni Reservation, except such offenses as may fall within the exclusive jurisdiction of Federal or State courts.

Section 6. The duties, jurisdiction and procedures of the courts of the Zuni Tribe shall be more fully prescribed by appropriate ordinances which will consitute the tribal law and order code, enacted pursuant to Article VI, Section 1(k).

ARTICLE XV-NOMINATIONS AND ELECTIONS

Section 1. The Zuni TriBal Council shall, by appropriate ordiance, establish procedures and regulate the conduct of all tribal elections, including the nomination of candidates for all elective offices of the tribe, the appointment of an election board, the registration of voters, the filling and posting of election notices, and absentee voting.

Section 2. Any qualified member of the tribe may become a candidate for any elective office of the tribe.

Section 3. The candidates for office of governor and lieutenant governor shall run for office as a team on a single ticket.

Section 4. All voting for candidates to office on the Zuni Tribal Council shall be by secret ballot, the form of which shall be established by ordinance of the Zuni Tribal Council.

Section 5. Any member of the Zuni Tribe who is eighteen(18) years of age, or older, who has registered to vote and who presents himself at the polls on election day shall be entitled to vote.

Section 6. The regular election of the Zuni Tribe shall be held every four(4) years on a date to be set by the Zuni Tribal Council, to be called and held during the period intervening between the end of Shalako and the beginning of the winter Desh'kwi. The first election under this constitution shal be held on a date to be set by the tribal council in 1970. The incumbent tribal council members, at the time of the adoption of this constitution, shall hold office until the expiration of the term for which they were elected, and until their successors are duly elected and installed on the first day after the winter Desh'kwi.

Section 7. The candidates for governor, lieutenant governor, and councilmen receiving the largest number of votes shall be elected for terms of four(4) years. Elected officials shall serve until their successors are elected and installed on the first day after the winter Desh'kwi. The two councilmen receiving the largest number of votes shall be known as the head councilman and lieutenant governor's councilman, respectively.

ARTICLE XVI-OATH OF OFFICE

All newly elected officers and members of the Zuni Tribal Council shall be required to take an oath of office, as shown below, at the time of their installation. Such oath shall be administered by the Head Cacique of the Pueblo and his aides.

OATH OF OFFICE

"Into your care we entrust our land and our people. Regardless of whether you are poor, or lack the oratory to express yourself fluently, you will, to the best of your ability, be the protector, impartially, for your people. The stranger who comes into our land will become as one of your people, regardless of race, color, or creed, and you will give unto them the same protection and rights as you would your own.

You will cherish and protect all that contains life; from the lowliest crawling creature to the human. By hastly work or deed you will refrain from hurting the feelings, both mentally and physically, of our people. In times when you, to the best of your ability and judgement, have resorted to every peaceful means of bringing reason to an individual, on a matter, and that individual, through stubborness, remains contrary to the point of disrespect for the office you hold, and would, through his action, be a bad example to his fellowmen, you will question him four times if he will continue to set aside peaceful intelligent reasoning. If his answer is yes the four times, then you may strike him with the flat of your hand, and four times if necessary."

ARTICLE XVII-VACANCIES, REMOVAL AND RECALL FROM OFFICE, SUCCESSIONS TO OFFICE

Section 1. Any member of the tribal council, judge, or elected officer of the Zuni Tribe who, during his term is convicted of any felony, shall automatically forfeit his office. Any member of the tribal council, judge, or elected officer found guilty of a misdemeanor involving moral turpitude, gross neglect of duty, malfeasance in office or misconduct reflecting on the dignity and integrity of the tribal government, may be removed from office if not less than five (5) members shall cas ballots in favour of removal at a legally called meeting. Before any vote for removal from office is taken, such member, judge, or officerchall be give a writing statement of the charges against him at least five (5) days before the meeting of the tribal council at which he is to appear, and he shall be given the opportunity to answer any and all charges at the designated council meeting. The decision of the tribal council shall be final.

Section 2. Upon receipt of a petition signed by at least twenty-five percent (25%) of those entitled to vote demanding recall of any member of the tribal council, or elected officer, filed with the secretary of the tribal council at least four (4) months before the expiration of such council member's or official's term of office, it shall be the duty of the tribal coucil to call a special election upon the question or recall. Such election shall be held not less than twenty-five (25) or more than forty (40) days from the filing of the petition. No council member or elected officer may be recalled unless at least two-thirds (2/3) of the voters casting ballots vote in favour of the recall, and unless at least thirty percent (30%) of those entitled to vote cast their ballots in the election.

Section 3. With the exception of the governor and the lieutenant governor, any member of the Zuni Tribal Council, who may resign, or may be removed from office, shall be replaced at a special election to be called and held by the Zuni Tribal Council in conformity with this constitution and ordinances of the tribal council. In the event the governor resigns, dies, becomes otherwise incapacitated or is removed from office, his unexpired term shall be filled by the lieutenant governor. The head councilman will succeed to the office of the lieutenant governor. An election will be called to replace the head councilman.

Section 4. If a member of the tribal council fails to attend four(4) legally called successive meetings of the tribal council or a committee thereof, of which he is a member, or any combination of tribal council or such committee meetings, he shall automatically cease to be a member of the tribal council. In such event, the tribal council shall declare the position vacant and the governor shall arrange for a special election to choose a successor to serve the unexpired term, unless such member:

a. Is excused by the tribal council, or
b. Is absent by reason of illness, or due to reasons beyond his control which are satisfactory to the tribal council.

Section 5. In the event of a vacancy, for any cause, in the membership of the tribal council, the unexpired term corresponding to the vacancy shall be filled by a qualified person in accordance with this constitution and in conformity with established tribal election procedures.

ARTICLE XVIII-INHERENT POWERS OF THE ZUNI TRIBE

Section 1. No provision of this constitution shall be construed as a limitation of the inherent residual soveriegn powers of the Zuni Tribe. Any such powers, not delegated to the representativetribal government by this institution, are retained for direct exercise by the people through referendum, as provided for herein, or for exercise by the tribal government following amendment of the constitutionl.

ARTICLE XIX-AMENDMENTS

Section 1. This constitution may be amended at an election which shall be authorized by the Secretary of the Interior upon request by the tribal council:

a. Whenever by majority vote of all members of the tribal council, the governing body of the tribe shall authorize the submission of a proposed amendment to the electorate of the tribe, or
b. Whenever a minimum of thirty percent (30%) of those entitled to vote, by signed petition, shall request such amendment.

Section 2. If, at such election, the amendment is adopted by majority vote of the qualified voters of the tribe voting therein, and if the number of ballots cast represents not less than thirty percent(30%) of those entitled to vote, such amendment shall be submitted to the Secretary of the Interior and, if approved by him, is shall thereupon take effect.

ARTICLE XX-REFERENDUM

Section 1. Upon receipt of a petition signed by at least thirty percent (30%) of those entitled to vote and filed with the secretary of the tribal council demanding a referendum thereon, any proposed or enacted resolution, ordinance or other action of the tribal council shall either be repealed by the tribal council or be submitted by it to the electorate for decision by the tribe in a general election to be held within thirty(30) days after receipt of the petition. The referendum shall be conclusive only if at least thirty percent(30%) of those entitled to vote cast their ballots therein.

Section 2. When a majority of the members of the tribal council shall request a referendum on any proposed or enacted resolution, ordinance or other action of the tribal council, the tribal council shall call an election within thirty (30) days thereafter at which those entitled to vote shall approve or disapprove, by majority vote, the ordinance or action in question; provided, however, that such approval or disapproval shall be effective only in the event thirty percent (30%) or more of those entitled to vote cast their ballots in such election.

Section 3. No referendum conducted pursuant to the provisions of Sections 1 or 2 above shall serve or abrogate, modify, or amend any properly approved contract or agreement with third parties.

ARTICLE XXI-RATIFICATION

Section 1. This constitution, when adopted by majority vote of the qualified voters of the Zuni Tibe, voting at an election authorized for that purpose by the Secretary of the Interior, in which at least thirty percent(30%) of those entitled to vote shall cast their ballot, shall be submitted to the Secretary of the Interior for his approval, and shall be effective from and after the date of his approval.

2

Constitutional Safeguards for Tribals and Tribal Administration in India

INTRODUCTION

India has a composite population. The Indian society lacks homogeneity in sop for as there exist numerous religious, cultural and linguistic groups. There are Hindus, Muslims, Christians. Paris, Sikhs Buddhists, Jains and others. The pattern of culture vary from place to place. There are Anglo Indian based on racial. religious and linguistic factors. Besides there are sections of people like the Scheduled Castes. The Scheduled Tribes and other backward classes. Who not only need protection from exploitation but even positive help from the state for amerlioation of their miserable lot. Even before India became independent there was a demand from many of the weaker sections of society for special provisions in the Constitution for the benefit of weaker sections based on the promise that these sections had been socially and economically discriminated against during the British times and therefore special steps were called for to help and improve the condition of these people vis a vis the forward cornrnunities.

The framers of the Constitution tried level best to safeguard the interest of the various minority groups whether based on religion or language, culture or socioeconomic factors so as to give them a sense of security. The scheduled tribes who. predominate in certain areas of the country like the North-Eastern region. the large parts of Madhya Pradesh. Bihar. Orissa and certain parts of Gujrat and the hilly regions of most states are those sections of the Indian population who still live in their tribal ways and observe their own peculiar customs and cultural norms. Their primitive way of Hvitlg. nomadic habits. love for drink and dance, and habitation. in remote and inaccessible areas. less affected by the forces of modernization, required special treatment from the framers of our Constitution in order to improve their economic and social position. Hence special provisions were for the development of these tribal groups made and they were classified as scheduled. Now the concern of us is how to keep a balance that on the one hand that their identity is their culture is not eroded and on the other hand bring them in to the main stream of national life. It is of interest to briefly upon these provisions as the enforcement of these require special administrative arrangements.

The framers of the Constitution were anxious to ensure the betterment of the Scheduled Tribes. Article 46 epitomizing the policy calls upon the state (Central & State government) to promote with special care the educational and economic interests of Scheduled castes and Scheduled tribes and protect them from social injustice and all forms of exploitation. It is comprehensive article comprising both the development & regulatory functions.

Protective Provisions

It is noteworthy that even provisions relating to fundamental rights have been qualified with reasonable restrictions in favour of Scheduled tribes. Article 15 prohibits discrimination against any citizen on grounds of religion, race, caste, sex or place of birth: but clause (4) thereof enables a State government to make special provisions for advancement ef members of Scheduled castes and Scheduled tribes. Article 16 provides for opportunities for all citizens in matters relating to employment or appointment or post in favour of Scheduled castes and Schedules tribes. Article 19 grants the rights of freedom or speech, assembly, associauon, union movement and residence throughout the country practice of any profession occupation trade or business. But for protection of the interests of Schedules tribes clause (5) permits reasonable restrictions on the exercise of rights of free movement, residence and settlement in any part of the territory of India, Article 23 prohibits traffic-in human beings Begar and other forms of forced labour: this has special relevance for Scheduled tribes. Reservational Provisions Reservation of seats for Scheduled caste and Schedules tribe communities has been provided for on the basis of population in the House of the People as per Article 330 and in the Legislative Assemblies of the states as per Article 332 for a certain length of time in the hope that in course of that time its need would disappear. In 1950 its validity was extended by another decade. The Constitution 8 Amendment Act 1959 extended all such reservations for ten years. Amendment Act further extended this period from 20 to 30 years and 45 Amendment Ac. Considering the present pace of progress. It does not seem likely that it would be feasible to dispense with reservation in the course of near future. But for reservation in legislatures the voice of these two weak communities would have remained muffled. Howsoever reservation in public services and posts as per Article 335 stands on a different footing. Such reservation in educational institutions has enabled members of these communities to register rise in the percentage of posts they have nailed.

Reservation are also provided to a lower extent in the allotment of houses by public institutions..in the provision of industrial loans grants in scholarship for the students of these sections and provision of special infrastructure facilities to the area in which these communities reside. However the tribal are not very articulate in protecting their interest and as consequence tribal interest are neglected. Much of the problems in the tribal areas are caused by the alleviation of tribal lands to non-tribal and the exploitation of the tribals.

The Constitution protects and guarantees cultural and educational rights of various sectors of the people vide Article 29. 30.. The Constitution provides for special staff for the protection of the interest of scheduled tribes (Article 338) and also for a commission to look in to the social educational conditions of these groups and to report to the Parliament on measures needed to improve these conditions. The Constitution 65th Amendments Act 1999 (Article 33R) provides for the establishment of National Commission for Scheduled Caste and Scheduled Tribes in place of special provision

Another constitutional provision is the one in relation to specification of Schedule tribes in Article 342. This empowers the Presidents to denote the tribes or tribal communities to be deemed as scheduled tribes. Such notification is in respect of state the President shall notify the Scheduled tribes within a state after consultation with the Governor or the state. This clause is important as it ensures national action to specify who the Scheduled tribes arc. The classification of these categories are state and a particular group may he classified as scheduled in one state and not in another depending on the social and economic condition of the group in the state. Development Provisions and Trihal Development Strategy

FOl the first time in the administration of the tribal people the Constitution placed the responsibility for their welfare on populo governments through the President and corners. For planned development availability of financial resources as per Article 275 and executive machinery as per Article 244 and the fifth & sixth schedule of the Constitution have relevance. The first provision of clause. (I) of Article 275 makes it incumbent to set aside out of the Consolidated fund of India for having given to the states so that the cost of schemes of tribal development and raising the level of administration in scheduled areas can he defrayed. Thus, there is no stint on financial resources, except as may be necessarily relative to over all availability Article 244, with the provision in the Fifth schedule enables a cleat frame of administration to concretisc the directives containeding Article 46. The term scheduled areas encompassed all areas the President of India notifes under the fifth schedule. The Governor has been made responsible for the peace and good government of scheduled areas. Under the fifth schedule a provision is made fur setting up a trihal advisory council which is consulted by the Governor in relation to his regulation making powers, Beside this Article 339(2) empowers the Centre to give directions to a State asking them to draw up and execute schemes tor the welfare of Scheduled tribes.

The fifth schedule contains provisions regarding administration and control of the Scheduled areas and Schedules tribes. There are eight States having scheduled areas. viz. Andhra Pradesh Bihar. Gujarat, Himachal Pradesh.. Madhya Pradesh. Maharashtra. Orrisa and Rajasthan; The Sixth.-... schedule contains provisions!; to the administration of the tribal areas in the stale of Assam Cachar Hills District and Karbi Anglong District), Meghalaya, Mizoram and Tripura protected by the inner line Regulations framed in 1872-73 prohibiting entry without a permit of Indian citizens from other parts of the Country as ell as foreigners. There are Autonomous regional council in these areas. They not only administer the various department and developmental programmes but also have powers to make laws on a variety of subjects e.g, land forest shifting cultivation village or town administration including village or town police and public health and sanitation inheritance of property and divorce and social customs. Under the clause (3) of the Fifth Schedule. The Governor is required to draw up annually a report on the administration the Scheduled areas-and submit it to the President. These provisions arc so strong and comprehensive that the Filth Schedule has been termed by some legal authorities as Constitution within the Constitution: Thus the Governors Report on the Scheduled areas carries special significance.

But its is unethical that these comprehensive provisions have however remained lesser operationalised. No attempt has been made even to elaborate as to what would constitute good government for these areas which was a special concern of the Founding Fathers. Most of the states have just made a flew regulations in respect of transfer of land and moneylending. The report of Governor ironically throws no light whatsoever on the State of administration of Scheduled areas ignoring the direction of the Constitution. Such reports have not evinced an interest in the Union Government. No attempt has been to assist the level of administration of the Scheduled areas and identity if, deficiencies therein by any state. No direction has been issued by the Union Government in exercise of its executive authority not with standing the grave concern expressed at all levels about the state of administration in the tribal areas which continues to be far from satisfactory resulting in intermittent unrest amongst the tribal people,

(The Tribes Advisory Councils are constituted in the state in accordance with clause (4) of the Fifth Schedule to the Constitution which provides that there shall be established in each slate having Scheduled areas, and if the President so directs also in-any State Scheduled Tribes but no Scheduled Area therein). The Tribes Advisory Council may consist of not more than 20 members of whom as much as three-fourth shall be representatives of Scheduled tribes in the Legislative Assembly of the State. It is significant to note that even before the Constitution was promulgated there were advisory Committees attached to some of their Provincial Government to assist them in the administration of the Tribal areas, but they played a very minor role and indeed were hardly noticed. But the situation has changed, now and in important mechanism.

The Constitution has given only tribal people this privilege according to which the beneficiaries are constitutionally desired to participate in their policy making enterprise. Though this idea was inserted 55 years ago in the Constitution it is the most modern theory of development which is now known as the people-centred approach to development. In people centred approach to development the needs of the people take precedence over the needs of the production system.

The Central themes of people-centred development are: (I) empowerment of people and (2) development of administrative process which responds 10 the needsof the people. Key elements In people-centred development are: (1) human growth and well-being, (2) equality (3) Self-reliance (4) participation and sustainability, 26th & 27th report of the commissioner. Sustainability is regarded as lasting quire, in a development I programme. A development programme can be sustained by: (1) creating a felt need among beneficiaries about the efficacy of the programme. (2) developing institutions which continually adapt. 0) Providing of resources, and (4) building support among political elites and community groups.

If Tribes Advisory Councils the function as desired by the Constitution development will be in accordance with the aspirations of the tribal people which IS propagated in the People Centred approach to development.

But when we examine its real working, we find that the various State Government are not serious about its utility. As per the guidelines issued by the Ministry of Welfare the tribes Advisory Council should meet at least twice a year-part of the State governments not to convene its meeting regularly. As such the very purpose of its formation is defeated. In Bihar. Himachal Pradsh. Maharashtra. Orissa and Tripura the Council is headed by the Chief Minister while in other States. It is handled by the Minister-in charge of Tribal development. It is therefore ethically desirable that a uniform practice should be followed in this regard.

LEGISLATIVE FUNCTIONS BETWEEN CENTRE AND STATES

The federal Indian constitutional edifice envisages division of legislative powers between the Union and the State governments. None of the three lists of the Seventh Schedule contains specific provision for legislation in respect of Scheduled areas or Scheduled Tribes.

It has been held by the Kerala High Court in Eacharan and one other versus the State of Kerala No, 3373 or 19(6) that if any law is to be made in respect of these two subjects alone. It can be done only by Parliament in exercise of its residuary powers as per Article 24R (I) read with entry 97 in List million list of the Seventh Schedule. This judgment related to a State which has no Scheduled area but is also relevant for states having Scheduled areas.

Mention has been made earlier of the far character of the provisions of the Fifth Schedule. It bears repletion that in accordance with sub paragraph.

(1) of para 5 of the Schedule the Governor of a state has been vested vast discretion for issue of public notification making it applicable subject to such exceptions and modifications that he may specify: the power conferred can have retrospective effect. It is noteworthy that this regulation making power contained in sub-paragraph.

(2) and the power to repeal or amend an act of Parliament or of a State Legislature contained in sub-paragraph.

(3) Require compliance with the procedure prescribed in sub-paragraph.

(4) and (5) making consultation with the Tribe Advisory Council of the state and the assent of the President. But there does not appear to be any such constraint of procedure as sub-paragraph (1) is concerned.

The regulation-making powers have been exercised by the Governors in many states for the business of moneylending in scheduled areas. combating alienation of tribal land. Liquidation of debt bondage, etc. In practice it is the state administration which take action for introducing regulations in the name of the Governor, in accordance with the spirit of the Constitution.

The overall position may be summed up by saying that laws on tribal affairs can be in the form of; (a) Central legislation or (b) regulations by the Governor, or (c) State legislation. In her words, legislation 011 tribal affairs is a joint responsibility of the centre and the Stales with a special role having been assigned to the Governor of a state. Now the question is, what approach should we follow with regards to tribal development?

Commenting upon the programme of development of the tribals. Nehru advised that we should approach the tribal people with affection and friendliness and go to them as liberating forces. They should be sure that we want to give them something and not to take away something from them. This is the best way to create psychological integration between tribals and others who may be traders, businessmen or administrators. There must not be drastic uprooting of tribals from their habitat. We have to understand tribals psyche andhave to give them due respect and honour their culture.

1. People should develop along the lines of their own genius and we should avoid imposing any thing on them but rather try to encourage in every way their own traditional ails and culture.
2. Tribals rights in lands and forests should be respected.
3. We should try to train and build up a team of their own people to do administration and development.
4. We should judge results by statistics or the amount of money spent but by the quality of human character that IS evolved.

Culture obviously must he a living moving thing always subject to change and Mr. Nehrus formula of developing the tribal people along the line of their own tradition and genius seem to put what was needed in a nutshell.

The Scheduled Tribes arc distinct racial and cultural entities. As such any new-comer percentage to tribal areas is apt to be bewildered by the difference in the nature or people there. The efficiency of a Public Official largely depends on the manner in which he behaves with the population. Insofar as these areas are concerned. However brilliant an officer may be he will be a failure unless he he haves in a sober and tactful manner with the population. There is one golden rule in dealing with tribals, namely behave like a gentleman and treat the tribals as one gentleman would behave with another.

The village administration in a tribal area is based mainly on respect for age. It is the oldest men in a village who will have the last say in any matter. Which is discussed. Age and experience are considered to be the most desirable qualities in those who administer them.

Tribals are usually desirous of being courteous therefore, they do not normally indulge in deliberate discourtesy. But a tribal when he is hurt about something and his feelings are ruffled can be extremely insulting. The officer should not mistake bluntness which a tribal possess in a large quantity fix discourtesy. Tribals are easy to win but arc still easter to lose. In democratic State like ours. It is essential that the common people and the administration should go hand in hand or this is the very essence true democracy.

CONSTITUTIONAL SAFEGUARDS

In India, the National Constitution of 1950 or any other Constitutional document does not define the word 'Minority'. The Constitution only refers to Minorities and speaks of those "based on religion or language". In the Constitution of India, the Preamble (as amended in 1976) declares the State to be "Secular", and this is of special relevance for the Religious Minorities. Equally relevant for them, especially, is the prefatory declaration of the Constitution in its Preamble that all citizens of India are to be secured "liberty of thought, expression, belief, faith and worship and "equality of status and of opportunity."

The Constitution of India has provided two types of safe-guards-general and specific to safeguard various interests of the minorities. In the first category are those provisions that are equally enjoyed by both groups. The provisions ensure justice-social, economic and political equality to all. The second category consists of provisions meant specifically for the protection of particular interests of minorities.

- people's right to "equality before the law" and "equal protection of the laws";
- prohibition of discrimination against citizens on grounds of religion, race, caste, sex or place of birth;

- authority of State to make "any special provision for the advancement of any socially and educationally backward classes of citizens" (besides the Scheduled Castes and Scheduled Tribes);
- citizens' right to "equality of opportunity" in matters relating to employment or appointment to any office under the State-and prohibition in this regard of discrimination on grounds of religion, race, caste, sex or place of birth.
- Authority of State to make "any provision for the reservation of appointments or posts in favour of any backward class of citizens which, in the opinion of the State, is not adequately represented in the services under the State;
- People's freedom of conscience and right to freely profess, practice and propagate religion-subject to public order, morality and other Fundamental Rights;
- Authority of State to make law for "regulating or restricting any economic financial, political or other secular activity which may be associated with religious practice", and for "providing for social welfare and reform";
- Authority of State to make laws for "throwing open" of Hindu, Sikh, Jain or Buddhist "religious institutions of a public character to "all classes and sections of the respective communities;
- Sikh community's right of "wearing and carrying of kirpans";
- Right of "every religious denomination or any section thereof-subject to public order, morality and health-to establish and maintain institutions for religious and charitable proposes, "manage its own affairs of religion", and own and acquire movable immovable property and administer it "in accordance with law";
- People's "freedom as to payment of taxes for promotion of any particular religion";
- People's "freedom as to attendance at religious instruction or religious worship in educational institutions" wholly maintained, recognized, or aided by the State;

- Right of "any section of the citizens" to conserve its "distinct language, script or culture"
- Restriction on denial of admission to any citizen, to any educational institution maintained or aided by the State, "on grounds only of religion, race, caste, language or any of them";
- Right of all Religious and Linguistic Minorities to establish and administer educational institutions of their choice; and
- Freedom of Minority-managed educational institutions from discrimination in the matter of receiving aid from the State.

Part IV of the Constitution of India, containing non-justifiable Directive Principles of State Policy, includes the following provisions having significant implications for the Minorities:

- Obligation of the State "to endeavor to eliminate inequalities in status, facilities and opportunities" amongst individuals and groups of people residing in different areas or engaged in different vocations;
- Obligation of State to "endeavor to secure for the citizens a uniform civil code throughout the territory of India";
- Obligation of State "to promote with special care" the educational and economic interests of "the weaker sections of the people" (besides Scheduled Castes and Scheduled Tribes; and
- Obligation of State to "take steps" for "prohibiting the slaughter of cows and calves and other milch and draught cattle".

Part IV-A of the Constitution, relating to Fundamental Duties, applies in full to all citizens, including those belonging to Minorities and of special relevance for the Minorities are the following provisions in this Part:

- Citizens' duty to promote harmony and the spirit of common brotherhood amongst all the people of India "transcending religious, linguistic and regional or sectional diversities; and
- Citizens' duty to "value and preserve the rich heritage of our composite culture".

Some other provisions of the Constitution having special relevance and implications for the Minorities are:

- Official obligation to pay out of the consolidated funds of the States of Kerala and Tamilnadu 46.5 and 13.5 lakh rupees respectively to the local "Dewasom Funds" for the maintenance of Hindu temples and shrines in the territories of the erstwhile State of Travancore-Cochin;
- Special provision relating to the language spoken by a section of the population of any State;
- Provision for facilities for instruction in mother-tongue at primary stage;
- Provision for a Special Officer for Linguistic Minorities and his duties;
- Special provision with respect to Naga religious or social practices, customary law and procedure, and "administration of civil and criminal justice involving decisions according to Naga customary law."
- Identical special provision for the Mizos; and
- Provision relating to continuation in force of pre-Constitution laws "until altered or repealed or amended by a competent legislature or other competent authority"

Part III of the Constitution gives certain fundamental rights. Some of these rights are common to all the citizens of India including minorities. These rights are enshrined in-

Article 14: This ensures equality before law and equal protection of law.

Article 15: This prohibits discrimination on any ground i.e. religion, race, caste, sex, place of birth.

Article 21: No person shall be deprived of his life or personal liberty except the procedure established by law.

Article 25: This ensures freedom of conscience and the right freely to profess, practice and propagate religion.

Article 26: This ensures a right to manage religious institutions, religious affairs, subject to public order, morality and health.

Article 29: Gives minorities a right to conserve their language, script or culture.

It provides for the protection of the interests of minorities by giving them a right to establish and administer educational institutions of their choice. The State is directed not to discriminate against minorities institutions in granting aid.

Article 350A: Directs the State to provide facilities for instruction in the mother tongue at the primary stage of education.

Art 164(1): According to this article in states of Bihar, MP and Orissa there shall be a Minister in charge of tribal welfare who may in addition be in charge of the welfare of the scheduled castes and backward classes.

Art 244(1): Regarding administration of scheduled areas and tribal areas-(1) The provisions of the Fifth schedule shall apply to the administration and control of the Scheduled areas and Scheduled tribes in any state other than the state of Assam, Meghalaya, Tripura and Mizoram. (2) The provisions of the sixth schedule shall apply to the administration of the tribal areas in the state of Assam, Meghalaya, Tripura and Mizoram.

Art 244(A): Formation of an autonomous state comprising certain tribal areas in Assam and creation of local legislature or Council of Ministers or both thereof. Parliament may by law form within the state of Assam an autonomous state comprising (whether wholly or part) all or any of the tribal areas.

Art 275: Provided that there shall be paid out of consolidated fund of India as grants-in-aid of the revenues of a state such capital and recurring sums as may be necessary to enable the state to meet the costs of such schemes of development as may be undertaken by the state with the approval of the Govt of India for the purpose of promoting the welfare of the scheduled tribes in that state or raising the level of administration of the scheduled areas therein to that of the administration of the rest of the areas in that state. Provided further that there shall be paid out of the consolidated fund of India as grant-in-aid of the revenues of the state of Assam sum capital and recurring.

Art 330: Reservation of seats for the scheduled castes and scheduled tribes in the House of People.

- Seats shall be reserved for scheduled castes
- The scheduled tribes except the scheduled tribes except the scheduled tribes in the autonomous districts of Assam
- The scheduled tribes in the autonomous districts in Assam.

- Art 332: Reservation of seats for scheduled castes and scheduled tribes in the Legislative Assemblies of the states.
- Seats shall be reserved for the scheduled castes and the scheduled tribes (except the ST's of autonomous districts of Assam) in the Legislative Assembly of every state.
- Seats shall be reserved also for the autonomous districts in the Legislative Assembly of the state of Assam.

Art 334: Reservation of seats and special representation in Legislative Assemblies and House of People to cease after fifty years.

Art 335: Claims of scheduled castes and scheduled tribes to service and posts-The claims of the members of the scheduled castes and scheduled tribes shall be taken into consideration consistently with the maintenance of efficiency of administration in the making of appointments to service and posts in connection with the affairs of the Union or of a state.

Art 338: National Commission for scheduled castes and scheduled tribes

Art 339: Control of the Union over the administration of Scheduled castes and Scheduled tribes.

Art 340: Appointment of a commission by the president to investigate the conditions of backward classes.

Art 341: Power of the President to specify the castes, races or tribes or posts of or groups within castes, races or tribes as scheduled castes.

Art 342: Power of the President to specify the tribes or tribal communities or parts of or groups within tribes or tribal communities as scheduled tribe.

Art 350(A): Facilities for instruction in mother tongue of a minority group.

Art 350(B): Special officer for linguistic minorities.

CONSTITUTIONAL SAFEGUARDS FOR DALITS

SAFEGUARDS IN THE INDIAN CONSTITUTION FOR SCHEDULED CASTES AND SCHEDULED TRIBES

The important Constitutional safeguards for SCs & STs are mentioned below:

Directive Principles of State Policy

Article 46 is a comprehensive article comprising both the developmental and regulatory aspects. It reads as follows:

"The State shall promote with special care the educational and economic interests of the weaker sections, of the people, and in particular, of the Scheduled Castes and the Scheduled Tribes, and shall protect them from social injustice and all forms of exploitation".

Social Safeguards

Article 17. "Untouchability" is abolished and its practice in any form is forbidden. The enforcement of any disability arising out of "Untouchability" shall be an offence punishable in accordance with law.

To give effect to this Article, Parliament made an enactment viz., Untouchability (Offences) Act, 1955. To make the provisions of this Act more stringent, the Act was amended in 1976 and was also renamed as the Protection of Civil Rights Act, 1955. As provided under the Act, Government of India also notified the Rules, viz., the PCR Rules, 1977, to carry out the provisions of this Act. As cases of atrocities on SCs/STs were not covered under the provisions of PCR Act, 1955, Parliament passed another important Act in 1989 for taking measures to prevent the atrocities. This act known as the Scheduled Castes and the Scheduled Tribes (Prevention of Atrocities) Act, 1989, became effective from 30.1.1990. For carrying out the provisions of this Act the Govt. of India have notified the SCs and the STs (Prevention of Atrocities) Rules, 1995 on 31.3.1995.

Article 23. Prohibits traffic in human beings and begar and other similar forms of forced labour and provides that any contravention of this provision shall be an offence punishable in accordance with law. It does not specifically mention SCs & STs but since the majority of bonded labour belong to SCs/STs this Article has a special significance for SCs and STs. In pursuance of this article, Parliament has enacted the Bonded Labour System (Abolition) Act, 1976. For effective implementation of this Act, the Ministry of Labour is running a Centrally Sponsored Scheme for identification, liberation and rehabilitation of bonded labour.

Article 24 provides that no child below the age of 14 years shall be employed to work in any factory or mine or engaged in any other hazardous employment. There are Central and State laws to prevent child labour. This article too is significant for SCs and STs as a substantial portion, if not the majority, of child labour engaged in hazardous employment belong to SCs and STs.

Article 25(2)(b) provides that Hindu religious institutions of a public character shall be thrown open to all classes and sections of Hindus. This provision is relevant as some sects of Hindus used to claim that only members of the concerned sects had a right to enter their temples. This was only a subterfuge to prevent entry of SC persons in such temples. For the purpose of this provision the term Hindu includes Sikh, Jaina and Budhist.

EDUCATIONAL AND CULTURAL SAFEGUARDS

Article 15(4) empowers the State to make any special provision for the advancement of any socially and educationally backward classes of citizens or for SC and ST. This provision has enabled the State to reserve seats for SCs and STs in educational institutions including technical, engineering and medical colleges and in Scientific & Specialised Courses. In this as well as in Article 16(4) the term 'backward classes' is used as a generic term and comprises various categories of backward classes, viz., Scheduled Castes, Scheduled Tribes, Other Backward Classes, Denotified Communities (Vimukta Jatiyan) and Nomadic/Seminomadic communities.

Article 330 provides for reservation of seats for SCs/STs in the Lok Sabha.

Article 332 provides for reservation of seats for SCs/STs in the State Vidhan Sabhas (Legislative Assemblies).

Article 334 originally laid down that the provision relating to the reservation of seats for SCs/STs in the Lok Sabha and the State Vidhan Sabhas (and the representation of the Anglo-Indian community in the Lok Sabha and the State Vidhan Sabhas by nomination) would cease to have effect on the expiration of a period of ten years from the commencement of the Constitution. This article has since been amended four times, extending the said period by ten years on each occasion. This provision was to expire in January 2000.

Service Safeguards

Article 16(4) empowers the State to make "any provision for the reservation in appointments or posts in favour of any backward class of citizens which, in the opinion of the State, is not adequately represented in the services under the State".

Article 16(4A). Nothing in this Article shall prevent the State from making any provision for reservation in matters of promotion to any class or classes of posts in the services under the State in favour of the Scheduled Castes and the Scheduled Tribes which, in the opinion of the State, are not adequately represented in the services under the State".

Article 335. "The claims of the members of the Scheduled Castes and the Scheduled Tribes shall be taken into consideration, consistently with the maintenance of efficiency of administration, in the making of appointments to services and posts in connection with the affairs of the Union or of a State".

Article 320(4) provides that nothing in clause (3) shall require a Public Service Commission to be consulted as respects the manner in which any provision under Article 16(4) & 16(4)A may be made or the manner in which effect may be given to the provisions of Article 335.

STATUTES AND LEGISLATIONS

There are a number of laws, both Central and State, which provide for safeguards to SCs/STs. Some of these emanate from the various Constitutional provisions. An illustrative list of such laws is given below:

- The Protection of Civil Rights Act, 1955.
- The Scheduled Castes and the Scheduled Tribes (Prevention of Atrocities) Act, 1989.
- The Bonded Labour System (Abolition) Act, 1976.
- The Child Labour (Prohibition and Regulation) Act, 1986.
- Acts and regulations in force in different States to prevent alienation of land belonging to SCs/STs. In some States such provision exists in the Land Revenue Code.
- Acts in different States for restoration of alienated land to SCs/STs.

CONSTITUTIONAL PROVISIONS

Constitutional rights and safeguards provided to the minorities in India

1. *Constitutional safeguards for religious and linguistic minorities of India*

Though the Constitution of India does not define the word 'Minority' and only refers to 'Minorities' and speaks of those 'based on religion or language', the rights of the minorities have been spelt out in the Constitution in detail.

2. *'Common Domain' and 'Separate Domain' of rights of minorities provided in the Constitution*

The Constitution provides two sets of rights of minorities which can be placed in 'common domain' and 'separate domain'. The rights which fall in the 'common domain' are those which are applicable to all the citizens of our country. The rights which fall in the 'separate domain' are those which are applicable to the minorities only and these are reserved to protect their identity. The distinction between 'common domain' and 'separate domain' and their combination have been well kept and protected in the Constitution. The Preamble to the Constitution declares the State to be 'Secular' and this is a special relevance for the Religious Minorities. Equally relevant for them, especially, is the declaration of the Constitution in its Preamble that all citizens of India are to be secured 'liberty of thought, expression, belief, faith and worship and 'equality of status and of opportunity.'

'Common Domain', the Directive Principles of State Policy – Part IV of the Constitution

The Constitution has made provisions for the Fundamental Rights in Part III, which the State has to comply with and these are also judicially enforceable. There is another set of non-justiciable rights stated in Part IV, which are connected with social and economic rights of the people. These rights are known as 'Directive Principles of State Policy', which legally are not binding upon the State, but are "fundamental in the governance of the country and it shall be the duty of the State to apply these principles in making laws". (Article 37). Part IV of the Constitution of India, containing non-justiciable Directive Principles of State Policy, includes the following provisions having significant implications for the Minorities:-

(i) obligation of the State 'to endeavour to eliminate inequalities in status, facilities and opportunities' amongst individuals and groups of people residing in different areas or engaged in different vocations;

(ii) obligation of State 'to promote with special care' the educational and economic interests of 'the weaker sections of the people' (besides Scheduled Castes and Scheduled Tribes);

'Common Domain', the Fundamental Duties – Part IVA of the Constitution

Part IVA of the Constitution, relating to Fundamental Duties as provided in Article 51 A applies in full to all citizens, including those belonging to Minorities. Article 51A which is of special relevance for the Minorities stipulates as under:-

(i) citizens' duty to promote harmony and the spirit of common brotherhood amongst all the people of India 'transcending religious, linguistic and regional or sectional diversities; and

(ii) citizens' duty to value and preserve the rich heritage of our composite culture.'

'Common Domain', the Fundamental Rights – Part III of the Constitution

The Constitution has provided a definite space for both the 'domains' i.e. 'common' as well as 'separate'. In Part III of the Constitution, which deals with the Fundamental Rights is divided into two parts viz. (a) the rights which fall in the 'common domain' and (b) the rights which go to the 'separate domain'. In the 'common domain', the following fundamental rights and freedoms are covered:

(i) people's right to 'equality before the law' and 'equal protection of the laws';

(ii) prohibition of discrimination against citizens on grounds of religion, race, caste, sex or place of birth;

(iii) authority of State to make 'any special provision for the advancement of any socially and educationally backward classes of citizens' (besides the Scheduled Castes and Scheduled Tribes);

(iv) citizens' right to 'equality of opportunity' in matters relating to employment or appointment to any office under the State – and prohibition in this regard of discrimination on grounds of religion, race, caste, sex or place of birth;

(v) authority of State to make 'any provision for the reservation of appointments or posts in favour of any backward class of citizens which, in the opinion of the State, is not adequately represented in the services under the State;

(vi) people's freedom of conscience and right to freely profess, practice and propagate religion – subject to public order, morality and other Fundamental Rights;

(vii) right of 'every religious denomination or any section thereof – subject to public order, morality and health – to establish and maintain institutions for religious and charitable purposes, 'manage its own affairs in matters of religion', and own and acquire movable immovable property and administer it 'in accordance with law';

(viii) prohibition against compelling any person to pay taxes for promotion of any particular religion';

(ix) people's 'freedom as to attendance at religious instruction or religious worship in educational institutions' wholly maintained, recognized, or aided by the State.

'SEPARATE DOMAIN' OF MINORITY RIGHTS

The Minority Rights provided in the Constitution which fall in the category of 'Separate Domain' are as under:-

(i) right of 'any section of the citizens' to 'conserve' its 'distinct language, script or culture';

(ii) restriction on denial of admission to any citizen, to any educational institution maintained or aided by the State, 'on grounds only of religion, race, caste, language or any of them';

(iii) right of all Religious and Linguistic Minorities to establish and administer educational institutions of their choice;

(iv) freedom of Minority-managed educational institutions from discrimination in the matter of receiving aid from the State;

(v) special provision relating to the language spoken by a section of the population of any State;

(vi) provision for facilities for instruction in mother-tongue at primary stage;

(vii) provision for a Special Officer for Linguistic Minorities and his duties; and

(viii) Sikh community's right of 'wearing and carrying of kirpans.

INDIA'S MULTI-CULTURALISM INTERWOVEN IN THE CONSTITUTION

The various Articles of the Constitution providing rights to the minorities, clearly and firmly point out to only one direction: that of a multi-religious, multi-cultural, multi-lingual and multi-racial Indian society, interwoven into an innate unity by the common thread of national integration and communal harmony. By the yardstick adopted by the framers of the Constitution and crystallized into its provisions the Indian Nation is not just a conglomeration of individual inhabitants of this State; it comprises of two distinct categories of constituents. The two-tier commonwealth of Indian Nation includes, on one hand, every citizen of India individually and, on the other hand, the multitude of religious, linguistic, cultural and ethnic groups among its citizens. The Indian Nation is an enormous coparcenary in which the individual citizens are also members of their own respective branches taking the form of religious, cultural, linguistic and ethnic groups. And all these groups, like all individuals, have the same Fundamental Rights to enjoy and the same Fundamental Duties to discharge.

PROTECTION OF WEAKER SECTIONS IN INDIAN PLURALISTIC SOCIETY

The social pluralism of India, as fortified by the unique Constitutional concept of secularism, raises the need for the protection and development of all sorts of weaker sections of the Indian citizenry – whether this 'weakness' is based on numbers or on social, economic or educational status of any particular group. The Constitution, therefore, speaks of Religious and Linguistic Minorities, Scheduled Castes, Scheduled Tribes and Backward Classes and makes – or leaves room for making – for them special provisions of various nature and varying import.

INDIAN GOVERNMENT, POLITICS IN INDIA, INDIAN CONSTITUTION

INDIAN POLITICS ENTERED a new era at the beginning of the 1990s. The period of political domination by the Congress (I) branch of the Indian National Congress came to an end with the party's defeat in the 1989 general elections, and India began a period of intense multiparty political competition. Even though the Congress (I) regained power as a minority government in 1991, its grasp on power was precarious. The Nehruvian socialist ideology that the party had used to fashion India's political agenda had lost much of its popular appeal. The Congress (I) political leadership had lost the mantle of moral integrity inherited from the Indian National Congress's role in the independence movement, and it was widely viewed as corrupt. Support among key social bases of the Congress (I) political coalition was seriously eroding. The main alternative to the Congress (I), the Bharatiya Janata Party (BJP—Indian People's Party), embarked on a campaign to reorganize the Indian electorate in an effort to create a Hindu nationalist majority coalition. Simultaneously, such parties as the Janata Dal (People's Party), the Samajwadi Party (Socialist Party), and the Bahujan Samaj Party (BSP—Party of Society's Majority) attempted to ascend to power on the crest of an alliance of interests uniting Dalits, Backward Classes, Scheduled Tribes, and religious minorities.

The structure of India's federal—or union—system not only creates a strong central government but also has facilitated the concentration of power in the central government in general and in particular in the Office of the Prime Minister. This centralization of power has been a source of considerable controversy and political tension. It is likely to further exacerbate political conflict because of the increasing pluralism of the country's party system and the growing diversity of interest-group representation.

Once viewed as a source of solutions for the country's economic and social problems, the Indian polity is increasingly seen by political observers as the problem. When populist political appeals stir the passions of the masses, government institutions appear less capable than ever before of accommodating conflicts in a society mobilized along competing ethnic and religious lines. In addition, law and order have become increasingly tenuous because of the growing inability of the police to curb criminal activities and quell communal disturbances. Indeed, many observers bemoan the "criminalization" of Indian politics at a time when politicians routinely hire "muscle power" to improve their electoral prospects, and criminals themselves successfully run for public office. These circumstances have led some observers to conclude that India has entered into a growing crisis of governability.

Few analysts would deny the gravity of India's problems, but some contend they have occurred amidst the maturation of civil society and the emergence of new, more democratic political practices. Backward Classes, the Dalits, and tribal peoples increasingly have refused to rest content with the patronage and populism characteristic of the "Congress system." Mobilization of these groups has provided a viable base for the political opposition and unraveled the fabric of the Congress. Since the late 1970s, there has been a proliferation of nongovernmental organizations. These groups made new demands on the political system that required a substantial redistribution of political power, economic resources, and social status.

Whether or not developments in Indian politics exacerbate the continuing problems or give birth to greater democracy broadly hinges on efforts to resolve three key issues. How will India's political system, now more than ever based on egalitarian democratic values, accommodate the changes taking place in its hierarchical social system? How will the state balance the need to recognize the interests of the country's remarkably heterogeneous society with the imperatives of national unity? And, in the face of the declining legitimacy of the Indian state and the continuing development of civil society, can the Indian state regenerate its legitimacy, and if it is to do so, how should it redefine the boundaries between state and society? India has confronted these issues throughout much of its history. These issues, with their intrinsic tensions, will continue to serve as sources of change in the continuing evolution of the Indian polity.

THE INDIAN CONSTITUTION & THE CONSTITUTIONAL FRAMEWORK

The constitution of India draws extensively from Western legal traditions in its outline of the principles of liberal democracy.

It is distinguished from many Western constitutions, however, in its elaboration of principles reflecting the aspirations to end the inequities of traditional social relations and enhance the social welfare of the population. According to constitutional scholar Granville Austin, probably no other nation's constitution "has provided so much impetus toward changing and rebuilding society for the common good." Since its enactment, the constitution has fostered a steady concentration of power in the central government—especially the Office of the Prime Minister. This centralization has occurred in the face of the increasing assertiveness of an array of ethnic and caste groups across Indian society. Increasingly, the government has responded to the resulting tensions by resorting to the formidable array of authoritarian powers provided by the constitution. Together with the public's perception of pervasive corruption among India's politicians, the state's centralization of authority and increasing resort to coercive power have eroded its legitimacy. However, a new assertiveness shown by the Supreme Court and the Election Commission suggests that the remaining checks and balances among the country's political institutions continue to support the resilience of Indian democracy.

Adopted after some two and one-half years of deliberation by the Constituent Assembly that also acted as India's first legislature, the Indian constitution was put into effect on January 26, 1950. Bhimrao Ramji (B.R.) Ambedkar, a Dalit who earned a law degree from Columbia University, chaired the drafting committee of the constitution and shepherded it through Constituent Assembly debates. Supporters of independent India's founding father, Mohandas Karamchand (Mahatma) Gandhi, backed measures that would form a decentralized polity with strong local administration—known as *panchayat* —in a system known as *panchayati raj,* that is rule by *panchayats*. However, the support of more modernist leaders, such as Jawaharlal Nehru, ultimately led to a parliamentary government and a federal system with a strong central government. Following a British parliamentary pattern, the constitution embodies the Fundamental Rights, which are similar to the United States Bill of Rights, and a Supreme Court similar to that of the United States. It creates a "sovereign democratic republic" called India, or Bharat (after the legendary king of the *Mahabharata*), which "shall be a Union of States." India is a federal system in which residual powers of legislation remain with the central government, similar to that in Canada. The constitution of India provides detailed lists dividing up powers between central and state governments as in Australia, and it elaborates a set of Directive Principles of State Policy as does the Irish constitution.

The 395 articles and ten appendixes, known as schedules, in the constitution make it one of the longest and most detailed in the world. Schedules can be added to the constitution by amendment. The ten schedules in force cover the designations of the states and union territories; the emoluments for high-level officials; forms of oaths; allocation of the number of seats in the Rajya Sabha (Council of States—the upper house of Parliament) per state or territory; provisions for the administration and control of Scheduled Areas and Scheduled Tribes; provisions for the administration of tribal areas in Assam; the union (meaning central government), state, and concurrent (dual) lists of responsibilities; the official languages; land and tenure reforms; and the association of Sikkim with India.

The Indian constitution is also one of the most frequently amended constitutions in the world. The first amendment came only a year after the adoption of the constitution and instituted numerous minor changes. Many more amendments followed, and through June 1995 the constitution had been amended seventy-seven times, a rate of almost two amendments per year since 1950. Most of the constitution can be amended after a quorum of more than half of the members of each house in Parliament passes an amendment with a two-thirds majority vote. Articles pertaining to the distribution of legislative authority between the central and state governments must also be approved by 50 percent of the state legislatures.

3

Indigenous Peoples Development Plan in India

INTRODUCTION

Tribal communities bear a disproportionate burden of vector borne diseases. For example, although tribals constitute only about 8% of the population, they account for about 30% of all cases of malaria, more than 60% of P. Falciparum, and as much as 50% of the mortality associated with malaria. National Family Heath Survey. 3 (2005-2006) data indicates that health outcomes for tribals are poor compared to the general population, and even when compared to Scheduled Castes. For example, a larger proportion of tribal women have a below-normal BMI as compared to their counterparts in the general population (46.6% versus 33%).

Not only do tribals have poorer health outcomes, their access to health services is also significantly worse: less than 20% of tribal women give birth in an institution as compared to 40% of women in the general population and 35% of Scheduled Caste women; and only about 31% of tribal children are fully immunized as compared to about 44% in the general population and 40% among Scheduled Castes. It is fair to conclude that their access to other health services would be equally poor, including to the services aiming to prevent and treat vector borne diseases.

In addition, tribals face other economic and social challenges when attempting to avail of health services: poverty, low levels of education, poor access to medical care, and isolation from the mainstream economy are the norm. Tribal communities have distinct languages, cultural behaviors and mistrust of outsiders;

and their knowledge of disease prevention and treatment is limited. A sample survey1 of K.A.P. about malaria carried out in a tribal area of Bastar district, which is a hyper-endemic area for malaria, predominantly P.falciparum, showed that understanding about the problem of malaria was poor amongst the tribals-only about 50% (ranging from 30% to 60%) of the respondents were aware about cause and signs and symptoms of malaria, breeding & resting habit of mosquitoes, usefulness of insecticidal spray and ill effect of mud plastering following residual spraying. Only 46% of the respondents were aware that malaria is caused by mosquito bite, the rest believed that it is caused by the wrath of God (20%), witchcraft (15%), strolling in a forested area (4%), eating stale food (2%), drinking bad water (1%), and about 10% of tribal people were ignorant about the mode of disease transmission. 50% of respondents were cognizant about the symptoms of malaria and the need to get their blood examined in case of fever. However, 50% revealed that in case of fever they would prefer to obtain treatment from tribal healers (20%), practice witchcraft (15%), use wild herbs (8%), use chili (4%), or turmeric powder (3%). 58% of the respondents were aware that mosquitoes rested in human dwellings, 30% believed that they lived in cattle sheds and jungles, and the rest did not know. The majority of respondents did not know the breeding place of mosquitoes. 60% were aware that spraying insecticides in the village was intended to kill mosquitoes, 20% believed that it killed house flies, and the rest did not know. 30% knew that mud plastering should not be done after insecticidal spraying; however, about 80% of the population did mud plaster their houses within a week of spray. 7% used smoke to drive away the mosquitoes or used Kuranji oil as repellent to prevent mosquito bites. Mosquito bednets or any other type of repellent were not used.

It is in this context that the VBDCP has developed and will implement a separate Indigenous Peoples Development Plan (IPDP). IPDP is necessary to improve the participation of tribal communities in sharing benefits and address any unintended effects that may increase their vulnerability.

BACKGROUND

Government of India (GOI) is committed to reducing the burden of vector borne diseases, and has pledged in the National

Health Policy (NHP-2002) to reduce mortality due to malaria, dengue and Japanese encephalitis by 50% by 2010; eliminate kala-azar by year 2010; and eliminate lymphatic filariasis by year 2015. This is in keeping with the Millennium Development Goal of halting and reversing the incidence of malaria by year 2015. In order to achieve this, GOI has undertaken under the National Rural Health Mission (NRHM) launched in April 2005 to (i) augment and ensure appropriate public health focus, peoples. orientation and ownership of public health programs; (ii) encourage community-based approaches to disease control; (ii) promote public-private partnership in service provision; (iv) involve local bodies and Panchayati Raj Institutions (PRIs); and (v) promote gender equity. These initiatives are intended to improve access to primary health care, thereby impacting the prevention and control of communicable diseases including vector borne diseases, reduction of infant mortality rate and maternal mortality ratio by 50% by year 2012 and promotion of healthy life styles.

GOI is planning a Vector Borne Disease Control Project (VBDCP), to be funded by the World Bank, as a nation-wide program within the overall framework of the NRHM over a period of five years. The project development objective is to: (a) increase the number of people benefiting from effective prevention, diagnosis and treatment services for malaria and other vector-borne diseases; and (b) strengthen central and state capacities for evidence based policy development, strategic planning, and program management for effective control of vector-borne diseases. The project would have two components: (i) Improving Access and Use of Services for Control of Malaria and Elimination of Kala-azar, and (ii) Policy and Strategy Development, Capacity Building and Monitoring and Evaluation.

It is foreseen that the implementation of the project will not have any adverse social impact on any group including those who belong to Scheduled Tribes. The project does not involve any land acquisition, use of forests or rehabilitation of land. All infrastructure development under the project will take place within the existing government activities. A Social and Beneficiary Assessment (SABA) of groups who live in predominantly tribal areas has been undertaken with a view to facilitate and ensure their free, prior and informed participation all through the project cycle and also to have a clearer understanding of various social, economic, cultural and health factors that help or hinder their accessing various components and activities under the project. The IPDP, as well as the Indigenous Peoples Planning Framework (IPPF) have been prepared based on the findings of the SABA, and these will form the basis for the preparation of districtwise plans for indigenous peoples access to VBDCP.

COVERAGE OF THE IPDP

The tribal population of the country, as per the 2001 Census, is 84.3 million, constituting 8.2% of the total population. The population of tribes had grown at the rate of 24.45% during the period 1991-2001. This is slightly more than the decadal growth rate of 22.66% for the nation as a whole. More than half the Scheduled Tribe (ST) population is concentrated in the States of Madhya Pradesh, Chhattisgarh, Maharashtra, Orissa, Jharkhand and Gujarat.

The terms.indigenous peoples., indigenous ethnic minorities, tribal groups, and.scheduled tribes. describe social groups with a social and cultural identity distinct from the dominant society that makes them vulnerable to being disadvantaged in the development process. By definition, IP refers to peoples living in an area within a nation-state, prior to the formation of a nation-state, but who do not identify with the dominant nation. This group has social, cultural, economic, and political traditions and institutions distinct from the mainstream or dominant society and culture. In India, IP with similar cultural characteristics are known as.Adivasis. in Hindi and are recognized as STs.

As per the Census 2001, STs constitute roughly 8.2% of India.s total population and the Indian Constitution has recognized about 573 communities as STs, which confers entitlements to affirmative action programs. However, the majority of tribal communities continue to be vulnerable even today in comparison to the general population and this is reflected in the socio economic realities and problems of these groups; 45.86% STs in rural areas having been categorized as living below the poverty line (BPL) and 34.75% in urban areas in 1999-2000. The Fifth Schedule of the Indian Constitution designates.Scheduled Areas. where more than 50% of the population is tribal. The Fifth Schedule covers Tribal areas in 9 states of India namely Andhra Pradesh, Jharkhand, Gujarat, Himachal Pradesh, Maharashtra, Madhya Pradesh, Chhattisgarh, Orissa and Rajasthan. The notified tribal districts of the country under Fifth Schedule are indicated below. It is noted that Bihar, Karnataka and West Bengal are not covered under this schedule.

Of all reported malaria cases in India during 2005, about 90% were in 11 states: Orissa, 22%; Jharkhand, 11%; Chhattisgarh, 10%; West Bengal, 10%; Gujarat, 10%; Madhya Pradesh, 6%; Uttar Pradesh, 6%; Karnataka, 5%; Assam, 4%; Rajasthan, 3% and Maharashtra, 3%. Practically all cases of Kala-azar reported in 2005 are from three states: Bihar, 70%; Jharkhand, 21%; and West Bengal, 9%. The 200 districts to be covered by the project include all of the above districts, as well as additional districts in these and other states with high endemicity of malaria and kalaazar. These 200 districts are in addition to the districts already covered by the GFATM.

ISSUES IN TRIBAL HEALTH

The SABA identified several important constraints to health seeking behavior amongst tribals. These include:

Inadequate Access to Services

There are delays that occur at various stages in the process of diagnosis and treatment of VBDs. The first is the delay in accessing appropriate care for the treatment of malaria. In many places fever cases do not reach a proper health care facility because of access problems. The patient will often be treated by a less than fully qualified practitioner who does not have access to chloroquine or other drugs for VBDs. The second delay is with regard to diagnosis of VBDs. This has to be done by a trained laboratory technician. When there is no facility for blood smear collection and transportation to the laboratory, delays occur. The third delay is in the commencement of radical treatment. This delay is due to factors like non-availability of personnel. Even after the blood smear is found to be positive, radical treatment is delayed because of delay in communicating to the patient or non-availability of medicine at the local level. In order to reduce the mortality due to malaria all these delays will have to be reduced to the minimum. The stipulation of radical treatment within 72 hours will be a challenge in the tribal setting.

Inaccessibility of health services due to difficult terrain or economic costs of seeking care are a major cause for the outbreak of malaria epidemics in tribal areas. The SABA assessed the various health facilities or providers available and accessed by tribals, their physical distance from the patients and the preferences of the patients while choosing between various services. It was found that tribals ranked government hospitals and health centres first as a source of care due to easy accessibility, availability of free services, as well as the belief that allopathic medicines work quickly and are thus effective. Malaria workers, pharmacists and village doctors were ranked second to fourth due to their availability. Female health workers and AWWs came next, followed by mission hospitals, vaidyas, and faith healers. Due to the high cost of treatment, private doctors were ranked the lowest. The distance and travel time between the hamlets and the testing centres was also an issue in certain sample villages, causing delay in collecting, transporting and testing the slides.

The focus group discussions with tribal communities undertaken during the survey revealed that, on an average, over one third of the respondents sought treatment of malaria during the first day of the illness while another one third within two days. It was also noted that spending time for treatment of ailments of self or family members means loss of income for the day for tribal communities and unless they are bed-ridden, the diseases are not taken seriously. It was observed that over 20% of respondents did not know the interval between the onset of malaria and taking treatment. Only around 10% of the respondents took traditional medicines for treatment of malaria. It was observed that the tribal communities are not always in favour of spraying inside the houses. Only around 10-15% of the respondents reported usage of nets and meshes in their homes. About 35% of surveyed villages in Madhya Pradesh and 65% of surveyed villages in Chattisgarh reported usage of bed nets provided by Government. The bed nets were provided at a cost to the community households @ Rs 10/-(BPL families) and Rs 20/-(APL families) and free for very poor families. In some villages, tribal communities reported little usage of bed nets. The purchase of bed nets from private sources was also reported. Bed nets were provided by the Forest Department and panchayats, in addition to regular governmental supplies through NVBDCP. Use of mosquito coil was noted to be less prevalent compared to smoke as a means of prevention of mosquitoes. No method was being used by over 30% of the respondents. Over 20% of the respondents slept outside their homes. There was a direct association between the sleeping habits and the literacy status of the respondents.

The majority of the community members stated that the health workers do not generally visit their homes. A sizeable proportion of the respondents (around 75%) indicated that insecticidal spray was not used in their area during the last one year. Only about 10-15% of the respondents indicated that they had their houses sprayed. Foul smell, respiratory problems and discomfort, lack of confidence in the usefulness of DDT as well as absence of advance information were cited as the reasons for not getting their homes sprayed. Around one third of the respondents indicated that they had their blood slides made with the onset of fever. Significantly, many indicated that they did not know the results of blood slide examination. No respondent could specify the type of parasite. P. Vivax or P.Falciparum. A small percentage of the respondents stated that they use impregnated nets. Majority of them got their nets from the government. A sizeable proportion of respondents claimed that they did not get free or subsidized impregnated nets from the government. A few reported purchasing the nets from private sources. It is found out that only people of the upper class and middle class use bed nets. Malaria workers believe that even if bed nets are freely distributed, unless serious promotional activities are taken up through NGOs, tribals may not use bed nets properly. Ready availability of medicated nets as well as availability of drugs through governmental sources are important given that the average monthly income of majority of respondents in the tribal communities visited was less than Rs 2000. The existing policy of free treatment for Early Detection and Prompt Treatment (EDPT) must be publicized and strictly adhered to.

Role of NGOs: The role of the NGOs is found to be minimal and insignificant in the sample villages covered in Madhya Pradesh and Chhattisgarh as well as in Andhra Pradesh and Orissa. Efforts are being made in Orissa to involve NGOs on a large scale including their association at PHC/DDC/FTD level. Integrated Tribal Development Agency, Andhra Pradesh has deployed four mobile medical clinics to extend VBD related services for isolated areas together with payment of honorarium to community health workers in inaccessible areas. The role of NGOs in anti malaria work is limited to participation in malaria month. There is no significant role observed of NGOs in preventive measures of VBDs like establishing, maintaining and distribution of larvivorous fish. The State Programme officials will need to motivate NGOs to get involved in areas like IEC, and working with volunteers and community and provision of financial resources for civil society engagement should be integrated into the project design. Field based data from the private/NGO sector should be incorporated into the District/State MIS. By and large, provision of VBD related services through hospital/mobile services by NGOs have not taken root in the states under coverage, except to some degree in Andhra Pradesh. There is a significant potential for involvement of mission/ faith based hospitals in the prevention and control of VBDs which at present is not extensive.

Poor Service Delivery

Inadequate Indoor Residual Spraying: Focal spraying is done based on incidence. But often spraying is delayed due to lack of money available to pay the spray workers at the PHC level. While indoor residual spraying is undertaken by health officials in some villages, coverage was variable and ranged from 30-80% of households in sample villages. Indoor residual spraying is not regular, and was not undertaken at all in as many as 50% of the villages during the last 1-2 years or more. Further, due to lack of advance communication of residual spraying, many households are not able to avail of spraying when it is undertaken in their village. Instead, tribal households resort to fumigation of neem leaves, bed nets and fogging, temofas/ganbusia spray and kerosene spray to control mosquito breeding. In addition, when a blood smear is found to be positive in a village, there is no effort to spray immediately. As per the guidelines, 400 square meter surrounding the house where the positive case is identified is to be sprayed. This is not always followed. Further, diagnosis takes more than 3 days and hence the disease can spread to other households. The tribal community members expressed speedier systems and better levels of service.

Non-Availability of Government Health Workers: ANM and/or AWW and/or MLV/Mitanins/MPW were reported to be available in majority of the villages covered under the survey. However, state-level data indicates that there is a shortage of MPWs as compared to the sanctioned strength in all the states included under the project. Overburden of work due to allotment of excess population was cited by most of them as the reason for MPWs to be irregular in their domiciliary visits. During FGDs, it was revealed that MPWs not only collect blood slides but give treatment as well in case of fever. Only a small proportion refers the cases to doctors without giving treatment. Nearly half of the community respondents revealed that MPWs did nothing to educate the people regarding illness (similar situation reported to exist with DDC/ FTD holders) and express their need for assistance on this issue. The ANM was reported to visit weekly in some cases but only monthly in others; in some villages, the ANM lived in the village itself. However, several of the villages included in the study reported the absence of a sub-center. In any case, with the caseload of the Reproductive and Child Health (RCH) project being high, it would not be realistic to expect the ANM to contribute significantly to the VBDCP. This causes a backlog of slides at the village level, leading to delays in diagnosis. The proposal to establish additional Fever Treatment Depots (FTDs) in remote/ inaccessible areas needs to ensure that they are effective in terms of collection of blood smears, administration of presumptive treatment, impregnation of bed nets, promotion of larvivorous fish etc. FGDs revealed that the tribals did not have a positive perception of the government health workers attitude to the mitigation, treatment and containment of VBDs in their villages. Though the Anganwadi Workers are given malaria drugs, they are not much interested in distributing these drugs because their main function is to take care of maternal and child health care. The PHCs function as dispensaries, where doctors are often appointed on contract basis. They are not actively involved in work related to malaria and other VBDs in the community. The priority programs of the PHC are immunization, family planning and tuberculosis. Only treatment of reported cases takes place at the PHC. Fever clinics and fever detection camps are not regularly planned and conducted, particularly during the monsoon months.

Inadequate number of laboratory technicians in PHCs: Though the position of laboratory technician exists in all the PHCs of sample villages, many positions had not been filled. In many PHCs, the services of the laboratory technician are available only for a few days of the week, as the technician has to take care of two or more PHCs. This also has led to delay in blood smear examination, diagnosis and treatment of malaria. In the absence of laboratory technician, the government may consider supply of rapid diagnostic kits to PHC to maintain the tempo of surveillance. There is currently a 5-7 day gap in some areas between taking of blood smear and reporting of results.

Ineffective surveillance: State data shows that active surveillance work is not effectively being undertaken as it was noted that most of the slides were collected from the patients who visited the sub-centre or PHC. There is a potential to strengthen the network from grassroots to institutions at state to gather information about outbreaks.

Lack of Demand for Services

FGDs with tribal community members conducted in sample villages in Madhya Pradesh and Chhattisgarh reveal that a sizeable fraction of the respondents were not aware of the causes, signs and symptoms of VBDs including malaria, breeding and resting habits of mosquitoes and usefulness of insecticidal spray. Most respondents fever as a symptom of malaria, as well as chills and rigor. Headache, weakness, vomiting, body ache and loss of appetite were also cited as symptoms of malaria. Enlargement of spleen during malaria was not known to the respondents. About 15% had no knowledge about even any one symptom of malaria. In particular, knowledge of the symptoms for other VBDs under the program is poor amongst tribals. Women were less aware of the signs and symptoms of VBDs compared to men; and awareness also varied with educational status. Majority of the respondents were aware that VBDs, including malaria, are spread by mosquitoes. Some respondents attributed spread of VBDs and particularly malaria to drinking contaminated water and contaminated food. Around 15% of the tribal respondents had no knowledge about the method of spread of malaria. The spread of malaria through blood transfusion was not known to the respondents.

Regarding the breeding of mosquitoes, about 50% were aware that mosquitoes lay eggs in dirty water while around 25% thought the mosquitoes lay eggs in any water collection while some thought they lay eggs in vegetation. The majority of respondents were in favour of drainage of water collection and removal of water collection to prevent the breeding of mosquitoes. The tribal population preferred the use of smoke for prevention of breeding of mosquitoes. Use of oils in drains was considered as an option by around 25% of the respondents.

Majority of the respondents knew about insecticidal spray and coils for killing mosquitoes. However, awareness of impregnated nets and their availability through governmental sources was not high. About 25% of tribal respondents were ignorant of the methods of diagnosing malaria and more than 75% about any diagnostic method for other VBDs. Use of blood slides for malaria diagnosis was known to around half of the respondents. This was largely influenced by the educational status and gender of respondents. Around 20% of the respondents were aware of chloroquin while the rest were not aware of choloroquin for treatment of malaria.

The awareness was low among illiterates and women. The awareness of the names of insecticides was observed to be low. DDT was the most common insecticide named by the respondents. The awareness of DDT, BHC, Malathion and commercial sprays was dependent on the educational status of respondents. ANM/AWW and doctors were cited to be the most common source of knowledge about malaria. This was followed by family members and to some extent by radio/TV.

Significantly, a sizeable portion of respondents did not cite newspapers or posters etc as sources of knowledge. Most respondents felt that malaria and other VBDs were not an everyday illness and that it was not self limiting that requires no treatment. Sizeable proportion of respondents agreed that insecticides used against malaria are effective. While some respondents were willing to get their houses sprayed, significant proportion of tribal respondents did not give an affirmative response. The general response to chloroquin as an effective medicine for malaria treatment was positive. Many respondents were not aware of other alternative drugs such as quinine and primaquine. There is also unfamiliarity with respect to the dosage and the treatment regimen. A significant proportion of respondents felt that VBDs including malaria should be treated even if the person has to buy prescribed medicine. Most of the respondents reported taking treatment in the event of malaria. However, knowledge of other VBDs was limited. The most common source for taking treatment of malaria was Health Centres and hospitals followed by qualified medical practitioners. Drug Distribution Centres (DDCs) and FTDs were the sources of treatment in a very small fraction of the respondents.

Despite low levels of awareness of the symptoms and treatment for VBDs, about 50% of the community members in the sample villages covered in Madhya Pradesh & Chhattisgarh expressed their willingness to pay for the medically treated bed nets, if supplied by the Government. There is no evidence of significant social marketing activity in the sample villages of four states covered in respect of stimulating the demand for drugs, ITNs and VBD related services in any of the four states covered during the study. Radical treatment is immediately started only in passive cases reported to PHCs. The doctors reported non-compliance of treatment regimen, with tribals taking low dosage and resorting to local herbal medicines. All these factors adversely affect the control of VBDs. There is a need for greater dissemination of information about the DDC/FTDs for treatment of fever and measures to instill confidence in them. IEC implementation strategies should be designed to align with the social and cultural setting of tribal communities for greater effectiveness.

Lack of Consultation

Community participation in the program is still very weak. The grassroots level functionaries are not equipped to involve the community in program planning and implementation. For example, when anti-malaria campaigns are organized at the village level, community members do participate. However, as many as 8 villages out of 20 sample villages (40%) in Madhya Pradesh reported that there was no anti-malaria campaign undertaken in their villages for a considerable time. Around 50% of the sample villages covered in Chhattisgarh did not have anti-malaria campaigns. Village health committees are already envisaged under NRHM and with the help of local NGOs/CBOs including faith based organizations, communities need to mobilized and involved in the planning and implementation of VBD control programs.

GOI has made efforts to motivate volunteers at the village level to run FTDs and DDCs. However, there is continual attrition of these volunteers as there is no provision for incentives for them to keep their interest alive. There is a need for constant interaction with the volunteers to upgrade their knowledge as well as recognition of their services, to enhance a sense of ownership of the program.

OBJECTIVES OF IPDP

The objectives of IPDP are as follows:

- Ensure that tribal/ST people affected by any subproject will benefit from the subprojects;
- Ensure tribal inclusion in the entire process of planning, implementation and monitoring of the subprojects;
- Ensure that the benefits of the subprojects are available to STs more than or at least at par with other affected groups
- Provide a base for the tribal groups in the area to receive adequate development focus and attention.

Consultation with Tribal Groups

Tribal groups/IP were consulted during the preparation of the IPDP (details provided in the SABA). They were informed of the mitigation measures proposed and their views were taken into account in finalizing the plan. The consultation was primarily in the form of focus group discussions with tribal communities in sample villages apart from special consultations with tribal women & children as well as local health functionaries, NGOs and community based organizations such as SHGs/Mahila Mandals, PRIs etc active in the project area and working on public health related programs/issues/campaigns. These discussions were coordinated and facilitated through mobilization of stakeholders and participation by the health officials of District Program Offices of NVBDCP. The wide ranging issues raised during the consultations were based on the check-list developed as a detailed questionnaire. The inputs elicited were both open ended and close ended. Ranking methods were used for qualitative assessment of responses related to certain issues. Following this, an analysis was conducted of the Strengths, Weaknesses, Opportunities and Threats (SWOT) faced by tribals when accessing health care. Key measures that were considered necessary to ensure that indigenous peoples receive social and economic benefits under the project are described as follows.

Action Plan for the IPDP

A range of interventions aimed at enhancing demand for VBD control services in tribal areas has been planned under the VBDCP. These interventions would address the social and economic constraints to health seeking behavior at the household and community level; as well as address some of the issues associated with limited access to services.

Increased Access to Services

There are several strategies for increasing access to health care services for tribals:

Public-Private Partnership (PPP): Private sector is not involved significantly in the control of malaria and other vector borne diseases. Currently, the Government is not trying to rope in the private sector in VBD prevention and control. There is a great deal of scope for expanding PPPs, as has been successfully demonstrated in many other centrally sponsored programs, such as the National Blindness Control Program and the Revised National TB Control Program. Several initiatives have been incorporated into the project: (i) networking with Registered Medical Practitioners and private clinics for sharing reports of malaria incidence and deaths to enhance accurate surveillance and response, particularly in tribal areas where availability of services through the government sector is poor; and (ii) organization of camps through public/private/NGO partnerships for the treatment of community owned bednets.

Involvement of faith healers/traditional healers and other informal service providers (ISPs) in whom the tribals have faith in the VBDCP is one way of increasing access to services. The ISPs need to be made aware of the correct practices for diagnosis and treatment measures being pursued by the Government, through well-designed short courses and sensitization programs, as well as appropriately designed IEC, in order that they are well versed with the magnitude of VBD prevalence and the treatment regimen. Reporting arrangements need to be developed so that ISPs can report the number of cases diagnosed and treated on a regular basis to the VBDCP; treatment kits would be distributed to them;

and referral arrangements will be worked out and communicated to the ISP in cases which do not respond to the accepted treatment regimen. Such strategies would be integrated into the overall BCC strategy for the project.

IMPROVED SERVICE DELIVERY

Increased availability of Staff: The project would enhance availability of staff at the state and district levels for specific skills such as BCC, financial management, procurement and M&E. In addition, it is proposed that vacant positions are filled with contractual staff in order to increase ove rall availability of service providers.

Shift from Target Based Approach to Need Based Approach: States practice a target based approach in blood slide collection, examination and treatment based on population figures. The migration figures are not taken into account and many times it is noticed that tribal population moves to nearby districts as daily wage labourers. Instead of a target being set up in the beginning of the year, it should be need based and the high risk districts should be identified and a clear cut special plan should therefore be developed in advance for implementation. The project would enhance the correct diagnosis and complete radical treatment of malaria in tribal and other project areas. Access to early diagnosis of PF based on RDKs will be implemented in 43 districts in the first year (many of these are tribal districts), an additional 105 in the second year and in all the 200 districts in the third year. Each district will be stratified according to the risk of PF malaria. In PHC blocks with SFR >= 2%, all fever patients will have an RDK for PF, except if a microscopy result can be available within 24 hours. In other PHC blocks an RDK will only be taken for patients at high risk. This selective use of RDKs will optimize cost-effectiveness.

Enhanced Demand

Social Mobilization Strategies: Efforts need to be made to include tribal communities while planning and implementing the VBDCP through appropriate social mobilization strategies. Women.s groups, including women.s health societies, local voluntary organizations and panchayat health committees should be encouraged to support local level VBD control programs in various ways. During the malaria month, PRIs should be involved in covering water collection areas and spraying activities. They should also be facilitated to support publicity initiatives for VBD control. Empanelment of NGOs active in health sector should be the basis for formulating a strategy at state and district levels for their continued involvement.

This should be a strategy rather than intermittent and ad hoc arrangements of their association in the VBD control program. All facilities within the framework should follow uniform reporting system and referral system. Outsourcing/franchising of discrete services (such as diagnostics) to NGOs/Private Sector should be explored. This will also include impact evaluation studies by an independent agency (to be hired as per set norms of the World Bank/WHO) to monitor behavior change in the community regarding use of ITNs, larvivorous fish, etc.

Social Marketing: Social marketing can play a lead behavior change role among high risk and vulnerable groups through provision of improved VBD services and promotion of better treatment seeking behavior; provision and promotion of high quality, targeted facilities in concert with targeted communication intervention.

The operational strategies should address certain critical issues: In order to expand the market in rural areas and urban slums, Social Marketing Organizations (SMOs) should be allowed to use government rural health infrastructure and other channels like ICDS, in addition to their own private distribution networks. Participation of the private sector should be promoted and publicprivate partnership should be encouraged at all levels, for a wider distribution of social marketing products. Participation of private health providers in the delivery of standard preventive services should be solicited, using commercial franchising techniques.

Government subsidies should gradually decrease for urban markets and non-essential products, so that public subsidy is targeted on the development of new markets (rural areas) and support of priority products. Specific interventions and free distribution should be designed for low-income (e.g. urban slums) and high-risks groups. Benchmarking funding and performance monitoring and evaluation mechanisms should be introduced. An ethics code for social marketing will also need to be developed and repression measures proposed to ban unfair marketing practices.

The SMO needs to ensure that people get the products and services that they need for basic and essential health care including prevention and control of VBDs, at reasonable cost to themselves, and to the Government. The SMO should not remain confined to the urban and peri-urban areas, but must reach out quickly and massively to rural households. Subsidies should be re-directed accordingly.

Behavior Change Communication: The project would strengthen capacity to plan and implement effective BCC/IEC. While doing so, several issues need to be addressed: (i) IEC material meant for tribal villages should not only be in the local language but should be prominently written in tribal dialect with emphasis on pictorial depiction to increase the visual impact of the campaigns to the target groups; (ii) local media such as wall writings, wall paintings and folk media should also be used. Generally, public announcements, drama/street plays/puppet shows, hospital and village meetings, health melas, songs etc could be a better means of communication for IEC than print media in view of the low literacy levels. These campaigns should keep in view the culturally and socially appropriate methods and traditional practices and beliefs of tribals which vary from place to place and community to community even within a given geographic region. It is noted that Mahila Mandals and religious ceremonies can be a media for carrying the IEC messages related to VBDs; (iii) there is a need to improve the outreach to the tribal communities through IEC with benchmarked activities and achievements with periodical assessment of their effectiveness. The periodic household surveys planned under the project would provide key information regarding changes in KAP with regard to VBDs.

School health programs and health education in schools may also be emphasized for prevention of VBDs in tribal districts not withstanding the low literacy rates, with children used as a resource in health education. Children may also be involved to throw larvivorous fish bags into water collection points. School children may be developed as.health volunteers working as neighborhood. Swyasthya Prahari.-through Child to Child approach.

Increased Community Participation

To augment community participation in the program: As envisaged under NRHM, several activities are aimed at increasing community participation in health programs. These include: activation of the Village Health Committees and involvement of a greater number of stakeholders particularly women and those from marginalized communities; appointing and training a woman from the community. Accredited Social Health Activist (ASHA), to play a key role in mobilizing people and supporting village health planning and action; enabling support to ASHA from the ANM, AWW, and village based functionaries of other departments; involvement of the ANM in village planning process made possible by provision of an additional worker at the sub-center. all these initiatives would contribute towards enhancing community participation.

Such a strategy has been used effectively in many countries facing endemic vector borne diseases. In Puerto Rico, for example, the use of community reporting has greatly enhanced the effectiveness of surveillance. The objective of the program was to change the public's perception about dengue and make them understand that it is an important and potentially fatal disease. The program sought to make the public understand that most transmission occurs in and around the home by a mosquito, that is there because of their bad habits, that the disease can be prevented, but that the ultimate responsibility for preventíon and control must be theirs, not the governments..

The community must be motivated to accept that responsibility. This "bottom up" approach was supported with community-based program is education. Different ethnographic segments of Puerto Rico were identified and effective methods of communication were developed that would motivate members of the different communities.

For example, a segment on DHF was written into a local television "novella" or "soap opera." Because of the popularity of the novella in Puerto Rico, this was a very powerful educational tool. The program in Puerto Rico has been developed on the assumption that in order to succeed, every segment of society must become involved and accept appropriate responsibility. This includes federal, state or provincial and local government agencies, business groups, civic organizations, youth, community, religious, and medical groups.

***Role of PRIs*:**

- PRIs should be involved in vector control programs such as distribution of larvivorous fishes, spraying operations, treating and distribution of bed-nets.
- Help Desks at PRIs, especially the health and education committees of local panchayat may be encouraged to identify the fever cases and direct them to sub-centres, DDCs, FTDs and malaria link volunteers (MLVs).
- PRIs may be given the responsibility to supervise the MLVs and their honorarium may be routed through them.
- PRIs may take an active role in distributing IEC materials widely in the community.
- PRI should play active role in all the activities during the VBD campaigns i.e. anti-malaria month, anti filarial campaign etc.

Role of community volunteers: In Chhattisgarh, community volunteers from hamlets are selected and trained for malaria work. They play a crucial role at the field level in terms of identifying fever cases, collecting blood samples and providing presumptive treatment. There is a need to review and revamp the current arrangements in this regard. Since the role of male health workers has been integrated with the general health systems it is necessary to enhance the capacity of MLVs for both active and passive surveillance, as required. The ASHA is an additional resource at the community level introduced under the NRHM. This resource can be effectively mobilized to increase outreach of services and IEC at the community level. The role of the ASHA has been spelled out in greater detail in Annex 1.

Inter-Sectoral collaboration: The extent and level of inter-sectoral collaboration is not seen to be coordinated and consistent both at the State and District levels. Through coordination with the Social Welfare Department, AWWs could be trained to identify fever cases and refer them to the ANM or other appropriate functionary for proper diagnosis and radical treatment. In some areas, tribal department is involved in providing facilities like providing space for clinics. Significant improvement in linkages with water and sanitation authorities will be needed to ensure that there is no water logging through public health engineering interventions. PRI are seen to play an important role in IEC, organizing health camps, supporting malaria workers with transport and increasing acceptance for spraying operations.

Gender Dimensions: Gender considerations would be incorporated into project planning and design by ensuring that consultations of the project field staff should include women and, depending on the cultural context, these consultations may have women facilitators consulting with women, separate from men. The household surveys would document changes in health status and health seeking behavior of women. However, due to the operational problems associated with disaggregating routine program data, this will not be undertaken under the NVBDCP.

ACTION PLAN FOR MITIGATION OF POTENTIAL ADVERSE EFFECTS ON INDIGENOUS PEOPLES

Integrated vector control is universally accepted as an effective tool for vector borne disease control program. Among the available vector control methods, chemical control is decisively superior over environmental and biological control strategies that have limited applicability in mitigating sporadic unpredictable outbreaks of vector borne diseases. Deployment of chemical control embraces the whole gamut of strategies, which include indoor residual sprays (IRS), different types of larvicides, insecticide treated nets (ITN) and an ever-lengthening list of household insecticide formulations for personal protection measures. Vector control measures recommended and practiced by the NVBDCP relies largely upon situation-specific chemical control strategies to ensure effective control4. Insecticides belonging to different groups are in use for interventions namely IRS, larvicides and ITN. A major impediment to this program has been the development of insecticide resistance by vector species, which necessitates frequent replacement of the existing insecticides in the control program with new insecticides having adequate human and environmental safety.

National Environmental Engineering Research Institute, Nagpur was commissioned to carry out studies for evaluating impact of indoor residual sprays, used for control of vectors of public health importance, on surrounding environment, including health of people residing in the areas in five states, viz. Mizoram, West Bengal, Karnataka, Haryana and Maharashtra in 2002. The salient findings indicated below point to some of the potential adverse effects of the spraying operations:

- Directorate of NVBDCP uses chlorinated hydrocarbons, organophosphorus compounds and synthetic pyrethroids for control of vectors of public health importance.
- In general, each of the pesticides, before and after spray, has shown impact on both liver and kidney of humans. The cholesterol level has shown abnormal values in both males and females. This might be due to pesticide exposure and its impact on lipid metabolism function of the liver. However, effect of alcoholism and drug intake, which shows variation in biochemical parameters with respect to liver and cholesterol metabolism, can not be ruled out.
- Similarly, serum enzymes, viz. acid phosphatase, alkaline phosphatase, AST, and ALT were noted to deviate from normal ranges after exposure to pesticides. Also, serum urea, creatinine and bilirubin levels showed abnormal concentrations on exposure to pesticides indicates indicating abnormality in either kidney or liver, or both.
- Statistically significant rise in the concentrations of the pesticides has been noticed in the blood, milk, animal tissue and environmental samples collected after the pesticides spray in majority of the cases. About 47% rise in the concentration of DDT was found in breast milk after spray, as compared to the same in blood of the female volunteers
- A few surface water samples did not satisfy the drinking water standards with reference to certain abiotic characteristics like nitrate, total iron, oil & grease and TDS.

In addition, the following issues need to be addressed as part of the mitigation plan:

Drug resistance: A few cases of drug resistance have been reported during the interaction with tribal communities but in view of the lack of verifiable data, it is not clear as to the degree and frequency of drug resistance in the districts covered in Madhya

Pradesh and Chhattisgarh. In Chhattisgarh, the documented chloroquine resistant areas are Wadraftnagar Block of Surguja District, Pondiupроро Block in Korba District, Gariband Block of Raipur District, Pakhanjoor Block of Kanker District.

Research on the particular vector and its bionomics and physiological aspects of resistance to insecticides may need to be undertaken.

In this context, research capacity of entomologists/biologists in the states may also be enhanced. Operational Research studies on drug resistance trends are among the measures advocated. To combat drug resistance in malaria, the NVBDCP drug policy recommends the use of combination therapy i.e Artesunate plus Sulfadoxine Pyrimethamine as a second line of treatment for *P.falcipuram* cases in chloroquine resistant areas.

Health risks from development projects: Health risks from development projects resulting from vector-borne diseases are triggered by development of water resources projects in the vicinity of project villages (such as irrigation and reservoirs). Such developments change the distribution and flow of surface waters, creating a favorable habitat for vector breeding. Human exposure to biting insects or contaminated waters provides the conditions necessary for an increased health risk.

Expensive mitigation measures then take the form of vector control through chemical application. Decisions about such development projects should require a health impact assessment procedure which could help reduce vector populations or prevent exposure. There is a need for interdepartmental coordination on this issue. This procedure, if advocated at the state level and adopted by the relevant interdepartmental agencies, would assist in the forecasting of the vectorborne disease implications of water resources development projects, covering the sub-sectors of irrigated agriculture and multipurpose reservoirs, assists the State Program office to identify:

- the specific vector-borne disease hazards which occur regionally and in different habitats;
- the vulnerable communities; and
- the capabilities of the health service to monitor, safeguard, and mitigate the vector-borne diseases.

Adverse Impact Mitigation Measures

The program will also improve the effectiveness of its vector control component by introducing micro-stratification of districts according to revised national guidelines based on epidemiological, and ecological data, to delimit areas and populations which would be targeted for selected interventions, i.e.IRS or ITNs. Furthermore, the program will systematize insecticide rotation for IRS to lessen the risk of insecticide resistance and ensure the implementation of good pesticide management practices. The use of IRS will be restricted to high risk areas, where ITNs are unacceptable for the population or there is other evidence for superior effectiveness of IRS and for the control of epidemics with a focus on quality and completeness of IRS coverage.

PROJECT MONITORING

Monitoring Arrangements: Monitoring mechanism would be strengthened at various levels.

At the macro level, GIS would be developed to (a) determine the geographical distribution and variation of diseases; (b) analyze spatial and temporal trends of diseases; (c) identify gaps in immunizations; (d) map populations at risk and stratifying risk factors; (e) document community health care needs and assessing resource allocations; (f) forecast epidemics (g) plan and target interventions; (h) monitor diseases and interventions over time; (i) manage patient care environments, materials, supplies and human resources; (j) monitor the utilization of health centres; (k) route health workers, equipments and supplies to service locations; (l) publish health information using maps on the Internet; and (m) locating the nearest health facility.

To maintain the use of effective drugs and get the desired impact, at least five units will monitor the quality of medicines and insecticides at different sites in the country. One unit in each state will be responsible for quality assurance of diagnosis. In addition, there will be an independent inspection agency monitoring the quality of pharmaceuticals by testing random samples.

A set of performance indicators has been agreed as part of the Results Matrix. This will be augmented with service data to be collected regularly from the district level, including in all tribal districts. For monitoring at the community/household level, three household surveys have been planned, of which the baseline has already been completed and for which baseline data is available. For monitoring of tribal patients tribal heads/elected representative may be involved/sensitized. Comparison of the Baseline and end line, process & impact indicators will allow project results and achievements to be measured. The functionaries were of the opinion that it is a difficult task to monitor the community based volunteers; therefore there is a need to strengthen the monitoring mechanism for the community based volunteers. This could be undertaken by PRI, considered to be crucial in the development of monitoring mechanisms as well as in all aspects of project planning and implementation at village level. ANMs should be more actively involved in VBD supervising activities at the village/community level, as well as involved in surveillance operations particularly infants, antenatal and postnatal cases.

Monitoring mechanisms: The monitoring and evaluation mechanisms should include arrangements for the free, prior, and informed consultation with the affected Indigenous Peoples. communities. The proposed project covers all districts included in the Fifth Schedule, and as such, the district-level data generated from routine monitoring as well as from the household surveys would provide adequate information on the impact of project interventions on tribal communities. Routine tracking of key elements of program performance would be undertaken through record keeping, regular reporting, surveillance systems and periodic surveys. A range of indicators has been identified for different reporting levels within the NVBDCP system. At national level, the monitoring efforts should focus on understanding and standardizing population based (including tribal communities) coverage for recommended interventions, through the GIS.

This would be augmented with periodic household surveys to collect data on key indicators, at baseline, mid-term and end-line. This would enable an evaluation of the impact of project interventions. At the state level, where efforts to implement interventions are functional, monitoring of program inputs (human resources, financing), processes (procurements and supplies, training) and outputs (services delivered by the NVBDC program) will be needed for understanding the complete picture of program activities for improved performance.

Management Information System (MIS): The directorate of Anti Malaria Program has recently developed software for MIS. This is a significant achievement for malaria control activities in the country. The software will provide substantial support for planning, surveillance, and monitoring activities of the program. Discussion forums and communication facilities for all users are provided in the website. Data can be analyzed even at sub-center level and one can even prepare maps from the data showing malaria prevalence village-wise which will be useful for early action. It is imperative that this software is installed in all the program states and districts with supportive training. There is a need to put in place mechanisms where in village level workers such as MLVs are actively involved in collecting blood smear samples and the data recorded is sent to PHCs/laboratories and to see that the laboratory technician document the outcome of the test, to ensure the accuracy of the data for MIS. Malaria cases treated in the private sector are not reported. Most of the non-poor fever cases are using the private health care, which go unreported to the government. As a result, not only the magnitude of the problem is unknown but also it affects taking preventive measures such as focal spraying. Therefore, mechanisms need to be evolved for instituting a system of reporting from major institutions in the private health care sector to feed into the MIS. Since malaria is a notifiable disease, the state government may insist on the private sector to report positive cases of malaria to the district health authorities. MIS using GIS at the New Delhi office should be extended to all states, so that village level information is available on the website for decision making as well for learning lessons from other states. The MIS should specifically evolve parameters of community involvement under the program which implies the level of community participation in the planning, implementation and maintenance of health services. Block Coordination Committees and Village Health Committees should be constituted for peripheral level collaboration and undertaking joint action including monitoring and evaluation.

Accessible Procedures to Address Grievances

Tribals have poor access to health services related to VBDs and there is also under utilization of health services owing to social, cultural and economic factors. Some of the problems of accessibility and poor utilization of health services unique to tribal areas are because of difficult terrain and sparsely distributed tribal population in forests and hilly regions; locational disadvantage of sub-centres, PHCs, CHCs; non availability of service providers due to vacant posts and lack of residential facilities; lack of suitable transport facility for quick referral of emergency cases; lack of appropriate HRD policy to encourage/motivate the service providers to work in tribal areas; inadequate mobilization of NGOs; lack of integration with other health programs and other development sectors; IEC activities not tuned to the tribal idioms, beliefs and practices; services not being client friendly in terms of timing, cultural barriers inhibiting utilization; non involvement of the local traditional faith healers and weak monitoring and supervision systems. In light of this, the project will adopt accessible procedures to address grievances through helpdesks at block and district levels. Where possible, such facility could be considered at village panchayat level. This facility would be widely publicized for enhancing access to the services of the project by tribal communities in terms of availing bed nets, medicines, blood slide examination, reporting of VBD cases, IEC material, seeking fumigation services or other biological control methods and for lodging any complaints for redressal. Institution of Village Health Committees with representation of tribal community members is another step in this direction.

Indigenous Peoples Planning Framework (IPPF) for Access to Vector Borne Diseases Control Project

The Indigenous Peoples Planning Framework (IPPF) is intended to guide selection and preparation of additional subprojects under the Program where impacts on tribal people are identified to ensure better distribution of the Program benefits and promote development of the indigenous peoples in the Project areas. The IPPF identifies the policy and procedural requirements together with the screening and planning procedures, which apply to sub-projects, components or investments that are to be approved during loan implementation.

Absorptive Capacity of Tribal Communities: The potential positive effects of such programs or subprojects on Indigenous Peoples are influenced by the absorptive capacity of tribal communities. Absorptive capacity is the capacity of the tribal community groups to reap the benefits from the project and/or adapt to the adverse impacts associated with the project. There are a number of critical factors needed to ensure that the benefits will flow to the people in the project areas. The first important factor is the availability and access to diagnosis and treatment. The second factor is the assured supply of drugs. The third factor is assuring preventive measures in tribal districts and villages. The fourth factor is the creation of awareness and knowledge among tribal communities on the vector borne diseases, prevention measures, symptoms, treatment regime, treatment facilities and program benefits. Unfortunately, the knowledge of the project beneficiaries is very low. In fact, the education level is also very low. restricting the capacity of the beneficiaries to absorb new knowledge and take advantage of the project benefits. It is very important to transfer knowledge to tribal communities as early as possible in the project through improved outreach services including training of local health workers, television, and other education and awareness programs.

Targeting: To ensure benefits flow to the intended tribal community members, robust data will be maintained through a well-designed GIS on the incidence and prevalence of VBDs in tribal areas. This will enable district and state authorities to target interventions based on need, and to bring on board additional support to the program in the form of PPPs with NGOs and other groups. An effective MIS would also enable program managers to track the availability of personnel, drugs and other supplies, and manage their deployment more effectively to meet the needs in areas where outbreaks have occurred.

Use of Insecticides: This project involves the use, storage, transportation, and disposal of insecticides and pesticides in various applications. The management of these insecticides requires stringent and systematic cradle to grave management, otherwise there could be direct environmental and public health implications. The proposed project will finance insecticides for control of malaria and other VBDs. In India the import, manufacture, sale, transport, distribution and use of insecticides is regulated under the Insecticides Act. While it is recognized that DDT is produced in India and is used in the vector control program, the Bank funds are not envisaged to be used for procurement of DDT. DDT use has been banned in the agriculture sector since 1989 and is no longer used in urban areas under the Urban Malaria Scheme (UMS) in favour of pesticides like Malathion and synthetic pyre thyroids. It is still used in rural areas of Madhya Pradesh and Chhattisgarh (and in other States) in indoor spraying applications (IRS) and it is important that appropriate guidance and training on safe handling is provided to the workers. Community awareness and information dissemination will play a key role in ensuring effective, focused and targeted use of DDT. This will require sound management and operational practices on the use and management of insecticides, including DDT, establishment of an institutional framework, capacity building, strengthening of technical guidelines, stringent monitoring of the supply and distribution chain, evaluation of behavioural changes and community awareness and advocacy.

Institutional Arrangements

Institutional arrangements (including capacity building where necessary) for screening projectsupported activities, evaluating their effects on Indigenous Peoples, preparing IPPs, and addressing any grievances.

Community participation, in the program by and large has not been very visible so far. Very few private practitioners were actively involved in the program. Participation of the CBOs/ NGOs was not significant. These aspects need to be looked into through village level mapping of the potential partners in terms of community organizations, private practitioners and NGOs for enhancing effectiveness of NVBDC program implementation through community mobilization and IEC efforts with decentralized funding mechanisms. There is also a need to train health sector personnel in the management and decision-making for integrated vector management which will include formulation of municipality level guidelines for the selection and evaluation of vector control options. Training of especially the grassroots functionaries should emphasize on enhancing counseling and communication skills of the functionaries, as counseling is a major issue for initiation of treatment at the right time and compliance with treatment. Thus there is a need to train them on social mobilization and motivation skills. Training should emphasize on the role of IEC activities.

Monitoring and Reporting Arrangements

Benefits monitoring has been incorporated in the Project Implementation Plan (PIP). The benefits monitoring plan would:

- Identify a few indicators of the achievement of the project output(s), purpose(s), and goal(s) for each component district-wise;
- Assess existing management information systems in terms of their adequacy in guiding the operation of the project for maximum effect;
- Specify indicators to monitor and evaluate the delivery and distribution of benefits to the tribal communities identified, and to identify adjustments required during implementation to meet the needs of tribal community groups more effectively;
- Field review missions to assess social dimensions and associated processes
- Encourage participation by adversely affected groups

An external independent monitoring agency will be engaged by the Directorate of NVBDC Programme to undertake independent external monitoring of the Plan. Reporting/ monitoring formats should be prepared for both internal and external monitoring.

Disclosure Arrangements

The EVBDCP should institute systems for disclosure of arrangements made and the results thereof (updated from time to time) in respect of IPP through appropriate formats for wider dissemination through their website.

4

Tribal Incorporation of First Amendment Norms in India

INTRODUCTION

As American culture becomes more individualistic, social and legal opposition has arisen regarding expansive judicial interpretations of First Amendment freedoms. According to this opposition, the courts have interpreted such freedoms in an almost exclusively individualistic light, with little regard for community interests and values. This debate over individual rights versus social and community interests has been raging for decades in the areas of pornography, crime prevention, and national security. In the case of constitutional protections granted to graphically violent video games, for instance, critics argue that courts should take a more balanced view of First Amendment freedoms, giving greater consideration to community interests in healthy child development and crime prevention, and less consideration to the rights of individual game distributors to sell their products to minors whose parents object to such games.

The First Amendment is a classic expression of the kind of western liberal political thought underlying American constitutional democracy. This political philosophy, in the classic sense, places great emphasis on individual freedom. Consequently, a strictly individualistic view of the First Amendment becomes almost inevitable. However, even within the borders of the United States, an alternate view and application of the First Amendment is emerging.

This article will examine how Indian tribal courts have incorporated First Amendment norms within tribal legal systems.

Given the more traditionally communal nature of tribal societies, Indian tribal courts have taken a slightly different approach to the kind of individual rights articulated in the First Amendment. As this article will demonstrate, tribal courts have elevated community interest and values when considering individual rights issues. Indeed, the ways in which those interests and values have been elevated may prove instructive to those who advocate a more balanced approach to First Amendment freedoms within the U.S. judicial system.

Indian tribes to protect certain individual rights. The article will first examine whether the First Amendment applies to Indian tribes, and then whether and how the Indian Civil Rights Act applies. In Part II, the article will analyze how federal courts have interpreted the Indian Civil Rights Act. Part III will survey Indian tribal court decisions concerning individual rights issues such as free speech, free press, and free exercise of religion. In the final part of the article, the analysis will turn away from reported tribal court decisions and focus on tribal political, social, and cultural issues relating to First Amendment-type rights. In this respect, the article will focus exclusively on the nine tribes of South Dakota, exploring how First Amendment-type issues have arisen within those tribes and how they have been resolved outside of the judicial system.

THE APPLICABILITY OF THE FIRST AMENDMENT TO INDIAN TRIBES

General Constitutional Applicability

The First Amendment to the United States Constitution states that "Congress shall make no law respecting an establishment of religion, or prohibiting the free exercise thereof; or abridging the freedom of speech, or of the press; or of the people peaceably to assemble, and to petition the Government for a redress of grievances." The question of whether this Amendment applies to Indian tribes depends first on whether the U.S. Constitution in general governs Indian tribes. In a series of cases stretching over more than a century, the Supreme Court has answered this question in the negative.

In Talton v. Mayes, the Court, presented with the issue of whether the Fifth Amendment to the U.S. Constitution applied to local legislation of the Cherokee Nation, recognized that the Amendment acted as a limitation only upon the powers of the national government. The controlling issue was whether the powers exercised by the Indian Tribe are derived from the Federal Constitution, or whether they are local powers not created by the Constitution, and thus not subject to the U.S. Constitution. Based on a long line of precedent, the Talton Court concluded that because tribal governments occupy a "semi-independent position," having exercised local self-government prior to the establishment of the Constitution, they are not subject to the limitations imposed by the Constitution. Thus, the Constitution does not apply to tribal governments when the powers being exercised are not federal powers. Moreover, this principle has been consistently reaffirmed since Talton.

In ruling upon whether the Equal Protection Clause of the Fourteenth Amendment applies to tribal governments, the Court in Santa Clara Pueblo v. Martinez, reiterated that because tribes were "separate sovereigns pre-existing the Constitution, [they] have historically been regarded as unconstrained by those constitutional provisions framed specifically as limitations on federal or state authority."

More recently, the Court in Nevada v. Hicks stated that "it has been understood for more than a century that the Bill of Rights and the Fourteenth Amendment do not of their own force apply to Indian tribes."

Judicial Rulings on First Amendment Applicability

Prior to passage of the Indian Civil Rights Act of 1968, few cases dealt with the specific issue of whether the First Amendment of the Constitution applied to Indian tribes. In Native American Church v. Navajo Tribal Council, the Tenth Circuit addressed the issue of whether an ordinance adopted by the Navajo Tribal Council prohibiting the introduction of, sale, use and possession of peyote in Navajo country violated the First, Fourth and Fifth Amendment rights of the Native American Church of North America and its members. Recognizing previous decisions holding that the unique semi-independent status of Indian tribes prevents the application of the Constitution to the tribal governing bodies, the court stated that "[i]t follows that the Federal courts are without jurisdiction over matters involving purely penal ordinances passed by the Navajo legislative body for the regulation of life on the reservation." Specifically referring to the First Amendment, the court acknowledged that the Amendment "applies only to Congress" and is "made applicable to the States only by the Fourteenth Amendment." Therefore, given that "Indian tribes are not states," the First Amendment does not apply to them.

CONGRESSIONAL IMPOSITION OF FIRST AMENDMENT NORMS ON INDIAN TRIBES

The United States Supreme Court and lower federal courts have repeatedly recognized that although tribes have the authority to self-govern when exercising their tribal functions, "all such rights are subject to the supreme legislative authority of the United States." Finding that "tribal members' basic constitutional rights [had] been denied at every level," Congress in 1968 passed the Indian Civil Rights Act (ICRA) as a rider to the Civil Rights Act of 1968. Aside from some notable exceptions, the ICRA follows the Bill of Rights of the U.S. Constitution. These individual rights, although not constitutionally imposed, became applicable to Indian tribes through congressional mandate. According to one scholar, "[t]he central purpose of the ICRA was to apply most of the provisions of the Constitution's Bill of Rights to tribal governments[.]"

THE INDIAN CIVIL RIGHTS ACT

The ICRA is composed of three sections: 1301, which provides definitions for "Indian tribe," "powers of self-government," "Indian court," and "Indian;" 1302, which sets out the constitutional rights protected under the Act; and 1303, which provides the remedy available for violations of the Act.

Section 1302 of the ICRA is known as the Indian Bill of Rights. The first subsection of this section largely parallels the First Amendment to the United States Constitution. In whole, it provides, "[n]o Indian tribe in exercising powers of self-government shall (1) make or enforce any law prohibiting the free exercise of religion, or abridging the freedom of speech, or of the press, or the right of the people peaceably to assemble and to petition for a redress of grievances[.]"

The only specifically-mandated remedy provided by Congress under section 1301 of the ICRA is one of habeas corpus, which "shall be available to any person, in a court of the United States, to test the legality of his detention by order of an Indian tribe." Even though the ICRA provided this limited federal remedy, federal courts initially "found that the ICRA had waived tribal sovereign immunity, and the courts regularly enjoined tribal governments and even awarded damages in ICRA cases." In 1978, however, the Supreme Court abruptly reversed this practice of creating jurisdiction for ICRA claims in federal courts. Declaring that "[t]ribal forums are available to vindicate rights created by the ICRA," Martinez put an end to federal court jurisdiction for ICRA civil violations.

THE GOALS AND PURPOSES OF THE ICRA

Motivating passage of the ICRA was the congressional belief "that the American Indian is the most neglected minority group in the history of this Nation." Seven years before its passage, the Senate Subcommittee on Constitutional Rights undertook an investigation of the legal status of American Indians, particularly "the problems [Indians] encounter when asserting constitutional rights in their relations with State, Federal, and tribal governments." Senator Sam Ervin of North Carolina, the primary sponsor of the legislation, asserted "that the rights of Indians were 'seriously jeopardized by the tribal government's administration of justice,' which he attributed to 'tribal judges' inexperience, lack of training, and unfamiliarity with the traditions and forms of the American legal system.'" The legislative history of the Act expressed "an intent to protect the individual rights of Indians while fostering tribal self-government and cultural identity."

Initially, the drafters of the ICRA envisioned imposing upon Indian tribes "the same limitations and restraints as those which are imposed on the federal government by the United States Constitution." However, this whole scale application of the Bill of Rights inspired much opposition, and eventually "a substitute bill that spelled out in specific terms the rights Indians would possess in their relationships with tribal governments" was offered and enacted.

Even after the ICRA was more narrowly tailored to fit the needs of Indian tribes, it continued to face opposition. As one scholar notes "[t]he ICRA was passed over the objections of many tribal governments, some of which felt the economic burdens of compliance would be too great and others... which felt their own cultural traditions were superior to 'white-man's justice.'" Opponents argued that the Indian Civil Rights Act was an "unnecessary intrusion on tribal sovereignty." In attempting to address these objections, the final version of the Act "indicates that the scope of the individual rights contained therein is to be determined by balancing them against the legitimate interests of the tribe in maintaining the traditional values of their unique governmental and cultural identity."

JUDICIAL INTERPRETATION OF THE ICRA

Pre-Martinez Cases

Soon after passage of the Indian Civil Rights Act, claimants began instituting suits in the federal courts alleging tribal government violations of the rights guaranteed under the Act, but only a couple of these suits involved section 1302(1) of the Act, which guaranteed rights similar to those found in the First Amendment to the U.S. Constitution. The first issue obviously to be settled was one of federal jurisdiction over these claims.

In Dodge v. Nakai (hereinafter Dodge I), the first case involving section 1302(1), the plaintiff brought an ICRA claim against an order removing the plaintiff from the Navajo Indian Reservation. In determining federal jurisdiction under the ICRA, the court concluded that "[b]ecause plaintiffs in this case assert rights purportedly guaranteed to them by [the Indian Civil Rights Act], this action is one arising under the laws of the United States, and this Court has jurisdiction under Title 28 U.S.C. [section] 1331." The court also found jurisdiction under Title 28 U.S.C. section 1343(4), stating that "this Court has original jurisdiction over 'any civil action authorized by law to be commenced by any person... under any Act of Congress providing for the protection of civil rights.'" Consequently, Dodge I found federal jurisdiction to hear the claims under the Civil Rights Act, "despite the failure of plaintiffs to seek redress in the Navajo Tribal Court."

Having settled the jurisdiction issue, the court in Dodge v. Nakai (hereinafter Dodge II) then went on to decide the case on its merits, which involved plaintiff's objection to having been removed from the Navajo Reservation for obnoxiously laughing in response to an Advisory Committee member's question. The court indicated that "[u]nder 25 U.S.C. [section] 1302(1), these individuals possess the right to express views as to the wisdom and propriety of the policies and programs adopted by tribal governmental agencies." It then held that the plaintiff's removal from the Reservation was unlawful under the Indian Civil Rights Act as an abridgment of both the plaintiff's freedom of speech and due process rights.

Federal court jurisdiction over ICRA claims was reaffirmed in Solomon v. LaRose. Dismissing the argument that jurisdiction cannot lie because the only remedy provided under the Act was for habeas relief, the court indicated that "[i]t does not follow that Congress intended [habeas corpus] to be the exclusive jurisdictional basis for enforcement [of the ICRA]. Such a finding would render nugatory the rights secured by provisions (1), (5) and (8) of [section] 1302." The court further explained that since 28 U.S.C. section 1343(4) also provided a jurisdictional basis to bring claims under the ICRA, a special provision within the ICRA was unnecessary.

In Big Eagle v. Andera, asserting jurisdiction over ICRA section 1302 claims, a federal court overturned a tribal disorderly conduct ordinance as vague and overly broad in violation of the ICRA. The court declared that "Indian citizens have the rights of freedom of speech and due process of law; since the enactment of 25 U.S.C. [section] 1302 these rights can be asserted against a tribal government just as any citizen can assert his or her rights against a state or municipal government." This broad recognition of federal court jurisdiction over claims brought under the ICRA, however, was short-lived and came to an end in 1978.

Santa Clara Pueblo v. Martinez

The Supreme Court's first opportunity to interpret the ICRA came in Santa Clara Pueblo v. Martinez. In Martinez, the respondent sought declarative and injunctive relief against the enforcement of "an Indian tribe's ordinance denying membership to the children of certain female tribal members." Because the ICRA did not "expressly authorize the bringing of civil actions for declaratory or injunctive relief to enforce its substantive provisions[,]" the Court had to determine whether such remedies were in fact available under the Act. The Martinez Court first considered the issue of whether the ICRA had waived tribal sovereign immunity for such lawsuits. It recognized that "a waiver of sovereign immunity... must be unequivocally expressed," but that "[n]othing on the face of Title I of the ICRA purports to subject tribes to the jurisdiction of the federal courts in civil actions for injunctive or declaratory relief." Consequently, the Court declared that "suits against the tribe under the ICRA are barred by its sovereign immunity from suit."

The Court then considered whether an action under the ICRA against the tribal officer could be heard in federal court. It recognized that providing a federal forum for such issues would interfere with tribal autonomy and self-government. Further, the Court demonstrated its recognition that

> Subject[ing] a dispute arising on the reservation among reservation Indians to a forum other than the one they have established for themselves, [may] undermine the authority of the tribal cour[T]... AND HENCE... iNfringe [sic] on the right of the indians [sic] to govern themselves.

Therefore, in an effort to prevent the unsettling of a tribal government's ability to maintain order as well as to respect tribal sovereignty and the plenary authority of Congress in this area, the Court refrained from granting federal jurisdiction for claims against tribal officials as well.

The Court further noted that the original ICRA legislation proposed a "de novo review in federal court of all convictions obtained in tribal courts." Such legislation was not adopted due to the harmful effects upon law enforcement within the reservation. According to the Court, the exclusive provisions of habeas corpus as a remedy for claims brought under the Act struck the perfect balance in avoiding unnecessary intrusions on tribal governments. The Court concluded by stating that

> [U]nless and until Congress makes clear its intention to permit the additional intrusion on tribal sovereignty that adjudication of such actions in a federal forum would represent, we are constrained to find that [section] 1302 does not impliedly authorize actions for declaratory or injunctive relief against either the tribe or its officers.

The message was clear: federal courts do not have jurisdiction to hear ICRA claims, unless the remedy sought is one of habeas corpus.

Post-Martinez ICRA Claims

Martinez put a halt to federal court jurisdiction over ICRA claims. Several federal court cases in which non-habeas claims under the ICRA were alleged were summarily dismissed on grounds of the sovereign immunity status of tribal governments. In 1980, however, the Tenth Circuit established the Dry Creek exception, which recognized a federal right of action for civil claims under the ICRA under limited circumstances. For the exception to apply, the plaintiff must demonstrate the following: that the dispute involves a non-Indian party, that a tribal forum is not available, and that the dispute involves an issue falling outside internal tribal affairs. More recently, however, the Tenth Circuit has restricted the holding in Dry Creek Lodge, and other federal courts have altogether refused to apply the Dry Creek exception. Therefore, jurisdiction for ICRA claims pursuing remedies other than habeas relief seemingly lies exclusively within tribal forums. Furthermore, "there is no judicial review and no appeal for tribal government decisions."

TRIBAL COURTS' INTERPRETATIONS OF THE INDIAN CIVIL RIGHTS ACT

Since the passage of the Indian Civil Rights Act, a number of tribal courts have construed the first section of the Indian Bill of Rights, which sets forth guarantees similar to those found in the First Amendment. One scholar who has studied these opinions indicates that, "[h]ere, more than in any other ICRA provision, the tribal courts have struck out on their own to develop ICRA doctrines that are independent of the federal case law." According to Professor Rosen, tribal courts have not applied the ICRA to tribal governments in the same way that federal courts have applied the First Amendment to state and federal governments. Under the ICRA, "tribal members do not have those same rights in their relationship to respective tribal governments" as do U.S. citizens regarding their state and federal governments. This is because "[t]he sovereignty of tribal governments, the perpetuation of the tribal culture and the need for self-government" plays a more important role in tribal courts. For instance, "[w]hile state and federal governments are required to remain neutral on issues involving religion, tribal governments, which are often theocratic, can and do promote religious practices and beliefs to preserve tribal culture."

As Professor Rosen observes, it is a "well-established doctrine that ICRA's statutory terms need not be ascribed the same meaning as their sister terms in the federal Constitution." Therefore, tribes are not required to apply federal constitutional law standards when analyzing claims under the ICRA. According to Professor Fletcher, "[t]he most critical element that tends to guide tribal court analysis of fundamental individual rights is whether the activity at issue is a distinctly Anglo-American construct versus a traditional or cultural construct."

In developing a doctrinal model for how tribal courts apply the ICRA, Professor Rosen has identified five different approaches. The "Tabula Rasa" approach is used when the tribal court "ignore[s] altogether the federal case law and proceed[s] to construe the provision wholly on its own." Under this approach, doctrines completely distinct from existing federal constitutional law doctrine can be applied. Rosen's second approach is "Incorporation," which is further divided into two subdivisions: "Stock Incorporation" and "Fitted Incorporation." This approach is "the polar opposite of Tabula Rasa" because "[u]nder [this approach], the tribal court completely incorporates the federal doctrine to the extent the doctrine has been developed[.]" Stock incorporation occurs, according to Rosen, when the tribal court "adopt[s] the federal case law without explanation." Fitted incorporation, on the other hand, occurs when "tribal courts actively fit the federal doctrine to the tribal context[.]"

The third approach, "Tailoring," is used when the tribal court adopts the federal standard for a particular Constitutional Law issue, but disregards all the precedent that contributed to the standard in its present form. Although the tribal court uses a federal standard, it tailored that standard to the case at hand, disregarding any previously-established factors articulated by the federal courts to apply that standard. Under Rosen's fourth approach, "Re-standardizing," the tribal court adopts the federal court's description of the underlying goal of the standard applied but does not affirmatively adopt the standard, thereby creating a different standard to reach that same goal. Finally, the "Re-Targeting" approach essentially replaces the goal of the federal standard with one that is more indicative of "tribal needs, values, customs, and traditions."

TRIBAL CONSTITUTIONS AND FIRST AMENDMENT TYPE RIGHTS

In a comprehensive review of tribal constitutions and their civil liberty guarantees, Professor Rusco found that twenty-two tribal constitutions had adopted the ICRA word-for-word. In terms of First Amendment-type rights, the majority of tribal constitutions contain a statement that protects, in a general fashion, "freedom of worship, conscience, speech, press, assembly, and association." Of the eighty-eight constitutions considered by Professor Rusco, eighty-five protected the freedom of religion, eighty-eight contained freedom of speech language, fifty-six included freedom of press or to write, eighty-eight protected the freedom of association and/or assembly (which was sometimes qualified with the word "orderly"), and thirty-four recognized the freedom of petition (sometimes specified as redress of grievances).

Professor Rusco also found that aside from the specific references to one or more of these First Amendment rights, "[a] number of provisions on religious freedom obviously were written specifically for the situation of the tribe[,]" as reflected by various references to Native religious beliefs or practices in such provisions. On the other hand, however, some constitutions veered away from the federal example and specifically limited certain freedoms, such as the freedom of expression and freedom of speech.

In a more recent study of tribal constitutions, Professor Carpenter determined that there are

> [A]t least four tribal constitutional approaches to the freedom of religion: (1) constitutions that track or incorporate ICRA, (2) constitutions that do not use ICRA but echo U.S. principles of individual religious freedom, (3) constitutions with unique language on religion, clearly expressing distinct tribal values and norms, and (4) constitutions that do not reference religion or related concepts at all."

Recognizing the differing ways in which federal and tribal courts protect religious liberty, Professor Carpenter argues that it is possible for tribes to "provide individual religious freedoms in ways that reflect tribal norms and enhance sovereignty."

TRIBAL CASE LAW

Freedom of Speech

Tribal court case law on individual rights issues is relatively limited, with the most recent decision that of Barnes v. Mashantucket Pequot Tribal Nation. In Barnes, after being fired by the Mashantucket Pequot Gaming Enterprise, plaintiff brought suit before the Mashantucket Pequot Tribal Court arguing that his termination was retaliatory and violated his freedom of speech. In rejecting this claim, the tribal court resorted to federal case law regarding both the elements of the claim and the standard of proof.

In a somewhat opposite approach, the Ho-Chunk Nation Supreme Court in Brown v. Webster stated that, with respect to a free speech claim, it "is not required to fully adopt the precedents established by the United States Supreme Court as to the United States Constitution. Rather, [it] must rely on the [Ho-Chunk] Nation's laws and perhaps, the Nation's common law or tribal law." The Ho-Chunk Nation Supreme Court chastised the trial court for failing to "look at legal issues in a fair and objective manner in light of tribal law and custom, rather than simply wholesale adopting the laws and precedents of the United States," and for neglecting to recognize "the importance of respect for one's tribe and the goals of that sovereign." Despite this admonition, however, the Ho-Chunk Nation Supreme Court did consider certain state court precedents deemed to be consistent with Ho-Chunk values. In LaPorte v. Fletcher, the Little River Band of Ottawa Indians Tribal Court rejected a free speech challenge to an employee's demotion from chief of police and to a tribal statute prohibiting employees from making certain statements to the media. Relying on federal case law precedent, the tribal court upheld the statute and allowed the demotion.

The Sisseton-Wahpeton Oyate Court entertained in Flute v. Labelle a defamation action in which an elected tribal leader sued the author of an unflattering letter to the editor. To determine whether the elements of libel were met, the tribal court applied federal and South Dakota constitutional law, and concluded that the defendant was liable for libel. In addition to granting nominal damages, the court also required the defendant to "write a retraction letter to the Tribal newspaper correcting the false impression she left with readers." Thus, although the court applied both federal and state common law to determine whether the elements of the cause of action were met, it "applied that law to fashion a tribe-specific remedy that severely limited the defendant's liability."

An appeal from a Hopi tribal order to exclude plaintiff from the reservation was heard in Monestersky v. Hopi Tribe by the Hopi Appellate Court. Holding that the tribe has the right to exclude members from the reservation, the court nonetheless indicated that a free speech claim was also implicated in plaintiff's exclusion from the reservation. In dismissing this claim, however, the court declared that "[i]t is well-settled that free speech is not absolute; for instance, one may not shout "fire" in a crowded theater, or engage in speech to incite violence."

In Fletcher v. Mashantucket Pequot Tribe, the Mashantucket Pequot Tribal Courtstrictly adhered to the language in the first subsection of section 1302 of the ICRA, which states, in pertinent part, that: "'No Indian tribe in exercising powers of self-government shall—(1) make or enforce any law... abridging the freedom of speech.'" In Fletcher, the plaintiff alleged that his employer interfered with his right to speak freely on matters of public concern by terminating him for trying to publish a book portraying life within the world's wealthiest Indian tribe as being "riddled with greed, racism and favoritism that is tearing itself apart." The court found the plaintiff's termination was not carried out through a promulgation or enforcement of any law, and that the ICRA did not apply.

A free speech issue in the context of an alleged retaliation occurred in Navajo Nation v. Crockett, where plaintiffs, who were employees of the Navajo Agricultural Products Industry (NAPI), claimed a free speech violation after being terminated for informing the Economic Development Committee of the Navajo Nation Council of possible NAPI mismanagement and misconduct. The Navajo Nation Supreme Court stated that "Navajo common law is the law of preference in the courts of the Navajo Nation[,]" and this is the law to be applied when adjudicating the plaintiff's free speech claim. The court acknowledged that "an individual has a fundamental right to express his or her mind by way of the spoken word and/or actions," but then limited this right by noting: "As a matter of Navajo tradition and custom, people speak with caution and respect, choosing their words carefully to avoid harm to others. This is nothing more than freedom with responsibility, a fundamental Navajo traditional principle."

Discussing how Navajo culture limited free speech rights, the court highlighted the ways in which individual rights were to be balanced against community interests and values: "For example, on some occasions, a person is prohibited from making certain statements, and some statements of reciting oral traditions are prohibited during specific times of the year." According to the court, "speech should be delivered with respect and honesty." In the employment context, pursuant to the Navajo tradition, the court stated that it is only appropriate to speak directly to one's supervisor if the employee has a complaint or problem with that supervisor. Moreover, the court stated:

> [U]nder the Navajo common law concept of nalyeeh, the employee should not seek to correct the person by summoning the coercive powers of a powerful person or entity, but should seek to correct the wrongful action by "talking things out." The employee should not seek a remedy from a stranger, but should rather explain the problem to the person or one of his or her relatives and ask that "things be put right."

Regarding the specific facts of the case in issue, the court explained that when an employee is bringing certain issues to management's attention, the employee shall abide by a few limitations: primarily, "[t]he employee must be respectful in his or her approach, and an initial inquiry with management to 'talk things out' is encouraged[;]" and if the employee provides a statement to a government committee, "the speech [and any documents provided] must involve matters of public concern and fall within the oversight authority of the committee."

Despite recognizing all these limitations on free speech rights under Navajo law, the court found that plaintiffs' speech was a matter of public concern, that they were speaking before an official body of the Navajo Nation Council, and that "NAPI's interest in promoting the efficiency of the public services it performs through its employees [is not outweighed by] the employees' right to free speech." The court then held that plaintiffs' free speech rights had been violated by NAPI. In its opinion, the court went to great lengths discussing the tribal cultural limitations placed on one's free speech rights; never once did the court cite to a federal case on the issue.

On the other hand, federal constitutional law was relied upon exclusively in Rave v. Reynolds, in which the court chose to "apply intermediate scrutiny where the tribe imposed nondiscriminatory restrictions on candidate eligibility" in an effort to prevent a "chaotic tribal caucus process." The tribal court struck down a tribal law limiting tribal members' attendance to only one electoral caucus, relying on two U.S. Supreme Court cases dealing with freedom of association in the national electoral context. On appeal, the tribal supreme court suggested that tribal law or community interests might preclude the application of federal constitutional law, "but no party chose to assert [such] alternative authority." After comparing the similarities between the tribal constitution's language and the First Amendment language, the tribal supreme court "adopted the federal 'sliding scale of scrutiny in election rights cases involving the right of political association depending on whether the election regulations in question severely burden political association rights or merely constitute 'reasonable nondiscriminatory restrictions.'" Applying the intermediate scrutiny standard, the court stated that the tribe had the burden of proving "an important governmental interest to justify the tribal statute." However, after finding that the purpose of the statute was to avoid a disorderly election process and that "voters could still write-in the candidate removed from the ballet," the court upheld the constitutionality of the statute. In doing so, "[t]he tribal court adopted federal constitutional law as an analog but recognized the particular tribal election circumstances that provided the requisite important governmental interest."

In Hopi Tribe v. Lonewolf Scott, the Hopi Tribal Court addressed a free speech claim by an individual who had been charged with injury to public property for unearthing part of the

Hopi-Navajo fence during a protest. The defendant argued that the charges should be dismissed for being unconstitutionally vague and overbroad, and because "the act of physically assaulting Hopi public property is conduct that is essentially protected activity." After holding that the statute was not facially vague, the court turned to the protected activity argument. It stated that this activity had nothing to do with speech, but rather that "defendants' actions constituted civil disobedience that resulted in physical damage[.]" In making this conclusion, the court cited federal case law, ruling that "[d]efendants' activities were not speech oriented, but were physical and allegedly destructive." The court then held that defendants' actions fell outside the protections of both ICRA section 1302(1) and the U.S. Constitution. Thus, in Lonewolf Scott, the court seemed to at least implicitly rely on federal precedent.

In Brandon v. Tribal Council for the Confederated Tribes of the Grand Ronde Community of Oregon, plaintiff contested his suspension from the tribal council for making a vulgar statement in response to his cousin's alleged provocation. The Grand Ronde Tribe court found that plaintiffs' conduct had "violated the tribal code." The court also stated that "[b]eing a tribal councilmember is a privilege, not a right, and councilmembers should be expected to conduct themselves at a higher level of restraint than other tribal members." In considering whether plaintiffs' suspension violated his free speech rights under the tribal constitution, the court cited federal law in asserting that "[t]he right of free speech and press do not entitle a person to talk or distribute written statements when, where, and how he/she chooses, with absolute protection from the consequences." Finding that the tribe "has compelling reasons to have interpreted the ordinance so as to limit the vulgar language that may be uttered by councilmembers in public," the court upheld the tribal code provisions at issue. In its decision, the court cited various federal authorities; it did not rely on tribal authority, nor did it discuss tribal tradition or custom in upholding the tribal code provisions.

Freedom of Press

Compared with the number of tribal court decisions on the issue of free speech, decisions on free press claims are almost nonexistent. Only one reported case in this area has been found. In Chavez v. Tome, the Navajo Nation Supreme Court heard

Chavez's allegation of libel against Tome, doing business as The Navajo Nation Enquiry. Chavez was an attorney in the Navajo Nation Department of Justice and had represented the Navajo Nation in a case on which the Enquiry had reported.

The Enquiry accused Chavez of lying to a judge, intimidating a judge, and bribing a judge to obtain favorable rulings. The Enquiry also reported that Chavez had been previously ejected by the Ute Tribe for causing problems throughout that community. The district court found Tome liable and ordered the printing of a retraction on the front page of three consecutive issues of the Enquiry.

On appeal, the Navajo Supreme Court stated that, "the United States Supreme Court has held that compelling a newspaper to print that which 'reason' tells them not to publish is an unconstitutional violation of the first amendment's guarantee of freedom of the press."

It also recognized that both the Navajo Bill of Rights and section 1302(1) of the Indian Civil Rights Act "guarantees the right of the press to be free of governmental intervention." The court further stated that "[t]he choice of material to be printed is a protected exercise of editorial control and judgment and the government is prevented from regulating this process." According to the court, under both the tribe's constitution and the ICRA, the tribal government cannot force the newspaper to print the retraction. In reversing that part of the district court's order, the Navajo Supreme Court appeared to rely on federal constitutional standards, rather than on tribal custom and tradition.

Free Exercise of Religion

As previously noted, the ICRA contains no establishment clause similar to that contained in the First Amendment. However, a few reported tribal court decisions have involved free exercise of religion claims. In Garcia v. Greendeer-Lee, the Ho-Chunk Supreme Court held that the religious freedoms of a nonmember employee of the Ho-Chunk Nation were not violated by tribe personnel policies disallowing paid leave for the employee to attend a Jehovah's Witness religious event. Under tribe policy, paid leave was provided only to employees who attended "certain tribe-specific religious events." This policy, according to the court, did not preclude the employee from practicing her religion, and thus did not violate her religious freedom.

In In re T.M.M., a mother of a cancer-stricken Indian child petitioned the Walker River Juvenile Court to order the cessation of "all allopathic treatment." She based this demand on her First Amendment freedom of religion—a claim dismissed by the court, holding that "[t]he U.S. Constitution does not apply to tribal governments." The court also denied any claim under the ICRA, stating that the "ICRA does not prohibit the Walker River Tribe from prohibiting her religion." Finally, the court ordered the child to remain in the care of the U.C. Davis Medical Center to continue his treatment.

Freedom of Assembly

Keeswood v. Navajo Tribe involved a group of people who gathered during a tribal council debate of a highly controversial Coal Gasification Resolution. Protestors who were arrested and criminally charged sued for "false arrest, false imprisonment, and use of unnecessary force by police in affecting the arrests." The court first ruled that the tribe's unlawful assembly statute could not be enforced because tribal members did not have adequate notice of the statute, due to its lack of publication.

The court further held that enforcement of the statute would violate the "Navajo peoples' right to freedom of communication." Moreover, the court stated that "constitutional law mandates that the right of assembly must be given the most liberal and comprehensive construction to protect the peoples' First Amendment Rights. To enforce the sanction of this law upon the facts of this case would put a chilling effect on our peoples' First Amendment Rights."

Considering the false arrest and imprisonment allegations, the court focused on the "sacredness of Free Speech and Assembly," as well as "the rights protected under the Navajo Bill of Rights, the [ICRA], and the United States Constitution and how essential it is to a free government."

Finding the defendants liable, the court cited to a federal court case and recognized that although the facts were distinguishable, "the principles of exercising great care to protect the peoples' First Amendment Rights are not any different."

FIRST AMENDMENT NORMS IN THE SOCIAL AND CULTURAL EXPERIENCES OF SOUTH DAKOTA TRIBES

THE EMPIRICAL STUDY DESCRIPTION

Five of the nine South Dakota tribes include First Amendment language in their constitutions. Those constitutions enumerating First Amendment rights include Crow Creek Sioux, Lower Brule Sioux, Rosebud Sioux, Sisseton-Wahpeton Oyate, and Standing Rock Sioux.

The Cheyenne River Sioux, Flandreau Santee Sioux, Oglala Sioux, and Yankton Sioux Constitutions specify no First Amendment rights. The empirical portion of this study will examine the kind of First Amendment-type issues that have arisen in the South Dakota tribes and how tribal government and society have treated such issues. The results of this study demonstrate that the ICRA allows "tribes to decide for themselves what individual rights mean in each tribal community."

STUDY METHODS

Law school researchers consulted with University of South Dakota faculty and personnel, who had experience in a variety of aspects of Indian law and social aspects, to help identify a broad range of regional Indian experts.

A large representative group of people was identified. In addition to the initial pool of more than seventy individuals, researchers asked interviewees to help identify other resource people that they thought might be helpful. The pool included Indians and non-Indians, education leaders, judicial representatives, Indian affairs reporters for both Indian and non-Indian newspapers, tribal college presidents, tribal authorities including chairpersons and council members, tribal attorneys, and Indian studies faculty.

Researchers then surveyed and interviewed this pool of experts and authorities on a number of First Amendment type issues. Authorities were asked about a number of subject matters, including their perception of how First Amendment norms impact the relationship between tribal governments and religion, censorship practices of tribes, practices that govern public access to tribal records and documents, and governmental relationship with tribal presses and libraries.

Furthermore, the research was not confined to personal interviews. Electronic databases and newspaper and magazine archives were also examined by the research group. Since, in South Dakota, both Indian and non-Indian newspapers report on tribal government concerns; researchers reviewed archives of newspapers and journals for First Amendments articles. Past and current volumes of the Indian Law Reporter were scrutinized for First Amendment cases, as were electronic databases such as The Social Science Research Network, which contains scholarly writings by social science experts, VersusLaw, which maintains a tribal court database, and Westlaw's Native American Law materials, periodical, and caselaw databases.

FINDINGS OF FIRST AMENDMENT SURVEYS

Indian Civil Rights Act (ICRA) Violations

No evidence was found of any First Amendment cases filed under the ICRA or the tribal constitution. Charles Abourezk, Supreme Court Justice for the Rosebud Sioux Tribe, says "unless a tribe adopts [the ICRA] and includes it as a tribal law it may not be enforced." He knows of no instance when the people have tried to enforce their First Amendment rights under the ICRA. An instance that involved a civil action to prevent a 1970 Sundance was mentioned by one expert, and an early twentieth century case concerning educating Indian children in sectarian schools, Reuben Quick Bear v. Leupp, was also mentioned, but it was prior to the ICRA. Overall the respondents did not see the tribes as enforcing "First Amendment rights under the ICRA."

Tribal Views of Religion and the First Amendment

Spirituality is a pervasive aspect of tribal culture; nearly all community and governmental events open with a spiritual ceremony or prayer. The prayer may be the traditional Lakota prayer or it may be offered as a Christian prayer, "both seem to be accepted."

Survey participants, tribal and non-tribal, view the tribes as supporting spirituality, but no one identified the tribes as having a tribal religion or sect. The tribes can give financial benefit or support to religion under the ICRA, but tribes tend to "support cultural programs that can be spiritual in nature" rather than financially supporting what would be perceived by white culture as organized religion. If financial support is lent, it is to Sundances.

Most tribes do not forbid participation of non-tribal members at religious ceremonies with the exception of the Cheyenne River Sioux Tribe which passed a resolution prohibiting the practice of native religion by non-natives. On occasion, the Holy Man or Medicine Man may deny participation of non-natives in a Sundance. Concern was also voiced about non-natives handling eagle feathers, but on the whole, non-tribal members are usually open to attend ceremonies including sweat lodge ceremonies. Tribal attorney, Mario Gonzalez, states that "tribal government is prohibited from denying any person the free exercise of religion under the 1968 Indian Civil Rights Act."

Censorship on Tribal Land

Tribal experts were questioned about censorship in such areas as: speeches that may have been sanctioned, restrictive practices of libraries, teacher or student speech policies or discipline, cultural or artistic exhibits that have been closed or censored, and defamation laws.

- Libraries and cultural exhibits: Any libraries on tribal land were identified as being school libraries and no respondents perceive the libraries as having restrictive practices. Cultural or artistic exhibits are also viewed as receiving little censorship. The only instance mentioned was a poster contest for young students that was closed down because the posters were "very critical of the non-Indian community." The school district shut the exhibit down; in this case the censorship was apparently from the non-Indian community with no action taken by the tribes.
- News sources: Tribal newspapers and radio stations have censorship issues that arise from time to time. Respondents mentioned it is difficult for people to travel long distances for tribal meetings so tribal newspapers and radio stations report government meetings and activities, and they also

enable people to register complaints against the government or tribal council members. Efforts are made by some of the "tribes to regulate libel and defamatory statements being made. But... there is a lively debate in the tribal newspapers and people are allowed to say whatever they want." While "there may [be] complaints or pressure" to censor statements, tribal governments do not act upon them.

The only instance of censorship is recalled by a South Dakota journalist who said that a newspaper was shut down on Pine Ridge land several years ago when the owner published a story that was considered libelous by most news authority since no substantiated sources existed." The story was never followed up, but the journalist believed the newspaper owner moved his operation. Community chairman of Rosebud, Todd Fast Horse, complained that he was sanctioned when the tribal newspaper would not publish his letter to the editor. He contacted the ACLU, but it declined to get involved.

- Schools: Speech and verbal expression in schools does not appear to be controlled by policy. No instances were cited of teachers or students being sanctioned by the tribes for inappropriate speech, however, one expert noted that speech in schools needs to be free of threatening language toward teachers or students. The only school policies for speech would be policies that maintain discipline and keep language from becoming disruptive "as any school should be able to regulate."
- General censorship complaints: Speech censorship or sanctioning is known to occur at tribal council meetings. Recently an impeachment complaint was filed against an Oglala tribal council member for comments that he made about soldiers in Iraq, but charges were dismissed. Tim Giago, owner of the Lakota Times, noted that he "often clashed with the tribe because he felt they were not giving the people the whole story." But the most commonly referred to instance of sanctioned speech centred on the former Oglala Sioux Tribal President, Cecilia Fire

Thunder, for speaking out in favour of abortion and an abortion clinic on tribal land. She was eventually impeached for her views. Another council member indicated that though speech may not be sanctioned, "someone could make an ethics charge" against a council member for speaking as though he was speaking on behalf of the whole tribe.

Accessibility of Tribal Meetings and Documents

An attorney for the Oglala Sioux Tribe states that the documents maintained by that tribe are of two types "purely tribal records and records from Public Law 93-638 contracts." Documents maintained by other tribes may vary, but tribal documents of any type are viewed as readily open to tribal members; although the ease of access varies from tribe to tribe.

Proceedings of council meetings are available to tribal members through newspapers, radio stations, Internet, or members can request the minutes from the tribal council secretary. Radio stations and newspapers are the easiest way to access council proceedings, but not all tribes have them.

Non-tribal members may have more trouble obtaining documents than tribal members. One expert notes that non-access may have "more to do with disorganization than it does with secrecy," and a non-tribal reporter stated that "it is just finding someone who is willing to help." There appear to be no policies restricting non-tribal members from obtaining copies of documents; in fact, a Rosebud Sioux council member states that all their documents were public.

While tribal meetings are open to the public, it may be difficult for members to travel to meetings from remote areas where the "poverty level can be pretty serious." The only time respondents mentioned that both tribal and non-tribal members are asked to leave a council meeting is if the council goes into executive session when personal matters are discussed. There are a few comments such as the one by a former staff writer for Indian Country Today, who states that councils seem to "go into executive session... quite often." While another expert says he hears complaints by tribal members about the "closed nature of tribal government[,] [he further noted that some kinds of things, like sunshine laws... they complain a lot about....".

Tribal Conflicts with First Amendment Norms and Values

A common tribal attitude and practice sees that speech practices should first reflect the custom and practices of the tribal communities, with First Amendment-type protections given somewhat less importance. According to one expert, "the First Amendment is more reflective of an individual's right, and it can totally disregard the community's rights.... [T]here are certain customs, especially respect for certain persons, that may run contrary to the First Amendment." Thus, although some customs may run contrary to First Amendment norms, the tribes may nonetheless continue those customs because of their importance and value to the community.

CONCLUSION

Even though Congress through the Indian Civil Rights Act mandated that tribal governments not infringe on First Amendment-type freedoms, the enforcement of that Act has been essentially left to tribal courts. In the relatively few decisions interpreting and applying the ICRA, tribal courts have taken a much more balanced view towards individual rights. Under this balanced view, tribal courts have been more willing to constrain individual rights for the sake of community interests and values. Thus, tribal courts have not taken a strict scrutiny kind of approach to restrictions on individual rights that federal courts have taken with respect to similar restrictions on First Amendment rights. The tribal court approach has been much more fluid and accommodating toward community interests.

This approach to the Indian Civil Rights Act reflects a broader tribal attempt to navigate in a more balanced way between individualistic and communitarian models. As scholars have pointed out, tribes are much more community based than is classic western society, out of which legal norms like the First Amendment have evolved. Under the tribal approach, more emphasis is put on the group. Whereas classical western society strives to protect the individual from the group, tribal society strives to protect the group from the individual. Consequently, tribal courts are more sensitive to balancing the interests of groups and individuals. Whereas western society may view society as a collection of atomized individuals, the tribal view is more community based and looks at individuals more through their relationships with the society at large.

Not only are there very few reported cases dealing with the ICRA, but the present study has also revealed the reason for that paucity of cases. Because tribal society is a more community based society, and a less individualistic one, it apparently generates much fewer individual rights type conflicts than does the more dominant U.S. society. Indeed, this has been shown through our study of the Indian tribes of South Dakota. Despite an exhaustive survey of groups and individuals associated with all those tribes, very few individual rights disputes were discovered. Therefore, a lack of individual rights cases in tribal courts are obviously the result of a lack of such disputes occurring within tribal society in general.

5

Constitution of the Comanche Indian Tribe

PREAMBLE

Invoking the guidance of Almighty God, we, the members of the Comanche Indian Tribe with faith in the purposes of our Supreme Being, with abounding pride in our ancient racial heritage and with the determination to promote, through united efforts, the general well-being of our tribe and to secure to ourselves and our descendants the rights, powers and privileges provided by law, do solemnly ordain and establish this organization and adopt the following constitution.

ARTICLE I-NAME

The name of this Organization shall be the "Comanche Indian Tribe."

ARTICLE II-PURPOSE

The purpose of this organization shall be:

Section 1., To define, establish and safeguard the rights, powers and privileges of the tribe and its members.

Section 2., To improve the economic, moral, educational and health status of its members and to cooperate with and seek the assistance of the United States in carrying out mutual programs to accomplish these purposes by all possible means.

Section 3., To promotes in other ways the common well being of the tribe and its membership.

ARTICLE III-MEMBERSHIP (Pursuant to Amendment V, adopt May 29, 1976)

Section 1. To define, establish and safeguard the rights, powers and privileges of the tribe and its members.

Section 2. To improve the economic, moral, educational and health status of its members and to cooperate with and seek the assistance of the United States in carrying out mutual programs to accomplish these purposes by all possible means.

Section 3. To promote in other ways the common well being of the tribe and its membership.

ARTICLE III-MEMBERSHIP (Pursuant to Amendment V, adopted May 29, 1976)

Section 1. The membership of the Comanche Indian Tribe shall consist of the following:

a) All persons, who received an allotment of land as members of the Comanche Indian Tribe under the Act of June 6, 1900 (31 Stat. 672), and subsequent Acts, shall be included as full blood members of the tribe.

b) All living direct descendents of allotees eligible for membership under the provisions of Section 1. (a) Of this Article born on or before the date of adoption of this constitution.

c) All children of at least one-fourth (1/4) degree Comanche Indian blood, as defined by and derived from Section 1. (A), born after the date of the adoption of the constitution to a member of the Comanche Indian Tribe; provided, that application for new membership has been submitted to the business committee supported as required by Section 2 of this Article.

Section 2. Application for new membership in the Comanche Indian Tribe under Section 1. (c) Must be supported by authenticated copies of birth certificate or other records recognized by state or federal recorders. All evidence so submitted shall be retained by the tribe to support the record.

Section 3. Any person eligible for membership in the Comanche Indian Tribe under the provisions of Section 1. Of this Article shall be considered a member of the Comanche Indian Tribe unless:

a) The person is an adult and submits in writing to the Tribal Chairman a statement of withdrawal from the Comanche Indian

Tribe and relinquishment of all rights of tribal membership, signed by him or her and attested by two (2) witnesses, which statement shall automatically effect a permanent withdrawal from membership in the Comanche Indian Tribe and a relinquishment of all rights and benefits thereunder; or

b) The person is at the time of the adoption of this constitution an enrolled member of another tribe or has in the past received and accepted or, if a minor, whose parents or legal guardian has received and accepted for said minor, material or monetary benefits as a member of another Indian Tribe and who fails or whose parents or legal guardian fails, if a minor, within ninety (90) days after the adoption of this constitution to declare in writing to the Tribal Chairman preference for membership in the Comanche Indian Tribe and at the same time in writing renounces membership in said other tribe; or

c) The person after the adoption of this constitution by his or her affirmative action or, a minor, by the affirmative action of his or her parents or legal guardian becomes a recognized or enrolled member of another Indian tribe with the full rights, privileges and powers of membership under the rules of said other tribe, which said affirmative action and subsequent recognition or enrollment shall automatically effect a permanent withdrawal from membership in the Comanche Indian Tribe and relinquishment of all rights and benefits thereunder; or

d) The person after the adoption of this constitution receives and accepts or, if a minor, his or her parents or legal guardian accepts for said minor, material or monetary benefits as a result of membership in another Indian tribe, which such receipt and

Section 4. Notwithstanding the provisions of Section 3. Of this Article, any person who meets the eligibility criteria in Section 1. Of this Article who as a minor accepted a material or monetary benefit as a member of another Indian Tribe or whose legal guardians accepted a material as a member of another Indian Tribe while the person was a minor, shall have the option of relinquishing their membership in the other tribe and becoming a member of the Comanche Indian Tribe not later than one year after they become an adult as defined by this Constitution, provided further that any person eligible for membership in the Comanche Tribe under this section who has reached adulthood prior to the approval date of this section must take appropriate action to enroll as a member of the Comanche Indian Tribe not later than 30 days subsequent to the adoption date of this section.

ARTICLE IV-ORGANIZATION AND OFFICERS

Section 1. The supreme governing body of this organization shall be the Comanche Tribal Council.

Section 2. In addition to the tribal council, there shall be elected a Comanche Business Committee.

Section 3. The elected officers of the tribal council shall be a Tribal Chairman, a Tribal Vice-Chairman, and a Tribal Secretary-Treasurer. In addition these officers shall serve in the same capacity on the Comanche Business Committee.

ARTICLE V-TRIBAL COUNCIL (Pursuant to Amendment I, adopted May 29, 1976, Amendment XI and Amendment XII, adopted April 14, 1979, Amendments XVIII and XIX, adopted September 29, 1984, and Amendments XXXI, XXXII, XXXIII, XXXIV, XXXV, XXXVI, adopted April 28, 1994)

Section 1. The Tribal Council shall consist of all members of all members of the Comanche Indian Tribe who are eighteen (18) years of age or older.

Section 2. There shall be an annual meeting of the tribal council on the third Saturday in April of each year at 1:30 p.m. to the Comanche Tribal Complex, Lawton, Oklahoma, or such other place as the business committee shall determine.

Section 3. In addition to the Annual Tribal Council meeting, the Tribal Chairman shall be required to call a special tribal council meeting in the following cases:

a) Upon written request by the Commissioner of Indian Affairs or his authorized representative; or
b) When he is so requested in writing by as many as three members of the business committee, setting forth the purpose of the meeting; or
c) When he is so requested by a petition signed by two hundred (200) eligible voters of the Comanche Tribe, setting forth the purpose of the meeting consistent with the constitution; or

d) Should the Tribal Chairman refuse to call and hold a meeting of the tribal council or neglect to do so for thirty (30) days after he is duly requested, the Commissioner of Indian Affairs or his authorized representative shall be authorized to call such special meeting and shall do so by notifying the officers and members of the business committee of the date thereof.

Section 4. Notice of all meetings of the tribal council, including the annual meeting, shall be given by the secretary-treasurer as follows:

a) By mailing a postal card or letter to each member of the business committee at least ten (10) days prior to the meeting date, stating the date, time, place and purpose of the meeting; and
b) By posting at a public place and inserting at least two (2) weeks prior to the meeting date a notice in two (2) local newspapers containing the same information as set forth above. Radio, television, or other media of notice may also be utilized depending on availability and at the discretion of the business committee.

Section 5. Voters of the tribe shall be members of the tribal council who otherwise qualify. All votes taken during tribal council meetings shall, at the discretion of the Chairman, be standing vote or ballot.

Section 6. No action shall be taken by the Tribal Council unless a quorum is present. A quorum shall consist of one hundred and fifty (150) eligible voters.

Section 7. Subject to the approval of the Secretary of the Interior or his authorized representative where applicable, the authority of the Comanche Tribal Council shall include and be exclusive with respect to the following:

a) To change, modify, alter or revoke membership rules.
b) To execute leases, contracts or permits for five (5) or more years with regard to property which is owned exclusively by the Comanche Indian Tribe, but this does not include any individually owned land or personal property.
c) To elect tribal officers and members of the business committee and to fill vacancies which may occur pursuant to Article VII.

d) To authorize the expenditure of funds which may be deposited to the exclusive credit to the Comanche Indian Tribe and of funds, which may be deposited to the joint credit of the Kiowa, Comanche, and Apache Tribes.

e) To select and authorize tribal delegation to transact business on behalf of the tribe. When travel is involved, the terms of the resolution shall include the purpose of the trip and the existence of the delegation's authority.

f) The salary for the Chairman of the Business Committee shall be established by the Tribal Council by the adoption of an annual tribal operating budget. Salary for all other members of the business committee shall be two hundred and fifty dollars ($250) per month.

Section 8. All minutes of the tribal council meetings shall be published in a manner to be determined by the tribal council.

Section 9. To hire an Administrator/Manager to administrate the tribal government. The Administrator/Manager shall be under the direction of the business committee. Members of the business committee shall not be an employee of the tribal government. Section 10. To hire an attorney to represent the tribe in legal matters.

ARTICLE VI-BUSINESS COMMITTEE (Pursuant to Amendment X, adopted June 10, 1978, Amendment XIII and Amendment XIV, adopted April 14, 1979, Amendment XX and Amendment XXI, adopted September 29, 1984, and Amendment XXIII, adopted June 29, 1985)

Section 1. The Comanche Business Committee shall be composed of seven (7) members of the Comanche Indian Tribe who are at least twenty-one (21) years of age, and be elected as provided in Article VII of this constitution.

Section 2. The business committee shall meet on the first Saturday of each month of each year at 10:00 a.m. In case of a legal holiday, the meeting will be held on the following Saturday. Special meetings may be called by the Tribal Chairman at his discretion; provided that such special meetings do not exceed a total of twelve (12) meetings per calendar year.

Section 3. Notice of all special meetings of the business committee shall be given by the Tribal Secretary-Treasurer by mailing a letter or postal card to each member of the business committee at least ten days (10) prior to the meeting date, setting forth the date, time, place, and purpose in general terms.

Section 4. No action shall be taken by the business committee except when a quorum is present. A quorum shall consist of five committeemen.

Section 5. At the beginning of each meeting of the Comanche Business Committee, the Tribal Secretary-Treasurer, or in his absence the acting secretary as may be appointed by the Tribal Chairman, shall keep a record in the permanent minute book of the names of those present and those absent. If a tribal committee is absent for four (4) consecutive regularly scheduled meetings of the business committee, the Tribal Chairman shall declare his seat vacant and so notify in writing the tribal committeeman affected and steps shall be taken to fill the vacancy pursuant to Article VIII, Section 1.

Section 6. All minutes of the business committee shall be published in a manner to be determined by the business committee.

Section 7. The duties, responsibilities and authorities of the business committee shall include the following:

a) To establish and maintain the tribal membership roll and to insure that the roll is available for inspection at all reasonable times.

b) To determine qualification of candidates nominated for office and to conduct election of tribal officers and business committeemen pursuant to the provision of Section 2, Article VII, of this constitution.

c) To execute leases, contracts or permits for periods not to exceed five (5) years with regard to property, which is owned exclusively by the Comanche Indian Tribe, but does not include any jurisdiction over individually owned land or personal property.

d) To develop annual budget for the financing of Comanche Tribal operations and to present such budgets to the tribal council for final consideration as to adoption or rejection.

   1) The proposed annual tribal operating budget shall be disseminated to tribal members forty-five (45) days prior to the annual meeting.

2) The budget shall be printed on a ballot in such a manner that each line item may be approved or disapproved by the tribal members.
3) The line items of the budget shall be approved or disapproved in the election of officers conducted subsequent to the annual meeting pursuant to Article VII, Section 2., in which tribal officers are elected.

e) To develop proposals which are in the interest of fulfilling the purpose of the Comanche Tribal Organization including, but not limited to, programs involving employment, health, education, public relations, social, recreational, and historical activities of the tribe. Such program proposals shall be presented to the tribal council for final consideration as to adoption or rejection.

f) To implement, administer, and report on progress of programs adopted by the tribal council.

g) To appoint such subcommittees as are needed to develop the proposals suggested herein or any other worthwhile endeavors, including delegation of such authorities to these subcommittees as in commensurate with their responsibilities.

h) To secure an audit of each fiscal year's financial activities relating to funds from all sources, to publish the audit of the prior year's funds in the tribal newspaper and two local newspapers at least sixty (60) days prior to each annual meeting, and to prepare for delivery to those attending the annual tribal council meeting a written annual report which shall contain a synopsis of varied activities of the business committee, the previously published audit and a forecast of activities proposed for the coming year. First audit funds shall come out of any monies available to the tribe for expenditures, including but not limited to the general budget fund or bingo fund. The audit shall be conducted by a reputable firm that is completely disassociated from any tribal member.

i) Such additional duties and/or responsibilities which may be assigned to the business committee by the tribal council by appropriate resolution approved in tribal council assembled.

j) To promulgate and enforce ordinances and codes governing law and order to protect the peace, health, safety, and general welfare on land determined to be within tribal jurisdiction subject to the approval of the Assistant Secretary for Indian Affairs or his authorized representative.

Section 8. The term of office for each officer and committeeman shall be for a period of three (3) years or until a successor is duly elected and installed in office. Each officer or committeeman shall be eligible to serve two (2) consecutive terms effective upon date of this amendment, present term being counted as one term. At the completion of the second consecutive term of office, an officer or a committeeman shall not be eligible for election to a position on the business committee until a period of three (3) years elapsed. In addition, an officer or committeeman who has completed tow (2) consecutive terms on the business committee shall not be employed within the Comanche Tribal governmental system until a period of three (3) years has elapsed. For the purpose of the section, any portion of a term shall be considered as one term.

ARTICLE VII-ELECTIONS (Pursuant to Amendment II, adopted May 29, 1976, Amendment VI, adopted June 10, 1978, Amendment XVII, adopted April 25, 1981, and Amendment XXI, adopted September 29, 1984)

Section 1. As soon as practicable after this constitution is adopted the Area Director shall call a tribal council meeting and shall hold and supervise the first nomination and election hereunder for the tribal committee and officers, as follows:

a) The Area Director may at his discretion delegate chairmanship of the initial meeting to an employee under his supervision. A Secretary for the proceeding may be provided by the Area Director from his staff or he may also designate this responsibility to a member of the Comanche Indian Tribe.

b) At the initial meeting of the tribal council shall nominate candidates for the office of the Tribal Chairman for (3) years, Vice-Chairman for three (3) years, Secretary-Treasurer for two (2) years, two (2) business committee members for two (2) years and two (2) business committee members for one (1). Nominations shall be made from the floor and accepted by the Chairman. Persons duly elected at the ensuing election shall serve for the terms stated above unless their successors are duly elected prior to the expiration of such terms. Thereafter, all terms of office shall be for a period of three years or until a successor is duly elected. The terms of officers and committeemen shall be subjected to the additional provisions of Article VI, Section 8.

c) A list of nominees shall be made a part of the official minutes of the proceedings of this initial organization meeting from which determination shall be made that all such nominees are officially qualified as candidates for office in accordance with the provision of Article IX of this constitution. The Area Director will be the final authority in making such determination as the qualifications of candidates for the initial election of officers and committeemen of the Comanche Indian Tribe.

d) Following the initial organization meeting, an election day shall be designated to elect the business committeemen and officers from among the candidates who were nominated during the initial meeting. This Election Day and polling places shall be declared by the Area Director. The election of committeemen and officers shall be by secret ballot. No absentee ballots will be considered at such election.

Section 2. At each annual Comanche Tribal Council meeting subsequent to the firs election of officers and business committeemen, under this constitution, candidates will be nominated to compete for election to offices being vacated by reason of expiration of term of office. Determination of reason of expiration of term of office. Determination of qualifications of nominated candidates and election processes shall be as described in Section1 (c) and (d) of this Article except that the Comanche Tribal Officers and Business Committeemen will assume the responsibilities assumed by the Area Director the first election under this constitution and except that absentee ballots shall be considered at all subsequent elections of officers and business committeemen. No election shall be held later than 60 days after the annual meeting. Because a valid election was not completed by the Comanche Indian Tribe within sixty (60) days after the 1980 Annual Meeting, the Anadarko Agency is authorized to conduct one (1) election for the tribe pursuant to rules and regulations as prescribed by the Anadarko Agency. The Anadarko Agency is further authorized to notice, call, and conduct a special meeting of the Comanche Tribal Council for the sole purpose of nominating candidates for the vacant or expired positions that will be filled pursuant to the election.

Section 3. Should an incumbent of the Comanche Business Committee accept a nomination at an annual tribal council meeting as a candidate for a different office, that individual shall be required to resign the business committee position, which he then holds. Although such resignation shall not be effective until the completion of the year's election processes. Nomination for candidates to fill the unexpired portion of such person's term of office shall be made at the same tribal council meeting, which be, accepts nomination for a different office.

ARTICLE VIII-VACANCIES AND REMOVAL FROM OFFICE (Pursuant to Amendment XV, adopted April 14, 1979)

Section 1. If a committeeman or officer of the tribe shall die or resign, be removed or recalled from office, his office shall be deemed vacant and the Tribal Chairman, or should this office be vacant, the Tribal Vice-Chairman, shall immediately call a meeting of the Comanche Tribal Council to be held within twenty (20) days for the purpose of filling such vacancy for the unexpired term, except that when such vacancy shall occur within four months of the annual meeting of the Comanche Tribal Council, the position shall remain vacant until the next election when provisions shall be made to fill the vacancy.

Section 2. The Comanche Tribal Council may at a meeting duly called specifically for the purpose, recall any officers or committeemen for neglect for duty or conduct that has brought disrepute upon the tribe.

Such a meeting shall not be unless a petition signed by two hundred (200) eligible voters of the Comanche Tribe requesting recall of submitted to the Tribal Chairman. The recall of only one officer or committeemen may be initiated per meeting called for purpose.

a) Following submission of an acceptable petition for a recall Tribal Council meeting, the Tribal Chairman shall require that a signed Bill of Particulars setting forth the elements of neglect or misconduct be submitted to the accused. The petitioner's representative shall provide proper evidence of receipt by the accused, the Tribal Chairman shall call an official meeting of the Comanche Tribal Council within thirty (30) days for the purpose of hearing and disposition of the case.

b) The format for the Tribal Council meeting shall be established as follows:

   1) Presentation of the Bill of Particulars against the accused by a representative of the accusers. This presentation shall be limited strictly to those specifics included in the Bill of Particulars as presented to the accused.

   2) The accused shall be given adequate opportunity to answer any and all charges of which he or she is accused. The accused may personally present or may choose to utilize the services of another to present this response.

c) Upon completion of these two presentations no further discussion shall be allowed and voting shall proceed immediately in a manner prescribed by this constitution.

d) A majority vote of those voting of the Tribal Council meeting shall be sufficient to effect recall providing a quorum is present. Should a quorum not be present the charges against the accused shall be declared null and void and no further action shall be taken on this petition.

Section 3. Any officer or committeeman who shall be found guilty by any State or Federal Court of a felony, a misdemeanor involving dishonesty or of accepting a bribe shall forfeit his office and such office shall immediately become vacant and be filled in accordance with Section 1. Of this Article.

ARTICLE IX-QUALIFICATIONS OF OFFICERS (Pursuant to Amendment XVI, adopted April 14, 1979)

Section 1. No person may seek tribal office unless he will be at least twenty-one (21) years of age at the time of his election and is a member of the Comanche Indian Tribe.

Section 2. No member of the Comanche Tribe who has been convicted of a felony, a misdemeanor involving dishonesty or of accepting a bribe shall be eligible to hold office.

Section 3. Any person recalled from office as a result of action by the Comanche Tribal Council in accordance with Section 2. Of Article VIII of this constitution shall forfeit the right to seek election to any position on the Comanche Business Committee for a period of three years beyond the expiration of the term of office in which the recalled person was serving at the time of recall.

ARTICLE X-BILL OF RIGHTS

Section 1. All members of the Comanche Indian Tribe shall enjoy without hindrance freedom of worship, conscience, speech, press, assembly and association.

Section 2. This constitution shall not in any way be construed to alter, abridge or otherwise jeopardize the rights and privileges of the Comanche Indians as citizens of the United States.

Section 3. The individual vested property rights of any member of the Comanche Indian Tribe, which shall include restricted lands and income therefrom as well as personal property, shall not be altered, abridged or otherwise affected by the provision of this constitution.

Section 4. Tribal members shall have the right to review tribal records, including those of any enterprise operated/funded in the name of the Tribe (including CERCO, Bingo and any other tribally operated/funded business) so long as the examination of the records is permitted within seven (7) days of the receipt of a written request for the review.

No charge or fee shall be imposed upon any tribal member in connection with the right to examine tribal records. No person or committee shall be authorized to deny any tribal member the right to make copies of tribal records except as required by Federal Statutes.

Section 5. No charge or filing fee shall be imposed upon any tribal member in connection with the right to petition which are provided for in this constitution. No person or committee shall be authorized to deny any tribal member the right to petition.

ARTICLE XI-AMENDMENTS Pursuant to Amendment III, adopted May 29, 1976)

Section 1. Amendments to this constitution may be proposed by a majority vote of the business committee or by a petition signed by two hundred (200) adult members of the tribe who are entitled to vote, and if approved by the Commissioner of Indian Affairs, shall be submitted to the voters of the Tribe, and shall become effective when ratified by a majority vote of those who cast ballots in an election called by the Commissioner of Indian Affairs.

ARTICLE XII-DUTIES OF OFFICERS Pursuant to Amendment VII, adopted June 10, 1978, and Amendment XXXVII, adopted April 28, 1994)

Section 1. The Chairman shall be the Chief Executive of the Comanche Indian Tribe exercising the authorities and powers as delegated to his office by this constitution and the Comanche Tribal Council. He shall preside at all meetings of the Tribal Council and the Business Committee and be the principal member of all tribal delegations. When so authorized by the Comanche Tribal Council, he shall sign necessary papers instruments for the Comanche Indian Tribe.

Section 2. The Vice-Chairman shall perform the duties of the Chairman in the event of the temporary absence or disability or the Chairman or when it is determined according to Article VIII, Section 2. That a hearing for removal of the Chairman is deemed necessary by the Comanche Tribal General Council.

Section 3. The Secretary-Treasurer shall preside in the absence of the other officers and shall keep the records, including financial records, of the organization, shall record and keep the minutes of the tribal council and business committee meetings in a permanent book, and shall be responsible for sending all notices of meetings as herein required.

He shall keep copies of all such notices and request for meetings together with a statement by him or another officer, as the case may be, that such notices were mailed and published as required herein and place the same in the appropriate permanent minutes book as a preface to the minutes of the meeting so called.

Section 4. Copies of all minutes of the tribal council and business committee meetings and resolutions shall be sent to the Anadarko Agency.

ARTICLE XIII-ADOPTION

Section 1. This constitution shall become effective when approved by the Commissioner of Indian Affairs and ratified by vote of the eligible voters of the Comanche Indian Tribe voting in an election called by the Commissioner; provided, that at least thirty (30) percent of those eligible to vote cast ballots.

ARTICLE XIV KIOWA, COMANCHE AND APACHE INTERTRIBAL LAND USE COMMITTEE (Pursuant to Amendment IV, adopted May 29, 1976)

The Comanche Business Committee shall designate members of the Comanche Business Committee to represent the tribe on the Kiowa, Comanche and Apache Intertribal Land Use Committee to transact business regarding property owned jointly by the three tribes. The representatives so designated shall be authorized to enter, on behalf of the Comanche Tribe of Indians, into leases, permits, easements, rights-of-way, contracts for development planning, and other transactions, excepted the sale thereof, relating to tribal lands commonly owned by the Kiowa, Comanche and Apache Tribes to the extent that the Comanche Tribal Council could so act.

ARTICLE XV-NEPOTISM (Pursuant to Amendment VIII, adopted June 10, 1978)

Section 1. A relative of a member of the Comanche Tribal Business Committee (to include wife, mother, father, son, daughter, sister, brother) shall not be employed within the Comanche Tribal governmental system.

6

Tribal Self-Rule Law and Common Property Resources in Scheduled Areas of India

Village-level democracy became a real prospect for India in 1992 with the 73rd amendment to the Constitution, which mandated that resources, responsibility and decision-making be devolved from central government to the lowest unit of the governance, the *Gram Sabha* or the Village Assembly. A three-tier structure of local self-government was envisaged under this amendment. The nationwide euphoria that greeted this about-turn in bureaucracy was seen again with the extension of the 73rd amendment to the *Scheduled Areas,* [through Provisions of Panchayats (Extension to Scheduled Areas) Act, 1996] [hereinafter PESA or Central PESA or the Tribal Self Rule Law as it is variously called). Scheduled Areas are those, which are under the Fifth Schedule of the Constitution of India where the tribal populations are predominant. It is also imperative to understand here that the founding fathers of the Constitution of India had envisaged a special scheme of administration in the scheduled areas where general laws would not be applicable unless the Governor deemed it fit to enforce such laws.

It was thought that these areas are inhabited with people who have resided on the basis of their own customary practices and traditional beliefs and culture and thus general laws of the land would be inappropriate with their customary laws and ethos. However, a decade later, there is a growing feeling that while the burden of 'management' of natural resources, has been devolved, 'control' over resources and land is still in the hands of the state.

This paper delves in some detail into the manner in which the States' have subverted the mandate of the Central Legislation through carefully using the wordings in law to make the implementation vague and ineffective especially in the context of 'community resources' in scheduled areas. The scheduled areas, which are notified by the President of India as the Tribal dominated areas, exists in nine states of India4.

THE COMING OF PESA (TRIBAL SELF RULE LAW)

A brief introduction of how the central law on PESA came into being and the consequent state mandate would be instructive here. The 73rd amendment to the Constitution and the subsequent enactment of Provisions of the Panchayats (Extension to the Scheduled Areas) Act, 1996 (PESA) aimed to operationalise decentralization in India, through the transfer of power to the *Gram Sabha* or the village assembly.

The PESA attempted to vest legislative powers in *Gram Sabha,* specifically in matters relating to development planning, management of natural resources and adjudication of disputes in accordance with prevalent traditions and customs. This significant legislation was expected to have far reaching consequences in the social, economic and cultural life of tribal people in Scheduled Areas. All the scheduled states were given one year to amend their respective Panchayat Acts to conform to the letter and spirit of PESA. Accordingly, most states have introduced some form of conformity amendments, which reflect their intent to conform to the spirit of PESA.

At a first glance the state conformity legislations and amendments seem to have generally reflected most of the provisions of the PESA, although a closer look establishes that almost all powers have been made subject to rules/further orders "as may be prescribed by the State Governments ". The control over prospecting of minor minerals, planning and management of water bodies, control and management of minor forest produce, prevention alienation of land are all subject to rules in force or as may be prescribed by the State. The fact that the enabling rules are not in place even more than eight years after the adoption of the central law on PESA suggests reluctance by the State Governments to operationalise the mandate of PESA.

There are four points that need particular emphasis here. *First* there are critical omissions of some of the fundamental principles without which the spirit of PESA can never be realized. *Secondly,* the state legislations, perhaps by design, twist certain words from the Central PESA that has resulted in powers being taken away from the *Gram Sabha*-the collectivity of all village adults where the need for empowerment is most critical for making local self-governance a reality in the Country especially in relation to managing common pool resources. *Thirdly,* even where it affirmed some provisions of the law in principle, their applicability was made subject to framing of rules/orders or "as may be prescribed." As stated earlier, such enabling rules are not yet in place in most cases. *Finally,* few rules and *prescriptions* began to surface in early 2000 primarily through revocable official circulars but which again have been totally inoperative because of the ambiguity and lack of clarity of these provisions. Thus it is not surprising that even these are waiting to be taken to the ground. The operative provisions being not in place, a promising radical law has been reduced largely to a paper law.

The above is exemplified in numerous ways especially in the context of community resources. The *Panchayats* (Institutions of Local Self-Government) at the appropriate level and/or the *Gram Sabha* have been endowed specifically with powers for management of local resources. For instance the *Gram Sabha* or Panchayat at appropriate level shall be consulted before making acquisition of land in scheduled area for development projects as well as before resettlement or rehabilitation of persons affected by such projects in Scheduled Areas. The use of the word 'consultation' under PESA instead of 'consent' significantly waters down the power vested with the Panchayat. Besides *Gram Sabha* and Panchayats have powers to prevent alienation of land in the Scheduled Area and to take appropriate action to restore any alienated land of Scheduled Tribe5. In this regard there needs to be a clear understanding of the nature and extent of powers that needs to be vested with the *Gram Sabha* and the various tiers of the Panchayats. The law is vague and ambiguous as will be demonstrated later in state specific examples. Further the ownership of forest based resources have also been granted though is a tendency to limit the local area of the *Gram Sabha* for the purposes of owning minor forest produce.

A central concern of the present paper is to highlight the conflicts arising out of the powers vested with the *Gram Sabhas* under PESA and the provisions contained in the various 'subject matter' State laws Under the PESA, the *Gram Sabha* or the Panchayats at the appropriate level has been vested with the mandatory powers to regulate on subjects such as minor forest produce, alienation of land, management of minor water bodies and control over local plans and their resources. On all these subjects there exist specific State legislation, which might impact the operation of the state variants of the PESA. Again when it comes to amending all the subject matter laws to give effect to PESA, the States response is varied.

THE STATE RESPONSE TO TRIBAL SELF RULE

There are also some glaring omissions in the State legislations when they are assessed for their conformity with the PESA. Some fundamental principles on which the PESA is premised such as state legislations on Panchayats shall be in consonance with customary laws, and among other things traditional management practices of community resources; the competence of *Gram Sabha* in safeguarding and preserving traditions and customs of the people and the community resources have been omitted from omitted from the conformity Acts for example in Rajasthan.

Let us now see some specific resources that have been impacted by the law on tribal self rule and the subsequent state legislations which include; management of minor water bodies, forest land especially relating to ownership of minor forest produce and tribal land alienation and restoration.

Minor Water Bodies

As per the Central PESA the power to plan and manage 'minor water bodies' exclusively vested with the Panchayat at Appropriate level (PAL) which in other words means that the Central law gives a discretion to the states to assign to any tier of the local self government such power in the best interest of the community. However, the first obstacle is on the definition itself. No legal definition of minor water bodies exists in the statute books. The states too have ignored it, whether by design or default is unclear. The Gujarat State in the Western India has given such power to the *Gram Panchayat* (Village Council). The State of

Himachal Pradesh in the north has assigned it to Village Council (*Gram Panchayat*) OR at Block Committee Level i.e. *Panchayat Samiti* OR District Council (Zila *Parishad*) level "as may be specified". The State of Rajasthan in the North West too uses the word " as may be prescribed" by the State. No such prescriptions are in place even after eight years. The Maharashtra Government completely ignores it. This ambiguous power devolution becomes further critical as there are a number of externally aided projects on water sheds and water users which are participatory based approaches and the state amendments completely ignores these developments in their enactments. The Participatory Irrigation Management laws enacted in states such as Rajasthan and Mahaharastra for instance where Water Users Associations have been created, Water Shed Committees that have been created instates such as Madhya Pradesh and Andhra Pradesh in the South has no linkage with the Local self Government units and more so in scheduled areas or tribal dominated areas.

Land Resources

Two critical land issues emerge in the context of the law on tribal self rule and the manner in which state conformity legislations on PESA has been enacted. One on land acquisition and the other on land alienation and restoration of illegally alienated lands. Note that land belonging to a scheduled tribe can be transferred to a non-tribal under the various Land Revenue Codes of the states and more so in tribal areas (read scheduled areas).

Land Acquisition

As regards land acquisition the power has been vested with the *Gram Sabha* or Panchayat at appropriate level (PAL) by the Central PESA. It mandates that there should be consultation before land Acquisition for development projects and before resettling or rehabilitating persons affected by such projects. The state of Gujarat for example has granted this power to higher level of Panchayat at the Block level (*Taluka Level*). The state of Himachal Pradesh mandates that the *Gram Sabha* shall be consulted before making the acquisition of land in the Scheduled Areas for development of projects and before re-settling or rehabilitating persons 'evicted' by such projects in the scheduled areas. Note the use of the word 'evicted' which limits the scope of this provision to evicted person only. The state of Madhya Pradesh in Central India states the *Gram Sabha* or the Panchayats at the appropriate level shall be consulted thus not deciding any particular tier but keeping it vague. At the same time the *Gram Sabha* in Scheduled Areas is also required to manage natural resources including land, water, forests within the area of the village in accordance with provisions of the Constitution and other relevant laws for the time being in force. Clearly there is an overlap and misdirection in terms of assignment of power to a specific level and simultaneous allocation of power on a very general basis. These are bound to give conflicting signals at the field level. In Maharashtra the power to consult before land acquisition has been granted to every *Panchayat* i.e at *Gram Panchayat; Panchayat Samiti* and *Zila Parishad* level (all tiers of local self government) —Provided that, every *Panchayat* shall consult the *Gram Sabha* before conveying its views to the Land Acquisition Authority concerned. Note here that there is a provision of 'conveying views' and without any clarity on what happens if such conveyed views are not taken into account. In Rajasthan the *Gram Sabha* or the Panchayati Raj Institution at such level, 'as may be prescribed' by the State Government, shall be consulted. Again there is total ambiguity in the manner in which the powers have been assigned.

Land Alienation

The powers of prevention of land alienation and restoration of illegally alienated land under the Central PESA has been vested both to the *Gram Sabha* and the Panchayat at appropriate level. One of the crucial reason why a necessary mandate to the *Gram Sabha* and any tier of local self government has been envisaged is the significance the Central Government attaches to certain subjects that are critical to the lives of the tribals. Land alienation is one such critical aspect among others in the context of common property resources. Different states have responded differently. While the Gujarat Government has only involved the District *Panchayat*. The Maharashtra Government has mandated that it shall be competent for every *Gram Sabha* in the Scheduled Areas to make recommendations through *Panchayat* having regard to the provisions of any law for the time being in force pertaining to transfer or alienation of land of the persons belonging to the scheduled tribes, be competent to make suitable recommendations to the Collector. Here again the precedence has been given to the already existing laws in the state rather than the spirit of the new law on PESA. The state of Rajasthan has not yet decided whether the powers would be assigned to Gam Sabha or the Panchayat at any appropriate level and again even if they decide "the power to prevent alienation of land in the Scheduled Areas and to take appropriate action to restore any unlawfully alienated land of a Scheduled Tribe *would* be in accordance with laws in force in the State". This seems to be somewhat as nebulous as the state Maharashtra as discussed earlier. The state of Madhya Pradesh has decided not to introduce this provision at all, the reasons best known to them.

Minor Forest Produce

Forest and forest based resources are yet another subject critical to the lives of the tribals. PESA recognizes this and thus responds most radically by granting ownership of minor forest produce to the *Gram Sabha* along with *Panchayat* at appropriate level. Again two critical legal issues emerge here. One the definition of minor forest produce and second the jurisdiction where such ownership rights would be exercised. Before these critical issues are discussed it would be instructive to assess the state's responses. The Gujarat Act has vested in the *Village Panchayat* minor forest produce found *(except found in the areas of National Parks or Sanctuaries)* in such area of a forest as is situate in the jurisdiction of that village. This essentially means that while the ownership rights have been granted but the area on which such resources exist is exempt. The Himachal Pradesh Act provides that the '*Gram Panchayat* or as the case may be *Gram Sabha*' shall have the ownership of minor forest produce within the local area *of the Gram Sabha*. Again which tier has been granted the ownership is not clear and what constitutes local area is ambiguous. The Maharashtra Act, empowers the *Gram Sabha* in the Scheduled Areas to issue direction to the *Panchayat* with regard to the exploitation and regulation of trading of minor forest produce, subject to provisions of the Maharashtra Transfer of Ownership of Minor Forest Produce in the Scheduled Areas, and the Maharashtra Minor Forest Produce (Regulation of Trade) (Amendment) Act, 1997. However, it does not transfer ownership. While the state of Madhya Pradesh Act has not transferred the power of ownership of minor forest produce under the State PESA at all the Rajasthan has made the local self-government units subservient to the executive initiated committees such as Joint Forest Management Commitees and Eco development Committees. As is obvious there is total reluctance from the state governments to give effect to this otherwise radical provision. It is well known that forest based resources are one of the most significant resource for tribal people in India and the reluctance by the States suggests that by excluding forest rich areas such as sanctuaries or by restricting the area to the local jurisdiction of the village or by making the *Panchayat* bodies subservient to the executive initiated committees such as Joint Forest Management Committees the states intention is to exclude the most important resource on which tribal life depends. What is most surprising that one of the most rich biodiversity and forested states of Madhya Pradesh in central India has completely ignored this provision.

Concluding Remarks

The various conformity legislations of the various tribal states in India supposedly giving effect to the most radical legislation in Indian legal history have proved that the spirit of a social welfare legislation can be totally marred by carefully selecting words and phrases in law that kills the soul while maintaining the body of a legislation. The law on tribal self rule which recognized for the first time the competence of a village assembly to manage its community resources, which recognized for the first time that a village where one resides is not always a homogeneous, population based entity but a social cohesive unit with its own self identity where people who have been ordinarily and traditionally residing for centuries with a common belief system and cultural traits apart from the manner in which they manage their natural resources. Despite such laudable objectives the states having scheduled areas have proved that it is too difficult to relinquish power in a bureaucratic power structure. Slight twist of words, maintaining ambiguity in legislative frame, and brazen omissions of fundamental principles on which a social, empowering legislation is based can override the basic intent of any well meaning law due to states' whim. But perhaps it is too late for states to undermine the significance of communities living close to natural resources on which they depend. It is only a matter of time when the nation-state would come about in their apprpach to realise that for any effective governance including managing our common pool resources they have to integrate communities closest to natural resources by a near total paradigm shift in their approach and not merely by some some ineffective sop in the garb of any social welfare legislation.

INDIAN TRIBES AFTER SIXTY YEARS

Of the 86 million tribals who are 8.4 percent of the population, 80 percent live in the Middle India belt of Andhra Pradesh, Orissa, Jharkhand, Chhattisgarh, Madhya Pradesh, Northern Maharashtra and Southern Gujarat. Around 12 percent or 10.2 millions live in the Northeast. The rest are spread over the remaining States (2001 census CDs).

Most tribes in Middle India come under the Fifth Schedule that accords protection to their land and culture. Some tribes in the Northeast come under the Sixth Schedule that grants them greater autonomy than their Middle India counterparts have. In response to their nationalist struggles, the Parliament amended the Constitution to allow the tribes of Nagaland and Mizoram to run their civil affairs according to their customary law. Most others do not have any special protection other than the laws preventing tribal land alienation (Barooah 2002).

It has not prevented land alienation, some of it legally through the Land Acquisition Act 1894 and the rest through devious means.

Tribal Displacement due to Refugee Rehabilitation

In West Bengal and the Northeast it began with the Partition when East Pakistani Hindu refugees either occupied or were rehabilitated on much land that the tribal communities owned according to their customary law. In West Bengal at least 230,000 hectares were used for refugee rehabilitation, 80,000 ha of it predominantly tribal common property resources (CPRs) that are considered State property according to the colonial land laws that continue to be in vogue in India.

They recognise only individual ownership. So the CPR dependants are not even compensated for the land they lose (Fernandes et al. 2006: 57). In Assam not less than 140,000 ha have been used for refugee rehabilitation, all but 6,600 ha of it predominantly tribal CPRs (Fernandes and Bharali 2006: 77).

Similar figures can be given from Meghalaya. The Chakma refugees displaced by the Kaptai dam in East Pakistan in the mid-1960s were resettled in Arunachal Pradesh. Much tribal land was used for refugee rehabilitation also in the Koraput district of Orissa, Bastar of Chhattisgarh and in Jharkhand.

DISPLACEMENT IN TRIPURA DUE TO REFUGEE REHABILITATION

Tripura in the Northeast is the worst hit.

After the first influx of refugees came the Hindu Bangladeshi immigrants. The State enacted the Tripura Land and Land Revenue Act 1960 that stipulated that only registered land would be recognised. Most tribals being illiterate did not register the community land they were living on for a thousand years according to their customary law (Bhattacharyya 1988: 97-98). So they were declared encroachers on the land that was their habitat for hundreds of years.

The land that was alienated from them was used to resettle the Hindu East Pakistani immigrants whose influx continues till today. Because of the influx, its tribal proportion has come down from 58 percent in 1951 (Sen 1993: 13) to 31 percent in 2001 (Census CDs 2001). The tribes have lost more than 60 percent of their land to the immigrants.

That is at the basis of the tribal insurgency in the State (Bhaumik 2003: 84-85).

Though most States have legal provisions to protect tribal land, the loss of individual land too has been high because in the fifth schedule as well as in non-scheduled tribal areas, those who control the political and administrative systems manipulate the land records in their own favour.

As a result, by official count 753,435 (40.77%) of a total of 1,848,000 acres of land in the tribal districts of AP were in non-tribal hands in the early 1990s. Studies put it at more than 50 percent (Laya 1998). Similar is the case in Orissa (Pradhan and Stanley 1999), Madhya Pradhesh (Mander 1998) and other States. In Assam because of changes in laws, the number of tribal blocks from which land cannot be alienated to nontribals has come down from 35 in 1947 to 25 in 2005 (Shimray 2006: 12).

Development-Induced Displacement

The legal way is the Land Acquisition Act 1894 that supersedes all other legislation and makes it possible for the State to acquire land under a public purpose that is yet to be defined. It recognises only individual ownership. What does not have an individual patta is State property (Ramanathan 1999: 20). It facilitates acquisition of tribal revenue and forest CPRs without even a notification and with no compensation. Many of their dependants are not even counted among the displaced (DP) and others deprived of livelihood without physical relocation (PAP). In Assam, for example, the State counts only 3.4 lakh DPs when the reality is more than 19 lakhs. Those excluded are CPR dependants, more than 50 percent of them tribal.

Studies on development-induced displacement 1951-1995 in Kerala, AP, Jharkhand and Orissa, 1965-95 in Goa and 1947-2004 in Gujarat show that more than 2 million ha of forests have been lost in these States. However, only 60 percent of the projects could be studied in Kerala, Jharkhand and Orissa and 80 percent in AP. The common revenue land could not be separated from forests in Assam and West Bengal. So much more has been lost in these States.

Besides, States like Chhattisgarh, Maharashtra and MP with large forest areas and a big tribal population have not been studied. Once they are studied and the figures for others like AP, Orissa and Jharkhand are updated, the total of forests lost in the whole of India will go up to at least 10 million ha. Most forests and much of the revenue CPRs lost are tribal habitat.

Needless to say, tribal displacement too is high. The DP/PAPs are tribal but they are 34.5% of the 16,729,392 persons whose caste-tribe is known. There are indications that around 50% of the DP/PAPs of Assam and 30% of West Bengal whose caste/tribe is not known are tribals.

Studies have not been done in Chhattisgarh, MP and Maharashtra that have a big number of tribal DP/PAPs. The caste/tribe of the DP/PAPs in Kerala and Goa was not got. The biggest past projects like Idukki and other dams in Kerala are in its tribal areas. So more than 10% of its DP/PAPs are bound to be tribals who are around 1% of its population. Also the Athirapally dam that the Centre has just sanctioned has a large number of tribals (Dutta 2007). Once all of them are counted, the tribal proportion for the whole of India is expected to reach 40%.

Tribals pay the highest price of national development because their regions are resource rich. 90 percent of all coal and around 50 percent of the remaining minerals are in their regions (Areeparampil 1996: 6). Also the forest, water and other sources abound in their habitat. Because of the extent of CPRs acquired, some (e.g. Singh 1989: 96) even think that in order to reduce its cost the project authorities deliberately choose the administratively neglected backward areas because their CPR component is high and compensation for their private land is low. The project cannot compromise on the technical components and on staff salaries. So it reduces the cost through this means.

Ensuring Availability without Access

The reason why the tribals and Dalits have not realised the hope of Dr Ambedkar is the economic growth based development paradigm and the neglect of the social sector. India has made much progress. The middle class has grown from around 30 millions at independence to more than 250 millions today (Desrochers 1997: 201-202). The country has developed a good industrial base and produces every item that it imported before independence. Literacy has grown from 14 percent to 64 percent. Its birth rate has declined from 49 to 32 and child mortality from 250 to 82. Life expectancy has gone up from 40 to 65 years (2001 census CDs).

On the other side, at least 350 million Indians go to bed hungry. They include a majority of the tribals and Dalits. One cannot deny that many positive measures have been taken in their favour. They are entitled to free education up to the university level. 7.5 percent of jobs in the government and in public sector enterprises and seats in the legislature are reserved for the tribals and 15 percent for Dalits. Special economic programmes and sub-plans are prepared for them. But that has not changed the situation of a majority of them because this approach only ensures that schools, hospitals and legal support are made available but they are not accessible to them. Access requires a social infrastructure of education and financial autonomy. It does not exist.

Their poverty prevents them from making use of these benefits (Kurien 1996: 26 28).

The contrast can be best understood by looking at the Asian Tigers who are presented to the world only as a success story of capitalism and Mainland China as socialist success. In reality their success lies to a great extent in their effort to combine the economic with the social sector. For economic benefits to reach the masses not less that 10% of the GNP has to be invested in the social sector i.e. education, health, nutrition and hygiene. That is what South and North Korea, Malaysia, Indonesia under Soekarno, Singapore and the two Chinas did. On the one hand, the State supported the building of an industrial infrastructure through the public sector or by supporting private investors. On the other, they invested 8 to 15% of their GDP on the social components. It is possible that in countries like South Korea and Taiwan it was a way of creating a class of consumers but it also prepared the masses for jobs in the system and to access the benefits of economic development (Colonel-Ferer 1998).

In Mainland China the endeavor was to lift the masses from misery to poverty. In Malaysia the Bhumiputra policy of reservations for the Malays went far beyond the Indian approach. The Malay leaders extended the reservations both to the public and private sectors at every level. They also made massive investments in the education, health, nutrition and hygiene of the Malays thus preparing them for jobs and to be consumers.

India, on the contrary, stopped at reservations in the public sector. Those who can enter a school get free education. Those who complete their studies can hope to get a job in the public sector. But no effort is made to create the social infrastructure required for them to gain access to schools or to remain in them when they enter. Thus, only a small minority has got its benefits. That can turn reservations into a vested interest of the elite and a political tool of the ruling parties. They were meant to be a tool of social transformation. That cannot happen with this approach.

The Development Paradigm

A large number of them have been impoverished during the last six decades because most planners view development only as economic growth and neglect the social components of education, health, nutrition and hygiene. The choice of the development paradigm is crucial to this contradiction. The colonial regime had robbed the country of its resources and had left it undeveloped and impoverished. However, when India launched its five-year plans it forgot that the development of the West was possible only because of the exploitation of the working class at home and of the colonies abroad. The colonialists turned the colonies into suppliers of raw materials and capital for the industrial revolution in Europe and captive markets for its finished products. That impoverished the colonies. Newly independent countries that followed this path were bound to impoverish some of their own communities for the benefit of their middle class since they did not have colonies to exploit. Indian planners were convinced that western development resulted from technology alone and chose precisely this path (Vyasulu 1998).

Its result is seen in its impact on most tribes who live in the resource rich backward regions. Their resources have been exploited in the name of national development and people have been displaced in order to acquire land for projects. As a result, India has made economic progress but it has paid very little attention to the subalterns in general and the DP/PAPs in particular.

Deforestation too has been high for industries and other development projects. Its net result is tribal impoverishment. More than half of them are malnourished, two thirds continue to be illiterate and live below the poverty line. Today globalisation adds to their woes. More land than in the past is being acquired to encourage investment by the Indian and foreign private sector which is eyeing mining land in Jharkhand, Orissa and Chhattisgarh. Thus, there will be more displacement than in the last 60 years, much of it tribal for mining in Middle India and dams in the Northeast (IW-GIA: 2004: 314). A list of 168 dams has been prepared for the Northeast. 48 of them are under active consideration of the Government of India (Menon et al. 2003), all of them in the tribal areas where the community owns land according to their customary law. Thus displacement will grow but they may not even be compensated for what they lose since the land laws that have come down from the colonial regime do not recognise their CPRs as their sustenance.

ATTACK ON TRIBAL CULTURE

The focus till now has been land loss and impoverishment. To the tribals land and forests are not merely economic commodities but are also the centre of their culture and identity.

They have built their economic, social and political systems and have developed sustainable management systems around them. Basic to their culture is equity i.e. ensuring that every family gets enough for its needs. Secondly, the resources are treated as renewable i.e. used according to need and preserved for posterity. Thirdly, as long as land and forests are community owned, the woman has some say in their management. All the tribes are patriarchal. So she is only has a higher social status than women do in other communities do but she is not equal to men. Her relatively high status depends on community ownership of their resources. These values are basic to tribal identity (Menon 1995: 101).

All of them come under attack and a total crisis enters their life when the resource is alienated from them. Once land alienation or deforestation causes a shortage of resources they fall in the hands of moneylenders. For sheer survival they abandon their tradition, absorb a new culture and begin to destroy forests and other resources that they had preserved till then for posterity. That causes more shortages, individualism enters their communities and equity that is central to their culture gets weak.

Because they destroy the resource for survival, the middle class that begins the vicious circle of their destruction, calls them enemies of nature (Bharali 2007). Poverty also forces many of them to fill the urban slums from which they are evicted in order to keep the city beautiful. During 2006 evictions took place in Ahmedabad, Delhi, Mumbai and other cities. Most of its victims are Dalits who are 65 percent of the slum dwellers in the major cities. But today there are also many tribals whom deforestation and displacement have impoverished and forced to fill the slums.

Also the relatively high women's status, the third base of their identity, gets weak. The whole tribe loses out but women and children suffer more than men do. The tribal woman's relatively high status as a productive member of the family depends on her work in the community owned land and forests and her role as the main decision-maker in the family. The man was in charge of society. Once these resources are lost, she ceases to be an economic asset. If jobs and land are given, they are in the name of men. So power passes from her to the man and to his son. She is reduced to being only a housewife. With it also her social status suffers. One of the tribal reactions is to internalize the male culture of the dominant society according to which her place is in the kitchen and she is not intelligent enough to take up other work. Children too suffer. Child labour increases among them. For example, because of impoverishment 56 percent of the families studied in Assam and 49 percent in West Bengal pulled their children out of school to turn them into child labourers.

Tribal Reaction

Many tribes have reacted to their exploitation, some of them peacefully and others violently. In the Northeast violent reaction began with Nagaland demanding sovereignty already before 1947. Mahatma Gandhi seems to have been sympathetic to their demand of self-rule but other national leaders did not understand the aspirations of Northeast India where most tribes belong to the Mongoloid stock. So the Naga leaders declared independence on 14th August 1947, a day before Indian independence. The nationalist struggle that began with it continues to this day. An agreement was reached in 1963 to create the State of Nagaland and recognise their customary law. Not much has happened after it. A cease fire is in place for a decade but negotiations do not seem to make progress. The positions have remained almost unchanged for sixty years. Neither the Naga leaders nor the Indian State seem to be ready for a compromise. The struggle has spread from them to some other tribes of the Northeast. The Mizo who made the same demand in the 1960s gained a State of their own and recognition of their customary law. That is where they stop.

Two major issues dogging tribal identity are the indigenous status and sovereignty. Those who demand sovereignty have not defined it till today. The State and those opposed to it interpret sovereignty and selfdetermination as independence and secession. That is the main reason why India has not signed Convention 169 of the International Labour Organisation that speaks of the sovereignty and self-determination of indigenous peoples. Very few consider it its main or only meaning. A few demand independence but most interpret it as high autonomy whose nature is yet to be defined. So the stalemate continues.

Some tribes of Middle India who demand sovereignty interpret it as control over their economy and administration because their struggles are by and large for the protection of their land and forests. This issue is dominant in most struggles be it against the Narmada dam in Gujarat, Koel Karo and the Netarhat test firing range in Jharkhand, Kashipur and Kalinga Nagar Orissa or against uranium mining at Domiasiat in the Khasi Hills of Meghalaya.

Most tribal leaders are aware that acceptance of this status can be a step in protecting their land and culture but have not developed a viable definition of either. Some like the tribes struggling against the Koel-Karo dam and the test firing range in Jharkhand have succeeded in stopping the projects. Others have been less successful. For example, many tribals who have been opposing land acquisition for copper mining at Kashipur in Orissa have been jailed. Some have been killed in police firing. Also the tribes who demanded a better deal when 6,500 hectares were acquired at Kalinga Nagar in Orissa were suppressed. Twelve of them died when the armed police opened fire on 2nd January 2006.

On the other side, the Fifth Schedule area won a major victory in 1996 by getting the Parliament to enact a law on their self-rule at the village level. It respects their traditional political systems and stipulates that the villagers be consulted before land acquisition. It is a beginning and much more has to be done.

One can probably end this section by quoting the Austrian anthropologist Haimendorf (1980: 1) who did a study of the tribals in the 1940s. After a second study of the same tribes in the 1970s he asked "How do you explain the fact that their communities that were self-reliant thirty years ago today need State subsidies? Their women had a high status three decades ago. How have they lost it today?".

The question is not about development but about its type. One is left with the impression that the colonial system continues in a new form. A resource and capital intensive form of development was attempted in a former colony. In this system the tribal and other resource rich areas came to be treated only as suppliers of raw materials whose benefits reached the urban middle class and the rural upper classes just as the colony was turned into a supplier capital and raw materials for the European Industrial Revolution and a captive market for its finished products. It was bound to impoverish the tribals and other rural poor to the benefit of another class.

Conclusion

The effort in this paper has been to look at the tribal situation in the context of their aspirations at independence. The development paradigm ignored these aspirations and that has resulted in greater inequalities. One sees signs of internal colonialism in the sense that the resource rich tribal regions are used as sources of raw material to the benefit of another class. This contradiction has got intensified after globalisation with the Indian and foreign private sector wanting more of their land and other resources.

None of those who get its benefits question the development paradigm that causes inequalities. But those interested in the their progress have to search for the type that combines economic growth with the development of every human community. This search has to begin with the tribal communities themselves. The rest can only support them. That does not seem to be happening. Many tribal alliances are formed but unity of all the tribes is yet to come. That is essential if as a group they are to demand their right to be human and equal.

7

NOGs Role of Indian Tribal Development

INTRODUCTION

The non-governmental or the voluntary organisations have been playing a crucial role in all the socioeconomic spheres, including that of the tribal peoples, in India. At one level, they can be termed as the 'means' by which the nation makes optimum use of its human resources. However, the mushrooming of voluntary organisations working in the field of rural development in recent years has generated widespread debate about their role, structure, programmes and performance. A unique feature of voluntary organisations is that they stimulate voluntary action among the target community and involve the progressive elements of that community.

In the present context of human resource development, voluntary organisations, in their functioning, have demonstrated the freedom and flexibility of working with a personal touch, a capacity for initiative and experimentation with novel programmes. Thus, voluntary organisations exercise full freedom in selecting localities for programme implementation and are free of bureaucratic hassles.

In the Indian context, the attributes of a tribe are that they live in relative isolation of hills and covered forests, and often in geographical areas inaccessible to the mainstream population. Tribes generally are groups without a written letter or script. Their sense of history is shallow or mixed with mythology, and in terms of their cultural ethos, language, customs, institutions and beliefs, they stand out from other sections of society.

In India, tribes have different names such as vanyajati, vanavasi, pahariya, adimajati, janajati, anusuchit jati and scheduled tribes — all of which mean the 'aboriginal'. India stands second interms of tribal population after Africa in the world. According to the 2001 Census, the total population of the tribals is 84.2 million, and accounts for 8.2% of the country's population. There are about 689 scheduled tribes speaking about 105 languages and 225 subsidiary languages. They have traditionally lived in about 15% of the nation's geographical area, mainly forests, hills and the undulating inaccessible terrain in plateau areas that are rich in natural resources. They have lived mostly as isolated entities for centuries together and this explains their politico-socio-economic backwardness.

However, we have to acknowledge that even before the freedom struggle a few voluntary organisations were active in the sphere of tribal welfare. They also played a significant role in the field of rural development and nation building and continued to do so. Many great personalities took initiatives to form such organisations, which at present, are performing a key role at the grassroots level in implementing various developmental works. Until such time that a genuinely democratic machinery of governance evolves, there will remain a strong urge for voluntary organisations to play a mediating role between the State and the people.

As early as 1871, the Bhil Seva Mandal came up in Gujarat. At that time, A.V. Thakkar was the moving spirit behind voluntary organisations committed to tribal development. By the time India got independence, he could establish more than 20 voluntary institutions in different parts of the country. Some other leaders in the Indian National Congress were also involved in tribal development activities.

Dr. Rajendra Prasad's Bharatiya Adim Jati Sevak Sangh helped a lot in shaping the tribal policy when the Indian Constitution at the drafting stage. Various approaches have been evolved in the country in the domain of tribal affairs; prominent among them are the voluntary agency approach, the political approach and the anthropological approach. These three approaches find support in three important policies: 1. Policy of Isolation 2. Policy of Assimilation and 3. Policy of Integration.

After Independence, the policy of integration was found to be the most suitable one. Also, Nehru's concept of tribal integration was reflected in the successive five-year plans. The policy of integration is the outcome of serious research activities undertaken by many social anthropologists in India.

Its main objective is 'social integration and cultural assimilation'. It was in the fifth five-year plan that the tribal sub-plan (TSP) approach was adopted. In order to fulfil the sub-plan objectives nearly 198 ITDAs and 257 MADA pocket, 78 clusters and 75 micro projects for primitive tribal groups (PTGs) were set up all over the country. Consequently, various strategies came into being. With the passage of time, it has widely been noted that the programmes and activities related to tribal development cannot be implemented by the governments alone. Thus, the significance of participation of the community and the role of voluntary organisations/NGOs was realised in this all-important sphere.

Objectives:

- To study the role of NGO's/voluntary organizations in tribal development.
- To study the budgetary allocations for tribal welfare.
- To analyse the amount spent for various developmental programs like vocational training centres and literacy programs.
- To study the tribal participation in the NGO sector.

Methodology

The present study used the literature available in different tribal welfare departments, government of India source on tribal welfare, its budgetary allocation and their analysis. A detailed analysis was made using budgetary allocations and their expenditure on the literacy rate improvement, vocational training and other welfare activities. An interpretation was made from the financial year 2001-02 to 2006-07 on the different developmental programs.

Voluntary Organisations are Necessary

1. to supplement government efforts in such fields where the administrative machinery has no reach

2. to fight against policies and actions which encourage exploitation of the helpless groups and render help to such social groups, including the tribal groups, to stand on their own feet to protect their ways of living and lifestyles.

A voluntary organisation can easily adapt itself to the needs of the people. A sensitive worker can assess each specific situation with sympathy and personal care. Thus, the gulf that arises between what should be done and what is being done as a result of some what inflexible operation of the administrative apparatus, can be bridged.

OBJECTIVES OF NGOS/VOLUNTARY ORGANISATIONS

Whatever the nature of NGOs/voluntary organisations, they play a key role in the upliftment of the weaker sections of society. The objectives of voluntary or non-governmental agencies include some or all of the following:

1. To create an awareness regarding participation in socioeconomic development
2. To create an able and efficient local leadership
3. To assist in the planned efforts to create socioeconomic infrastructural facilities
4. To facilitate the process of expanding employment opportunities
5. To induce appropriate persons to set up small scale productions and
6. To make the tribals give up the pre-agricultural technology and seek better education.

ROLE OF NGOS/VOLUNTARY ORGANISATIONS

NGOs/voluntary organisations have a long history of active involvement in the promotion of human welfare and development. They come up with a mission to serve a human cause, spontaneously-voluntarily and without any compulsion or control, to fulfil certain needs of specific groups of people. These organisations are flexible and possess the virtue of humanitarian service with concern. Voluntary action is the soul of social action as this medium secures active involvement of the people from policy making to implementation of programmes. Their activities cover a diverse range of functions in the welfare sector. The programmes of voluntary organisations are strictly service-oriented, professional in nature and specialized in functions. The essential feature of voluntary action is that it fixes the problem. It starts to not only to solve a problem but also to prevent the occurrence of it. Voluntary action, thus, ultimately aims at creating a situation conducive to the development of potentialities in individuals, groups and communities so they can find solutions to their problems and realise their ultimate goals.

Regarding the role and nature of voluntary organisations, there appears to be two different views. Some are happy with the functioning of such organisations and plead for their increasing role. According to them, these organisations should be given ample scope to serve people. For, the government agencies, crippled as they are with bureaucratic complications and rigidity, have failed to work satisfactorily. Others hold that it is undesirable to give undue importance and authority to voluntary agencies as there is a great possibility of institutionalizing the chances.

In this context, the suggestion is that the voluntary organisations should be given ample scope to work in collaboration and cooperation with the government agencies and subject to strict government scrutiny and monitoring. The need for involving the NGOs in rural development was highlighted and acknowledged by various official committees set up by the Government of India. One of these was the Balwant Rai Mehta Committee (1957) which in its report emphasized that during the implementation of community development schemes more and more emphasis should be laid on NGO's/VOs. The Dhebar Commission in its report on the scheduled areas and Scheduled Tribes opined that the principle of active and purposeful participation of people at all levels could best be served by assigning an important role to non-official organisations. It is necessary in any democratic framework to take up some of the nation-building activities under non-official auspices.

The report of the committee on Panchayat Raj Institutions (1973) appreciated the role of voluntary organisations in the development of rural and interior areas. The committee reiterated that these organisations could be particularly involved in conceiving projects and schemes. They can be of great help in creating strong public opinion in support of measures of social change. The Sivaraman Committee set up by the Government of India also recommended involvement of voluntary organisations in planning and implementation of the integrated rural development programmes. Thus, there exists a widespread agreement among all the concerned that voluntary organisations have an important role to play in the overall development of the rural areas.

WELFARE OF THE SCHEDULED TRIBES

The Ministry of Tribal Affairs is the key governmental agency with respect to the welfare and development of the tribal peoples all over the country. It is the responsibility of the ministry to reach the target groups, particularly the tribals living in remote and inaccessible areas. The objective is to bring them into the mainstream of development by assisting them to overcome their social, psychological and educational backwardness. Capacity building is the key factor here. Such training would equip them to employ their capabilities to their fullest potential thereby reducing their reliance on others and achieving self-sustenance to the maximum extent possible – which is the ultimate goal of the government.

The NGOs supplement the efforts of the State in ensuring that the benefits reach the maximum number of people. In certain cases, voluntary organisations are in a better position to implement the governmental schemes in a more efficient manner than the administrative machinery. This is primarily attributable to the highly committed and dedicated human resources that are available with the voluntary organisations. The role of NGOs was in the reckoning since the first five-year plan. Many organisations have done commendable job in tribal areas and are still active. Since the last two decades, there has been an exponential growth in the number of NGO/VOs approaching the ministry of tribal affairs for financial assistance.

It has been felt that along with few very dedicated and committed voluntary organisations/non-governmental organisations a large number of other organisations have also come up that want to grab public funds for their narrow and selfish interests. The ministry would take all the possible steps to curb the entry of such voluntary organisations/non–governmental organisations in the field of tribal welfare. The Ministry of Tribal Affairs feels that some organisations solely depend on aid from the government. This situation has to change. The voluntary organisations should aim to expand their effort on the support from the government and thereafter establish other support systems that could free them from financial constraints.

It should be the intention of the organisations to obtain support of other sources for their work. This can happen after they establish themselves with the support of the government and prove their usefulness to society, at large. If the impression that NGOs can support themselves financially gains ground, then the support of corporate houses and even the community would follow as a natural consequence. Contribution, both in kind and cash, would come easily once their credentials are firmly established. Additional resources, if necessary, could also be mobilised. Voluntary organisations should make all possible efforts to involve the community in their work. Community participation helps in building confidence among the people and in providing feedback for further improvement and reorientation of the programmes. Thus, the long-term interests of the tribal communities can be served. The Ministry of Tribal Affairs endeavors to provide full advantage of all schemes to the non-governmental organisations/ voluntary organisations that have absolute credentials in the field of tribal welfare. It also wants to promote new groups with brilliant ideas and new strategies for the speedy development of the targeted people.

It has been the constant endeavor of the ministry to identify the voluntary organisations/non-governmental organisations which have an all India character and known for their selfless service and facilitate them with some preferential treatment with regard to sanction of new proposals and relaxation of certain norms and conditions relating to release of annual grants. In this direction, the ministry has identified a few such organisations and categorized them as "Established Voluntaries Agencies (EVAs)"

The following organisations have been identified as the EVAs by the ministry:

1. Ram Krishna Mission and its affiliated organisations

2. Akhil Bharatiya Banavasi Kalyan Ashram
3. Bharat Sevashram Sangh and its affiliates
4. Bharatiya Adim Jati Sevak Sangh
5. Seva Bharati & its affiliated organisations
6. Vidya Bharati and its affiliated organisations
7. Swami Vivekanand Youth Movement

Schemes in the Voluntary Sector

There are three on-going schemes with the ministry, which are open to participation of the voluntary and non-governmental organisations. The schemes are:

1. Grant–in–aid to voluntary organisations working for welfare of scheduled tribes (GVWST).
2. Educational complex in low literacy pockets for the development of women's literacy in tribal areas (ECLP)
3. Vocational training centres (VTC)

In addition to the said schemes, the ministry has an exclusive programme for non-governmental organisations with regard to the development of primitive tribal groups (PTGs)

Objective: The prime objective of the scheme is to provide for an overall improvement and development of the target group i.e., the scheduled tribes though voluntary efforts in the fields of education, health & sanitation, environment, drinking water and legal services as well as the need-based socioeconomic upliftment efforts. It also supports other relevant activity deemed appropriate and having a direct impact on the target group. The scheme is under implementation since 1953-54.

Salient features: The grants are provided to the non-governmental organisations on their application in prescribed formats, in the form of supporting projects that meet the objectives of the scheme. The NGO's are required to maintain separate accounts in respect of the grants released to them, which are open for inspection by all appropriate officers/agencies of the government. The NGO is also required to maintain separate accounts of Grant-in-Aid audited by the Government Auditor or a Registered Chartered Accountant and submit complete set of copies of Audited Statement of Accounts as prescribed by the Ministry. The grants are generally made in two installments every year subject to satisfactory performance of the NGO. Activities of the NGOs are monitored as per the established provisions of the Financial Rules besides field inspection by the Ministry or the State Government officials or by any other agency designated by the Ministry.

Funding Pattern: Funds are granted – to the extent of 100 per cent – directly to the Non-Governmental Organizations working in the Scheduled Areas based on the recommendations of the State Governments and the Union Territories. The non-governmental organizations are supported to the extent of 90 percent of the project cost for projects in areas other than Scheduled Areas. However, the Ministry of Tribal Affairs has the discretion to assist even up to hundred percent.

Schemes of Educational Complex in Low Literacy Pockets

The Scheme was introduced in 1993-94 in 136 districts with less than 10 per cent literacy rate among tribal women. It is being implemented through:

1. Non-Governmental Organizations
2. Institutions set up by the Government as Autonomous Bodies and
3. Registered Cooperative Societies.

Objectives: The primary objective of the scheme is the promotion of education among tribal girls in the targeted districts of the country. The secondary objective is to improve the socioeconomic status of the economically backwards and the illiterate tribal masses.

Coverage: The scheme covers 136 districts with less than 10 percent literacy among ST women spread over 14 States namely Andhra Pradesh, Bihar, Chattisgarh, Gujarat, Jharkhand, Madhya Pradesh, Orissa, Rajasthan, Tamil Nadu, Uttar Pradesh, Uttaranchal and West Bengal.

Procedure for Release of Grant-in-aid and Funding Pattern

1. The extent of assistance under the scheme would be 100% in all cases.
2. In the event of the Ministry of Welfare itself executing any element of the programme i.e. engagement of consultants,

for project formulation, monitoring and evaluation, as well as expenses towards cost of training of NGO functionaries, etc, full cost shall be borne from the budgetary provision of the scheme.

3. Under the programme, while predefined cost heads are stipulated at the project formulation stage, each implementing agency shall submit a detailed project proposal clearly bringing out the programme modalities and individual expenditure heads. Ministry of Welfare while approving the project shall indicate the extent of support to the project as a whole as well as to each component of the project against which re-appropriation to the extent 20% of the total grant shall be permissible.

Salient Feature: Educational complexes can be set up in rural areas in the notified districts and can have classes up to V with provision for up-gradation up to Class XII provided they have sufficient accommodation for classrooms, hostels, kitchen, and garden and for sporting facilities. These educational complexes impart not only formal education to tribal girls but also train students in agriculture, animal husbandry and other vocations and crafts as to make them skilled for leading a better life. The teaching from classes I to III is imparted in tribal dialects of the area and women with proficiency in tribal dialect are engaged as teachers. The strength of students for each class is fixed at 30, however a maximum of 10 more students, if available, in the locality are admitted as day scholars.

PERFORMANCE OF THE SCHEMES

It can be concluded there is not much increase in the amount spent for the tribal welfare through Grant-in-aid. In the year 2001-02 an amount of 27 crores was allocated but only eleven crores was spent. In the following years all most all the allocated amount was spent completely but there no increase in the budget allocation.

Establishment of Ashram Schools

The Ashram schools have played an important role in raising the literacy levels of the scheduled Tribes. They provide the necessary environment conductive to learning. The schedule is in operation since 1990-91.

Construction of Girls Hostel for scheduled Tribes

The main objective of the scheme is to ensure adequate enrolment of scheduled Tribes girls in educational institutions, particularly at the school stage. The scheme of girls' hostels for scheduled tribes has been in operation since the Third Five Year Plan.

Construction of Boys Hostel for Schedule Tribes

The main objective of the scheme is to ensure adequate enrolment of Scheduled Tribes boys in educational institutions, particularly, at the high school level. The scheme of Boys Hostel for Scheduled Tribes has been in operation since 1989-90 under the Centrally-sponsored scheme of Establishment of Boy's Hostel in Tribal Sub-Plan areas.

Schemes for Primitive Tribal Groups (PTGs)

Objective: There are certain tribal communities that are having low levels of literacy, declining or stagnant population, and pre-agriculture level of technology and are economically backward. There are 75 such groups in 15 States/UTs that have been identified and categorized as the Primitive Tribal Groups (PTGs). Each of these groups is small in number, differentially developed with respect to one another, of remote habitat with poor administrative and infrastructure back up. Therefore, they are in urgent need of support from the government as well as the non-government agencies. Their protection and development at par with other tribal groups has to be accorded utmost priority.

The problems and needs of PTGs are quite different from other scheduled tribes. Since they constitute the most vulnerable among tribal groups, States/UTs have been requested to allocate requisite funds and plan special schemes for their socioeconomic development. However, there are areas/activities, which though very crucial for the survival, protection and development of PTGs, are not specifically catered to by any existing scheme. Funds under this scheme should be used for such activities.

Scope: Such provisions/activities should not be identified only at the central level as they may differ from State to State and within a State from project to project (ITDA). However, funds under the scheme could be used for helping the beneficiaries of the project to cope with extremely adverse situations that threaten their very survival and protect them against various forms of exploitation thereby bringing them to a stage from where they can demand and receive specific assets and services.

The activities under the scheme may include measures such as awareness generation and confidence-building, training for skill development of tribal youth, self help groups and provision of services/inputs not covered by any existing scheme. In terms of beneficiaries, the scheme can cover maximum number of the PTGs.

Implementing agency: The scheme will be implemented through integrated tribal development projects (ITDP)/Integrated Tribal Development agencies (ITDAs), tribal research institutes (TRI) and non governmental organisations having requisite skills and determination. The State government concerned will be responsible for proper execution, implementation, supervision and coordination of the scheme, including selection of NGOs.

Terms& Conditions

1. The financial assistance as provided under the scheme should be utilized for the purpose it has been sanctioned and for the welfare of the members of the Primitive Tribal Groups
2. The financial assistance given to ITDPs/ITDAs and TRIs would deemed to be given to the state governments concerned and rules and regulation governing the grant in aid to States/UTs will apply to them.
3. The implementing agency shall allow the representative of the Ministry of Tribal Affairs or the State government to monitor or evaluate the actual working of the scheme.
4. The private agencies (NGOs) shall furnish a certificate to the effect that they accept the grant sanctioned to them subject to terms and conditions laid down by the Tribal Affairs Ministry. They should also furnish a bond with two sureties in the name of the competent authority signed by an office bearer duly authorized by the Board of Directors of the agency for the actual implementation of the scheme and submit accounts of the grant sanctioned by the ministry.

The expenditure incurd was not the total amount sanctioned. For example in the year 2002-03 an amount of 7 crores rupees was allocated but only 6 crores was spent. It is nearly the same spending in the next three following financial years.

Vocational Training Centres

Objectives: There is a great need for vocational training centres in tribal areas where the Left wing extremism is on the rise. Large-scale unemployment has been stoking rebellious tendencies among the tribal youth in such areas.

The extremism is manifestation of frustration and lack of faith in the present pattern of development. It is necessary that both the State and Central governments should make efforts to wean away the tribal youth from disruptive activities. Establishing vocational training institutes and creating a wide range of employment opportunities can be the way forward.

The amount spent for vocational training centres is very less and also the amount being spent on such programs is being reduced. In the year 2002-03 though the amount that was sanctioned was 3 crores, only 2.3 crores was spent. This trend continued in the following years.

Non-governmental organisations shall meet the following requirements:

1. It is a registered body under an appropriate Act so that it gets a corporate status. A legal personality and a group liability have to be established for its activities.
2. It has an appropriate administrative structure and a duly constituted managing/executive committee
3. The aims and objects of the organisations and programmes in fulfillment of those aims and objects are preciously laid down and
4. The organisation is initiated and governed by its own members on democratic principles without any external control.

Procedure for Release of Grant-in-Aid

1. Under the scheme, 100% Central assistance will be given to States/UTs/NGOs for setting up and running of vocational training centres.

2. In the event of ministry of welfare itself executing any element of the programme i.e. engagement of consultants for project formulation, monitoring and evaluation as well as expenses towards cost of training of NGO functionaries etc. full cost shall be borne from the budgetary provision of the scheme.
3. Under the programme while no predefined cost heads shall be stipulated at the project formulation stage, each implementing agency shall submit a detailed project proposal clearly bringing out the programme modalities and individual expenditure heads. Ministry of welfare while approving the projects shall indicate the extent of support to the project as whole as well as to each component of the project against which re-appropriation to the extent of 20%of the total grant shall be permitted.

Conclusion

In India, we have a pluralistic society as opposed to a monolithic culture. The voluntary organisations cater to the needs of our cultural plurality. If we would like to avoid concentration of power in the hands of a few, we must retain this multi-ethnic character of a free society and make full use of it. Voluntary organisations can serve as 'power breakers'. Efforts should be made to prepare people for a new kind of society through voluntary work. When the State's resources are limited, voluntary action would bring forth additional resources and cover the areas hitherto uncovered by the State. In view of their flexibility in operation, ability at experimentation and innovation, pioneering spirit and other such qualities, voluntary organisations can continue to work for better standards, better methods and better forms of organisation. There is an argument that at the empirical-existential level voluntary agencies are nothing but the stooges of the ruling elite and the corporate sector, mainly of the capital finance variety. In this new role, voluntary organisations have created a crisis that begs a comprehensive solution.

However, given the circumstances in terms of administrative or governmental reach, especially in the implementation of welfare schemes for the tribal peoples, we for once cannot deny the positive role of the non-governmental organisations. There are many areas yet to blink the state's radar. They are either very remote or inaccessible. In such a situation, the concerned and committed civil society groups have no other alternative but voluntary approach. The role of NGOs in the fields of education, health, sanitation, housing and particularly agriculture has not been a wide ranging one. We shall hope they would expand their area of action.

TRIBAL DEVELOPMENT IN INDIA

The Scheduled Tribes (STs) according to the 1991 Census account for 67.76 millions representing 8.08 per cent of the country's population. They are spread across the country mainly in the forest and hilly regions. More than 70 per cent of the ST population is concentrated in Madhya Pradesh, Maharashtra, Orissa, Bihar, Andhra Pradesh, West Bengal and Gujarat. The essential characteristics of these communities are primitive traits, geographical isolation, distinctive culture, shyness of contact with communiies at large and backwardness.

The founding fathers of the Indian constitution were aware of their problems. Therefore, they made special provisions for their protection and development. The main safeguards include promotion of educational and economic interests and their protection from social injustices and all forms of exploitation. The constitution protects the general rights of all Indian citizens to move freely, settle anywhere and acquire property. It also permits the States to make reservation in public services in case of inadequate representation and requiring them to consider their claims in appointments to public services. The constitution provides special representation for the STs in the Lok Sabha and State legislative assemblies till 25th January, 2010 (Arts, 330, 332 and 334) and enjoins the setting up of separate departments in the States and National Commission at the Centre to promote their welfare and safeguard their interests (Arts 164 and 338). Special provision for administration and control of Schedule Areas and Tribal Areas (Art. 224, Fifth and Sixth Schedules) and grant-in-aid to the States to meet the cost of such schemes of development as may be undertaken by them for promoting the welfare of the Schedule Tribes or raising the level of Schedule Areas (Art. 275 (1) are also guaranteed. Later on with a view to effectively deal with the crimes against the Scheduled Tribes two special laws, viz., Protection of Civil Rights Act, 1955 and the Scheduled Castes, Scheduled Tribes (Prevention of Atrocities) Act 1989 were enacted.

Special economic development of the Scheduled Tribes and protection against their exploitation has been an important agenda of the Government. To ensure that the constitutional mandates listed above and translated into various policies and programmes and put into effective action, high priority for the welfare and development of Scheduled Tribes right from the beginning of the First Five Year Plan (1952-57 is being accorded. Recognising their special problems the principles of *Panchsheel* have been adopted in the welfare and development of these communities so as to ensure an understanding of their culture and traditions and an appreciation of the social, psychological and economic problems with which they are faced. An important landmark was opening of 43 Special Multipurpose Tribal Blocks (SMPTBs) during the Second Five Year Plan, later called Tribal Development Blocks (TDBs), each having about 25000 people as against 65000 in a normal block. An amount of Rs.15.0 lakh per SMPTB was contributed by the Central Government. Further, an important step in this direction was taken during the Fourth Five Year Plan when six pilot projects in Andhra Pradesh, Bihar, Madhya Pradesh and Orissa were set up in the Central sector. A separate Tribal Development Agency was established for each project and an amount of Rs.2.0 crore was allotted to these agencies. Commissions and Committees appointed by the Government to review the tribal situation brought to its notice that the percolation theory had not helped the tribals in getting their due share and the backward classes sector had substituted general sectors instead of supplementing them and viewed that much more was still needed to be done to bring up the STs on par with the general population of the country.

TRIBAL SUB-PLAN

The Fifth Five Year Plan marked a shift in the approach when the Tribal Sub Plan (TSP) for direct benefit of the STs was launched. The Tribal Sub-Plan for the Scheduled Tribes was designed to channelise the flow of outlays and benefits from the general sectors in the plans of the States and Union Territories (UTs) and Central Ministries in proportion to their population both in physical and financial terms. It is an umbrella under which all schemes implemented by the States and Central Governments are dovetailed for addressing different needs of the Scheduled Tribes.

It is basically an area development programme with focus on tribals under which infrastructural development and family-oriented programmes are undertaken. The strategy has been successful in garnering larger flow of funds for the development of Scheduled Tribes from Rs. 759 crore during the Fifth Five Year Plan to about Rs. 16902.66 crore by the end of the Eighth Five Year Plan (1992-97).

The Ministry of Tribal Affairs, besides providing Special Central Assistance, which is an additive to the Tribal Sub Plan of the States and UTs and grants under Article 275 (1) of the Constitution for raising the level of infrastructure in the Scheduled Areas and economic development of the Scheduled Tribes to the level of general population, is also implementing various Centrally-sponsored and Central sector schemes under which financial assistance ranging from 50 per cent to 100 per cent is given to the States and UTs for construction of hostels and coaching of ST students for competitive examinations, upgradation of their merit, research and training, setting up of *ashram* schools, vocational training centres, village grain banks, educational complexes for ST girls in low literacy pockets and development of primitive tribal groups. Besides, non-governmental organisations (NGOs) have also been involved in the development of STs. Their developmental and financial needs are being taken care of over and above the credit available through priority sector lending of banks and other institutions by the NSFDC.

With the prime objective of providing marketing assistance and remunerative prices to tribals for their minor forest produce (MFP) and surplus agricultural produce (SAP) and to wean them away from exploitative private traders and middlemen, the Tribal Cooperative Marketing Development Federation (TRIFED) was set up by the Government in the year 1987. The TRIFED has ensured remunerative prices for the MFP to tribals.

While these achievements are a matter of some satisfaction as various development plans, policies and programmes have brought forth a perceptible improvement in the socioeconomic status of the Scheduled Tribes a lot more needs to be done with concerted focus on the issues crucial to improve their status on par with the rest of the population. These are: prevention of land alienation from tribal to no-tribal, review of National Forest Policy and Forest (Conservation) Act 1980, taking into consideration symbiotic relationship the tribals are having with forest, provision of clean drinking water and medical facilities, effective rehabilitatiion of the tribals displaced on account of setting up of development projects and legal measures to crub the activities of money lenders and traders by effective implementation of laws and regulations. Women play a significant role in tribal society: their empowerment with upgradation of their skills is one of the issues to be addressed urgently. To look into these issues and further focus attention on the development of tribals the Government has set up separate Ministry under the charge of a Cabinet Minister. The Government is working hard towards a new social order based on social equality and social harmony.

RESOLUTION ON TRIBAL PROBLEMS

The 18th congress of the Communist Party of India (Marxist) reaffirms its firm pledge to organise ceaseless struggles of people of the scheduled tribes against all forms of exploitation, social oppression and discrimination, which have intensified in the neo-liberal regime.

The NDA government, far from addressing the real problems of the tribals, had implemented the provision contained in the Forest Act of 1980 to evict them from their own traditional habitat. The Forest Act provisions, which are anti-tribal, have to be withdrawn.

In response to the militant revolts of the tribal people, colonial rule was forced to enact legislation to prevent the alienation of tribal people from their land. However, this legislation proved altogether ineffective and that legacy continues today. The fraudulent transfer of the land of tribal people to non-tribals has intensified after the mining sector has been opened up to corporate plunder. There has been massive eviction of tribal people from their land in order to handover the land to private corporations, Indian and foreign. There are more than 84 million people of the scheduled tribes in India today; more than 15 per cent of them have been displaced without any comprehensive programme of rehabilitation in order to make way for development projects such as dams, manufacturing industries, and mines. The traditional access of the tribal people to forest and minor forest resources has made them victims of the contractor-forest official nexus. These circumstances have forced many Adivasi people into contract labour gangs and even to bonded labour and many atrocities are being committed on them.

Illiteracy, poverty, ill-health, malnutrition, hunger and starvation continue to be higher among the scheduled tribes than among any other section of the population. The designation of criminal tribes by the British of certain communities, though formally annulled in 1952, continues to be used by the police administration, who treat these communities as 'habitual criminals'. The identities of the scheduled tribes of India – their culture and languages – and the status of tribal women today are under serious threat. Only the Left-ruled states stand as an exception — be it with regard to the question of land, or, those of culture, language, regional autonomy and extension of the Scheduled Areas Act. If not for the intervention of CPI(M) members of parliament, *Santhali* would never have been included in the Eighth Schedule of the Constitution.

The tribal problem of the North-East is of a somewhat different nature. Successive central governments have ignored the development needs of the region, particularly with respect to the building of infrastructure. Due to the spread of education in North East states, a good number of educated unemployed tribal youth are not getting any avenue for future employment and are thereby frustrated. These frustrated youth are becoming victims of certain divisive forces who are channelising them towards insurgency in the region. In many cases, they are aided and abetted by the agencies connected with imperialist forces, which are very active in destabilising our country.

The capacity of our Party to emerge as the party of the toiling scheduled tribes is illustrated nowhere so well as in Tripura and West Bengal. Against heavy odds in Tripura this year, the CPI(M) and its allies won all the 28 seats in the Tribal Area Autonomous District Council, winning 72 per cent of the popular vote. In West Bengal, in all Adivasi-dominated areas, the CPI(M) has won the overwhelming majority of seats at every level of representation – parliament, assembly, zilla parishad, block and gram panchayat.

The 18th congress of CPI(M) resolves to forge the unity of all toiling sections in the tribal areas in the struggle to realise the 13-point tribal people's charter of demands formulated in the last Party congress and at the All-India Tribal Convention held at Ranchi in November 2001. The congress calls upon all sections of tribal and non-tribal people to launch countrywide struggles to force the government of India to implement the following urgent demands of the tribal masses of our country without further delay.

- Scrap the infamous Tribal Policy Document prepared by the NDA government and stop the eviction of tribal people from the land they have been living from time immemorial.
- Restore land by fresh enactment which got alienated from the tribals by fraudulent means and ensure all loopholes that permit fraudulent transfers are plugged;
- Enforce the Samata judgement of the Supreme Court and the provision of the Panchayat Extension Act in the 6th Schedule Areas. Amend the Fifth and Sixth Schedules of the Constitution to provide more autonomy to these areas;
- Amend the Forest Conservation (Amendment) Act of 1988. The degraded land should be distributed among the tribals with financial assistance from government for horticulture.
- Implement a comprehensive rehabilitation package for displaced persons before undertaking any essential development project in tribal areas in consultation of local people.
- Provide wage employment, institutional credit, universal school education, health facilities, safe drinking water and food security through universal public distribution and social welfare schemes in tribal areas.
- Implement reservation policies for all categories of education and employment.
- The government should come forward to maintain distinct identity of indigenous tribal art and culture and allocate funds for its proper promotion.
- Proper identification of de-notified and nomadic tribes of our country are made and constitutional safeguards to be ensured. Appropriate govern ment aided programmes are to be taken up earnestly for their socioeconomic upliftment.

8

Tribal Children's Right to Education in India

ISOLATED COMMUNITIES AND IGNORED CLAIMS: TRIBAL CHILDREN'S RIGHT TO EDUCATION IN INDIA

Indigenous communities of India are commonly referred to as tribal or *adivasi* communities and are recognised as Scheduled Tribes under the Constitution of India. Although the Constitution does not define Scheduled Tribes as such, it designates these communities as those which are scheduled in accordance with Article 342 of the Constitution. According to Article 342 of the Constitution, the Scheduled Tribes are the tribes or tribal communities or part of or groups within these tribes and tribal communities which have been declared as such by the President through a public notification. The criteria followed for specification of a community, as scheduled tribe are indications of primitive traits, distinctive culture, geographical isolation, shyness of contact with the community at large, and backwardness. At present, 533 tribes in India have been notified under Article 342 of the Constitution with the largest number of 62 tribes belonging to the State of Orissa.

SOCIO-ECONOMIC AND DEMOGRAPHIC PROFILE

As per the 1991 Census, the Scheduled Tribes (ST) account for 67.76 million representing 8.08 percent of the country's population. Of this, 1.32 million (1.95%) belong to Primitive Tribal Groups (PTG) who are more marginalised than the ST population. The ST population is estimated to have reached 88.8 million in 2001 which is 8.6% of the country's total population in 2001. The

Scheduled Tribes are spread across the country and reside mainly in forest and hilly regions. The proportion of Scheduled Tribes within general population varies across States/Union Territories and indicates heavy concentration in certain parts such as Mizoram (94.7%), Lakshwadeep (93.2%), Meghalaya (85.5%), Dadra and Nagar Haveli (78.9%). States of Kerala (1.1%), Tamil Nadu (1%) and Uttar Pradesh (0.2%) have a low percentage of Scheduled Tribe population in comparison to the general population. Since Independence, the percentage of ST population has steadily increased following the growth in general population.

It is also important to note that a large majority of tribals in India are landless and do not have a sustainable source of livelihood. The 1991 Census figures reveal that 42.02 percent of the Scheduled Tribe population were main workers (those who were employed for more than 183 days in the preceding year) of whom 54.50 percent were cultivators and 32.69 percent agricultural labourers.

Thus, about 87 percent of the main workers from these communities were engaged in primary sector activities. While a majority of those employed do not receive even the statutory minimum wages, tribal women are found to be doubly exploited since they are paid even less than the tribal men. It is thus not surprising that poverty is widely prevalent among tribal population in India. Even when the overall levels of poverty for tribal population have reduced between 1993-94 to 1999-2000 from 51.94% to 45.86% among the rural tribal population and 41.14% to 34.75% among the urban tribal population, two important trends can be observed. Firstly, the rate of decline in poverty among the STs is much lower than that among the general population and secondly, the gap between poverty rates among tribal and general population is widening. A number of Scheduled Tribes living below poverty line have been provided economic assistance to enable them to rise above the poverty-line. However, this assistance has decreased from Rs. 9.98 lakh during 1999-2000 to 8.81 lakh during 2000-2001.

The sex ratio among the STs, although significantly higher than the general population, has been slowly declining. While there were 982 tribal females for every 1000 tribal males in 1971, the 1991 Census shows that there are only 972 females for every

1000 tribal males. This could be indicative of their poor access to health services.

Educational Status of Tribals in India

. Tribal children, like several marginalised groups of children in India, are trapped in an intergenerational vicious cycle of poverty, illiteracy and deprivation. This is evident in extremely poor adult literacy rates which are reproduced as low education levels among the children from ST communities. This section presents some key data points on educational status of ST communities as a whole as well as schooling status of tribal children. The literacy rate of Scheduled Tribes is abysmally low at around 29.60 percent, as against the national average of 52.21 percent. A review of literacy rates among ST population in comparison with that of the general population indicates a growing gap between literacy rates of these two communities.

It is also important to note that the 1991 literacy rates for STs are almost equal to the literacy rates of the total population in 1971!

Female literacy is another significant indicator of educational development within any social group. Research studies have shown the importance of female literacy and education in uplifting the socioeconomic parameters of a given society. In the context of tribal women in India, illiteracy is so highly prevalent that their engagement with the mainstream society is seriously limited. While more than three-quarters of ST women are illiterate, 77 districts in India have tribal female literacy rates lower than ten percent and 14 districts have less than three percent tribal female literacy rate.

Inter-state differences in the literacy rates of tribal population is evident with tribes from North Eastern States of India showing high literacy rates. The highest literacy rate among tribals in Mizoram (82.73%) is attributed to a spread of Christian missionary educational institutions and a strong matrilineal family system among the Khasi and Garo tribes belonging to the State. Low literacy rates are seen among the tribals from Madhya Pradesh (21.54%) and Orissa (22.31%).

The above data shows that the gross enrolment ratio for Classes 1-5 and Classes 1-8 has declined from 1990-91 to 1999-2000 for the total population, but in the case of ST population it has decreased for Classes 1-5 (except for girls) but has improved for Classes 1-8. But there still remains an almost five percentage point gap between the enrolment of ST girls and non-ST girls wherein less than half of ST girls are not even enrolled in schools. Yet, this large scale enrolment of ST children in schools has been on account of wide scale government efforts to universalise education and a growing demand among the tribal communities to access formal education system, perhaps as a means to achieve inclusion in the mainstream. However, this has had its own ramifications. While schools as institutions and teachers as critical agents have remained fundamentally unchanged, the school atmosphere has not always become conducive to accept 4 and retain these children in schools. As we shall see later in this paper, tribal children's school experience is an important variable which determines whether the child continues to be in school or decides to drop out.

The problem of drop outs persists among all categories of children in India. However, in the context of children studying in Classes 1-10 the gap between the ST and total population in reduction of drop-outs has widened from 1990-91 to 1998-99. The reduction in the drop out rates could be because of various incentive schemes run by the State Governments for education of ST children such as those providing free books, uniforms and scholarships in government schools. But schemes such as those providing for hostels for ST boys and girls are not implemented fully by the States owing to lack of financial resources and therefore fewer ST children pursue high school education. The policy of reserving special seats for ST students at higher education levels is not widely availed since a large number of ST students do not even reach those levels and drop out at lower levels of school education. Even the *Ashram schools* (residential schools for ST boys and girls) started by the Government in 1990-91 are poorly maintained and sometimes lack even the basic facilities. Given the low levels of literacy among the ST population, several children from these communities happen to be 'first generation learners' and in the absence of State support for helping them cope with studies, very many children drop out of the schools.

This disproportionately low representation of ST children at higher levels of education compounds the existing disparities among Indian society. Lack of proactive governance in favour of the STs is not linked only to lack of resources. Governmental indifference and lack of political will are largely responsible for the callous state of affairs. The unutilised amount for tribal welfare for the years 1998-20011 for all the states combined was Rs. 40546.46 lakhs. States with high proportion of ST population also had high amounts of unutilised funds with Bihar (Rs. 8113.26 lakhs), Jharkhand (Rs. 4742.62 lakhs), Madhya Pradesh (Rs. 4721.61 lakhs) and Gujarat (Rs. 3721.72 lakhs) topping the order.

The School Experience

At school, the experiences of tribal children range from discrimination to a sense of complete alienation. Students from ST communities encounter a series of obstacles including commuting long distances to school in hostile environmental conditions, abuses and discrimination from teachers and fellow students from non-tribal backgrounds, difficulty in comprehending the language of instruction and negotiating space for themselves which was denied historically.

Children's denominational identities have always affected their school experiences. Ideally, the school teacher must play a vital role in supporting the struggles of first-generation learners. But it is found that although there is formal inclusion in the mainstream education system in the sense that children are officially enrolled, the teachers are often found to question the 'educability' of tribal children, revealing that nothing much has changed in the perceptions held about the 'other' by teachers who are generally drawn from mainstream social groups.

Research shows that tribal children are often subjected to overt discrimination by non-tribal upper caste school teachers who view them as 'slow learners' unable to learn despite several repetitions; as 'unclean' and are therefore given tasks of sweeping and swabbing the schools unlike non-tribal upper caste children who may be asked to fetch water or lock the school. Teachers also demean tribal children by calling their parents 'drunken', with no interest in schools and education. Untouchability is also found to prevail in schools, where upper caste teachers and students refuse to drink water from the same tap as the tribal children before washing it thoroughly. Even play activities and school transactions are sometimes segregated on the basis of these identities. The tribal children are repeatedly subjected to verbal abuse at the hands of upper caste teachers and this has a critical impact on the way these first generation students view themselves as learners.

Since the tribal languages are distinctly different from the medium of instruction in schools (which is usually the respective State language) tribal children often find it extremely difficult to cope with their studies and homework. This lack of language skills acts as a serious impediment when the teacher is a non-tribal and makes no effort to link the two linguistic experiences for the child. Aspirations among tribal children are also low considering that there are not many formally educated persons in such communities. The inability to secure jobs amongst tribals who have completed formal education have lead some to get disillusioned with the education system and question the futility of spending several years struggling to get educated. Some consider school educated children as unfit to carry out their hereditary occupations thereby rendering them 'useless' in their traditional lives. Yet, the motivation of a large number of tribal children to walk hours to reach school, tolerate the rebuke of teachers and fellow students, their efforts to identify with a language and curriculum that is alien to their own life worlds and their struggles to break free of their historical marginalisation is definitely striking.

A QUESTION OF TRIBAL RIGHTS

In several societies, children's rights are intrinsically linked to respect for human rights and it would be almost impractical to separate rights of children from those of their families and communities. Fulfilment of third generation of rights i.e. group or community rights is often imperative considering that it is not children's rights alone but those of an entire community which are under extreme risk. By bestowing children from such social groups rights that are not enjoyed by their families or communities, superficial lines get drawn between children and their families or communities while making a farce of realising children's rights. It also presumes that children's rights can be respected while the rights of their parents and communities are persistently violated. However, as we shall see below, children's rights remain unfulfilled so long as the position of their social group is not improved. In the Indian context too, tribal children's rights are more likely to get realised if rights of tribal communities are holistically recognised and fulfilled. The following problems faced by tribal communities in India make it extremely difficult for tribal children to gain entry and sustain within the mainstream education system.

Displacement: Forced or voluntary eviction of tribals from their homes and habitats has been a serious problem since Independence. Large scale projects such as large dams, power plants, industrial units, large mining projects undertaken on tribal lands for the 'larger public good' very often provide little to the displaced communities. For years, questions have been raised about the unsatisfactory manner in which they have been rehabilitated. Research shows that between 1951 and 1990, a population of 21.3 million persons have been displaced in the states of Andhra Pradesh, Bihar, Gujarat, Maharashtra, Madhya Pradesh, Rajasthan and Orissa. Of this, 8.54 million are tribals (40 percent of the total) and of those only 2.12 million (24.8 percent) tribals have been resettled so far.3 In the absence of appropriate rehabilitation, displaced communities are uprooted and forced to migrate to newer areas. While they may settle down on forestlands in the new villages or in urban slums in case they migrate to cities, their settlement is considered illegal and they are therefore denied even the basic civic amenities. Children belonging to families of displaced tribal families are never able to continue schooling even if they were enrolled initially, and usually end up in wage employment in order to support the family's fresh set of challenges.

Land Alienation: Among tribal communities, land and its natural resources are sacrosanct and hold significant place in their socio-cultural and religious life. It is also the main source of livelihood and Minor Forest Produce (MFP) is known to help several communities to survive.

Given the vulnerability of tribal communities in India, several of them have had to part with their treasured resource for reasons ranging from acquisition of land for public purposes, encroachments by non-tribals or 'outsiders', forcible evictions, etc. The Ministry of Rural Development data shows that as many as 4.65 lakh cases of alienation of tribal land covering an area of 9.17 lakh acres were registered in the states of Andhra Pradesh, Assam, Bihar, Gujarat, Himachal Pradesh, Karnataka, Madhya Pradesh,

Maharashtra, Orissa, Rajasthan and Tripura in January 1999. Of these, only two lakh cases were disposed in favour of 1.56 lakh tribal families covering an area of 5.31 lakh acres. Among the states, land alienation is high in Andhra Pradesh (2.79 lakh acres), Madhya Pradesh (1.58 lakh acres), Karnataka (1.30 lakh acres), and Gujarat (1.16 lakh acres). An absence of political and administrative will to identify and hand over alienated land back to the tribals is considered to be a major obstacle in ensuring that the tribal communities get what is due to them. While on the one hand, tribals continue to loose their land to so-called large developmental projects, without being compensated or restored with lands adequately, questions are being asked about the so-called benefits of these projects percolating to the tribals themselves. In fact, due to lack of education and vocational training amongst tribals, projects set up in tribal areas rarely absorb the local tribals in employment. In many cases, tribals migrate at different times of the year to find employment. Children from such migrating families are either never enrolled in schools due to frequent transfers, or end up discontinuing education for the period that they are away which has an adverse impact on their educational attainments.

Conclusion

Tribal communities in India have been historically deprived of access to resources and opportunities, including the opportunity to get educated. The present efforts of the Indian government to bring these children into formal schools fails at two levels. Firstly, because it is not able to enrol all tribal children and provide them access to good quality functional schools. In some states, the government has started providing alternate schools run by untrained local youth which is opposed by many education activists, since it is a poor and sub-standard system given out to those who are already marginalised. Secondly, even when tribal children are enrolled into schools, the education system besides doling out some incentives does not do much to improve the school environment which will treat these first-generation learners with respect and dignity. Instead, tribal children are made to put up with an offensive and insulting climate that continuously discriminates and alienates. For such historically deprived communities, providing access to education is simply not enough, the government has to take a proactive role in creating overall conditions and opportunities that will facilitate their transition and breaking of the intergenerational cycle of poverty and illiteracy. A sensitive cadre of teachers and bureaucracy is definitely required to make the difference.

At another level, educational deprivation must be seen in the context of overall deprivation of the community and hence emphasis must be placed on improving the situation of tribal communities in general. Restoring land and livelihoods, empowering women, providing basic civic amenities such as fuel, water and sanitation are preconditions to advancements of rights of tribal children. Unless the government undertakes urgent steps to address these issues, its proclamations on child rights would remain examples of empty rhetoric and its actions would effectively continue to exclude those already sidelined. Following the increasing gap between the rich and the poor in the country, the gap between the tribal and non-tribal children is also widening rapidly, thereby further isolating the isolated. Respecting their claims at the outset should set the ball rolling in the right direction.

EDUCATION OF THE TRIBAL GIRLS IN ORISSA A STUDY ON ATTITUDE AND LANGUAGE OF INSTRUCTION

Geographically, Orissa in Eastern India is divided into two parts: the coastal belt near Bay of Bengal, and the hilly regions. Orissa has a total population of 3,68,04,660 according to the census of 2001. The total number of persons in the scheduled tribe population is 81,45,081 (male-40,66,783, Female-40,78,298). The tribals are the indigenous auto-ethonous people of the land who occupy the relatively more inaccessible regions of forests and hills.

As a result, we find tribes who, for centuries, lived far away from the mainstream in their relatively isolated, inaccessible, less fertile and less agriculturally productive regions of forests, hills and mountains. During the British India period, with the introduction of land rent system, the immigrants, Jagirdars and zamindars (landlords), forced many tribals to pay high rents or to render unlimited amount of forced labour. Such exploitation further forced many tribals to settle in more inaccessible regions of hills, thus isolating themselves from the mainstream.

TRIBES IN ORISSA

There are sixty-two tribal communities speaking various tribal languages as mother tongue in Orissa, as recognized by the Indian Constitution under article 342 of Section 4.

These are (1) Bagata, (2) Baiga, (3) Banjara, Banjari, (4) Bathudi, (5) Bhattoda, Dhotada, (6) Bhuiya, Bhuyan, (7) Bhumia, (8) Bhumij, (9) Bhunijia, (10) Binjhal, (11) Binjhia, Binjhoa, (12) Biror, (13) Bondo Poraja, (14) Chenchu, (15) Dal, (16) Desua, Bhumij, (17) Dharua, (18) Didayi, (19) Gadaba, (20) Gandia, (21) Ghara, (22) Gond, Gondo, (23) Ho, (24) Holva, (25) Jatapu, (26) Juang, (27) Kandha, Gauda, (28) Kawar, (29) Kharia, Kharian, (30) Kharwar, (31) Khond, Kond, Kandha, Nanguli Kandh-Sitha Kandha, (32) Kisan, (33) Kol, (34) Kolah, Loharas, Kol Lohras, (35) Kolha, (36) Koli, Malhar, (37) Kondadora, (38) Kora, (39) Korua, (40) Kotia, (41) Koya, (42) Kolis, (43) Lodha, (44) Madia, (45) Mahali, (46) Mankidi, (47) Mankirdia, (48)Matya, (49) Mirdhas, (50) Munda, Munda Lohra, Munda Mahalis, (51) Mundari, (52) Omantya, (53) Oraon, (54) Parenga, (55) Paroja, (56) Pentia, (57) Raiuar, (58) Santal, (59) Saora, Savar, Saira, Sahara, (60) Shabar, Lodha, (61) Sounti, and (62) Tharua (Taradutt, 2001).

STATUS OF TRIBAL WOMEN IN ORISSA

The tribal women have a peculiar position and status in the tribal society. In some tribal societies, matrilineal and matriarchal systems exist. Most of the tribal organizations have clearly defined areas of work among the males and the females. Although the work domain assigned to woman is important in terms of sustenance of the family, yet viewed from the value rating of work, they are relatively low in the hierarchy of work domains (superior-inferior domain) (Ambasht 2001).

Tribal women in Indian society have been contributing positively to the local economy by participating actively along with men in the pursuit of economic activities to earn livelihood. In reality, women are seen to do more hard work in the fields than women. They participate in all agricultural operations except ploughing. They work in all sectors of indigenous cottage industries, tribal arts, and production of artifacts.

In other words, they share major responsibilities in the production process. The division of work is heavily loaded against the tribal women, because, in addition to an equal or greater burden in the economic production process, she has to take the sole responsibility of household chores, which is a stupendous task. Child-rearing is also her sole responsibility. Tribal women working in the fields carrying child in the back is a common sight in the tribal areas. Nowhere will one find a tribal man carrying the child on his back while he works on the field. This kind of division of labour places women in a disadvantageous position compared to their non-tribal counterparts.

Among the non-tribals, except in few urban cases, men look after the financial aspects while women look after the household aspect and remain under the control of men. In the market place, tribal women are seen as vendors as well as buyers especially in the weekly market, a scene normally not found in non-tribal communities.

The tribal woman has the freedom to choose her husband and often dates with boys without any restriction. Premarital sex is also prevalent in some community.

This arrangement is conspicuous by its absence in non-tribal counterparts. Whereas her parents, due to the dowry system followed in marriage, consider the non-tribal girl as an economic liability, the tribal girl is considered as an economic asset. The concept of 'bride price' justifies this. A tribal groom has to pay bride price to the bride's father on marriage for the economic loss the father is going to face.

AIM AND OBJECTIVES OF THE PRESENT STUDY

In spite of the tribal woman's freedom to chose her groom, free access to market place, and relative egalitarianism in their relations with men, the rate of enrollment in primary or secondary schools and dropout rates are alarmingly high. The enrollment at the University is almost nil.

This paper aims to find out if there is any gender discrimination in tribal education. If yes, why it is directed only towards education? I hypothesize that, apart from reasons such as the language policy and faulty education system, the tribal women are also burdened with work in the fields and homes, and this last condition is mainly responsible for their low rate of education.

SAMPLES

The tribal girls between the age 11-14 years from various tribal villages, their parents and teachers in the tribal schools of various tribal areas are selected randomly as samples. All the tribals are agricultural farmers and only twenty five percent of the teachers are tribals.

TEST/TOOLS AND MEASURES-OBSERVATION AND INTERVIEW

This study is based on visit to various tribal areas and interviewing of the tribal girls, their parents and teachers. The interviews are recorded with the help of tape recorders and then were analysed to draw conclusions and suggestions.

Acccording to Indian Child: A Profile 2002 published by Department of women and child Development, Ministry of HRD.

Enrolled scheduled tribe school going population (1999-2000) in Orissa are as follows.

	Total	Males	Females
6-11 years	10,18,000	6,59,000	3,59,000
11-14 years	1,99,000	1,19,000	80,000

Enrolled ratio scheduled tribe (1999-2000) in Orissa (%) are as follows

	Total	Males	Females
6-11 years	99.69	129.97	69.83
11-14 years	41.13	49.54	32.84

The above data shows that among the 6-11 years enrolled, the tribal female ratio in percentage is 69.83, and that among the 11-14 years, the ratio drops down to 32.84 percent. This clearly gives the disadvantageous position of the tribal girls (11-14 years) in education.

During the interviews, the respondents (tribal girls and parents) were asked questions about their views on education. They were asked to give their thinking as to whether (i) education is needed for better living, (ii) whether they want to move out to the city in search of better economic conditions and comforts, (iii) whether they are contented in their present style of living, since apart from poverty, many die due to uncared medical attention and unhygienic conditions, (iv) whether their traditional system of education, popularly known as 'youth dormitory' where young boys and girls get training together or separately, for their roles in adult life, but do not provide any kind of literacy skills, are preferable to modern systems of education, (v) Whether girls should be educated, (vi) whether girls should go to offices and work, (vii) whether the present practice of 'bride price be stopped,' (ix) what do they think of the teachers and their attitudes, and (x) whether they find the present curriculum sufficient.

The teachers were also interviewed. Unfortunately, the non-tribal teachers do not go to their schools. They stay in the city and come to get their salary once in a month, as they know after a few years they will be transferred. Among the tribal teachers, all were Santals, who are more progressive in their thought. Out of the forty recruited teachers in these schools that I visited, only three tribal teachers were present on the day of the interview. They were asked questioned like

(i) What are the causes of the low rate of attendance in the schools specially among girls?
(ii) Whether they like to teach in the tribal school?
(iii) Whether they feel tribals need education?
(iv) Whether the infrastructure provided are sufficient,
(v) Whether increase in the amount of scholarship and incentives by the government will attract more tribal girls to study,
(vi) Whether they find the language of the dominant majority of the state difficult to comprehend and learn,
(vii) Whether the language used in school as medium of instruction is the reason for dropout,
(viii) Whether they should be taught in home language initially to create motivation,
(ix) Whether the present syllabus is satisfying,
(x) Will they students develop positive attitude to education if sufficient study materials are supplied to them..

RESULTS

Almost 97% of the tribal girls and their parents felt

1. Tribals are the gifts of their god. It is their god who wanted them to stay in isolated places and lead an isolated life happily. They are content about the way they live.
2. There is no need for the girls to go to school and waste their time. In fact, girls are needed for home and field. Hence, they have no time for studies. Even if school scheduke is changed to evening hours, they cannot come to school as they have to do house work.
3. City people are crooks who constantly exploit them. Hence they want to be away from them.
4. The youth dormitories are practical in the sense that they teach how to live in adult life, unlike modern education, which is only theoretical.
5. The boys may get education and work in offices and become officers but not the girls. So, if they have a choice, they will send their sons to get educated,but not their daughters.
6. The teachers are rude and look down upon the tribal children as uncivilized people. This also causes a wide gap in teacher-student relationships.
7. The school language and teaching curriculum are not favorable to the tribal girls.
8. If they are taught in mother tongue, may be some girls will go to schools.
9. The traditional system of 'bride price' should not be abolished.
10. After all, a girl child is a blessing to tribal parents.

THE FINDINGS OF THE INTERVIEW HELD WITH THE TEACHERS

All the tribal teachers felt-

1. Tribal people are uncivilized, unaware of the value of education.
2. The non-tribal teachers do not come to schools and teach, and they are rude whenever they come to their school.
3. The school languages, that is, Oriya, English, Hindi/ Sanskrit, are difficult to learn for the tribals, who speak different tribal languages at home.

4. There is no proper environment to study at home.
5. Tribal girls cannot go to the hostels as they are needed at home and field.
6. Although government has many programmes to uplift the tribals, due to various other factors, they are not implemented.
7. If the course is taught in mother tongue, some girls may study.
8. If the school timings are changed to evening and the school holidays and dates for the examinations are changed to suit the local situations (during times there is no sowing, harvesting, etc.), may be, some more girls would join schools.
9. Moreover, massive awareness of the programmes should be implemented.

CONCLUSIONS AND SUGGESTIONS

The study revealed that the tribal girl child is viewed as a security and asset to the family, and so, the parents do not allow the girls to study. Although the tribal boys are also not given adequate opportunities, comparable to those available to boys in the plains, they are still given a choice in the tribal society. The parents would like to give their sons better education. If the school language is changed into mother tongue and the syllabus is in tune with tribal culture, such as stories of tribal heroes who fought for India's freedom struggle are included, or modes such as story telling, showing video films, etc., are added, it will generate more interest for the pursuit of education.

The tribal teachers who understand the tribal language and culture must be posted in tribal schools. They should be given incentives to try to generate motivation among tribal girls and their families about the value of education, especially girls' education. The government must organize mass awareness programmes. The teachers and government must try to encourage gender equitable values and the role of men in household activities may be encouraged and taught as part of the curriculum as well so that the boys and men also share the household activities and the tribal girls get time for studies.

EDUCATION OF TRIBAL CHILDREN IN INDIA

The Janshala Programme is a collaborative effort of the Government of India (GOI) and five UN agencies - UNDP, UNICEF, UNESCO, ILO and UNFPA – to provide programme support to the ongoing efforts towards achieving Universal Elementary Education (UEE). Janshala, a community based primary education programme, aims to make primary education more accessible and effective, especially for girls and children in deprived communities, marginalised groups, Scheduled Caste/ Scheduled Tribes/minorities, working children and children with specific needs. A unique feature of Janshala is that it is a block-based programme with emphasis on community participation and decentralisation. The blocks have been selected on the basis of different indicators such as low female literacy, incidence of child labour, and concentration of Scheduled Tribe (ST) and Scheduled Caste (SC) populations.

TARGET GROUP AND PRIMARY BENEFICIARIES

The GOI and the UN system recognize that certain sections of the population remain marginalised. Therefore it is the goal of the Joint GOI-UN System Education Programme to target girls and the marginalised population of children in selected areas and to improve their attendance and performance in primary education. Children who are marginalised by the formal education system are usually scheduled tribes, scheduled castes, working children, those belonging to minorities, disabled children, and children in remote areas. Girls from these groups are severely marginalised.

Coverage

The Programme is being implemented in nine States of India-Andhra Pradesh, Jharkhand, Chhattisgarh, Karnataka, Madhya Pradesh, Maharashtra, Orissa, Rajasthan and Uttar Pradesh-with a total of 139 blocks including ten cities under the Programme. The Programme covers nearly three million children, and 58,000 teachers in 18,000 schools. Out of 139 blocks more than 75 blocks have substantial tribal population. The proportion of tribal children is 33% of the total target group children in the project area.

Education of Tribal Children

The Indian Constitution assigns special status to the Scheduled

Tribes (STs). Traditionally referred to as adivasis, vanbasis, tribes, or tribals, STs constitute about 8% of the Indian population. There are 573 Scheduled Tribes living in different parts of the country, having their own languages, which are different from the one mostly spoken in the State where they live. There are more than 270 such languages in India. According to the 2001 census, the tribal population in India is 74.6 million. The largest number of tribals is in undivided Madhya Pradesh (16.40 million), followed by Orissa (7 million) and Jharkhand (6.6 million).

There were 16 million ST children (10.87 million of 6-11 years and 5.12 million of 11-14 years) as of March 2001, out of the total child population in India of about 193 million in the age group of 6 to 14 years *(Selected Educational Statistics – 2000-01, Government of India)*. Education of ST children is considered important, not only because of the Constitutional obligation but also as a crucial input for total development of tribal communities.

An important development in the policy towards education of tribals is the National Policy on Education (NPE), 1986, which specified, among other things, the following:

- Priority will be accorded to opening primary schools in tribal areas;
- There is need to develop curricula and devise instructional material in tribal languages at the initial stages with arrangements for switchover to regional languages;
- ST youths will be encouraged to take up teaching in tribal areas;
- *Ashram* schools/residential schools will be established on a large scale in tribal areas;
- Incentive schemes will be formulated for the STs, keeping in view their special needs and lifestyle.

The NPE, 1986 and the Programme of Action (POA), 1992, recognized the heterogeneity and diversity of the tribal areas while underlining the importance of instruction through the mother tongue and the need for preparing teaching/learning materials in the tribal languages. A working group on Elementary and Adult Education for the Xth Five Year Plan (2002-07) emphasized the need to improve the quality of education of tribal children and to ensure equity as well as further improving access.

The interventions being promoted in States under Janshala include:

- Schools, education guarantee centres and alternative schools in tribal habitations for non-enrolled and drop-out children;
- Textbooks in the mother tongue for children at the beginning of the primary education cycle, when they do not understand the regional language. Suitably adapted curriculum and the availability of locally relevant teaching and learning materials for tribal students;
- Special training for non-tribal teachers to work in tribal areas, including knowledge of tribal dialect;
- Special support to teachers as per need;
- Deploying community teachers;
- Bridge Language Inventory for use of teachers;
- School calendars in tribal areas appropriate to local requirements and festivals.
- Anganwadis and Balwadis or crèches in each school in tribal areas so that the girls are relieved from sibling care responsibilities;
- Special plan for nomadic and migrant workers;
- Engagement of community organizers from ST communities with a focus on schooling needs of children from specific households;
- Ensuring sense of ownership of school committees by ST communities through increasing representatives of STs in VECs/PTAs etc. Involving community leaders in school management;
- Monitoring attendance and retention of children;
- Providing context specific intervention e.g. Ashram school, hostel, incentives etc.

Universalizing Access

One of the challenges in providing education to tribal children relates to setting up school facilities in small, scattered and remote tribal habitations. The majority of the Scheduled Tribes live in sparsely populated habitations in the interior and in inaccessible hilly and forest areas of the country. Nearly 22 per cent of the tribal habitations have populations of less than 100 while more than 40% have population of 100 to 300. The rest have population of 300 to 500 *(Sujatha, 2000).*

RELAXED NORM FOR SETTING UP SCHOOLS

One of the reasons for poor access to schooling in tribal areas before the 1980s was the high norm on population, number of children and distance for opening new schools. Most of the states have relaxed these norms to enable setting up schools even in small tribal hamlets. This, along with other measures has improved access in tribal areas. For instance, Andhra Pradesh has relaxed norms to set up schools in habitations even with 20 school-age children. Some states have lowered the population size norm, especially for tribal areas. EGS centres can now be established even with 15 children. In remote tribal habitations in hilly areas of North Eastern states and Jammu & Kashmir, EGS schools can be opened with only 10 children.

The *Sixth All India Educational Survey (1993)* showed that 78 per cent of the tribal population and 56 per cent of tribal habitations have been provided primary schools within the habitation. In addition, 11 per cent of the tribal population and 20 per cent of tribal habitations have schools within less than 1 km radius. About 65 per cent of rural habitations covering 86 per cent of the total rural population have primary schools within the habitation or within a distance of half a kilometer, as against 56 per cent of tribal habitations with 79 per cent of tribal population. Mizoram and Gujarat have the highest percentage of population and habitations covered by primary schools within the habitations. Up to 95 per cent of the tribal population and 85 to 90 per cent of the tribal habitations in the states are provided with schooling facilities within the habitation.

QUALITY IMPROVEMENT

Most of the states recognize the need to address issues related to teachers' attitudes, medium of instruction, textbooks and materials, curriculum and pedagogy and teaching-learning process in tribal areas. An increasing number of researchers strongly advocate the use of the mother tongue or home language as medium of instruction in early stages of education. This assumes greater significance in the context of education of tribal children because their mother tongue is often quite distinct from the prominent languages in the state or regional languages. ST children face problems wherever teachers do not speak their dialect at all. From the perspective of language, it is desirable to have a local teacher from the same tribal community (Jha & Jhingran, 2002).

Although research evidence has demonstrated the positive consequences of bilingual or multilingual schooling on cognitive development and social interaction processes, tribal children would require special programs to be able to cope. The Constitution of India allows the use of tribal dialect (mother tongue) as the medium of instruction if the population of the tribe is more than 100,000.

Assam was the first state to prepare teacher training modules and separate teaching learning materials for the Bodo tribal language in 1995. Bodo is also a medium of instructions in some districts of Assam. The work on tribal language materials was undertaken through DIET staff and BRC/CRC coordinators who belonged to the tribal community. Resource material in Bodo language has been prepared and all workbooks at primary stage have been translated/adopted in Bodo language. In Golpara district, Garo medium workbook has been translated/adopted and distributed in the schools.

Most of the states have taken up activities for quality improvement of tribal area schools. One of the issues identified by the states was the problem faced by tribal children whose home language was very different from the regional language, which was the medium of instruction at the primary level.

In Madhya Pradesh teachers' handbooks called Bridge Language Inventory (BLIs) have been prepared in 3 tribal languages viz. Gondi (Shahdol and Betul district), Kuduk, (Raigarh) and Bhili (Dhar). Identified teachers were given training in using BLISs in their classrooms. The teaching-learning package called *Dham Dhama Dham* was translated into Gondi and supplementary reading material, *Kopal*, was developed for tribal children. The class I textbook *Bharati* has been translated into tribal languages. Supplementary TLM for tribal children has been developed in Jhabua district using local cultural form i.e. folk tales, songs, proverbs, riddles, to make the learning process interesting. In all,

450 teachers of 311 schools have been trained to use the supplementary materials.

Researches have underlined the need to develop culturally sensitive programmes of school education that can ensure the dignity of tribal groups by providing them with economically viable options for life *(Sinha & Mishra, 1997)*. Some attempts have been made for linking curriculum with the local needs of the communities. Such curriculum would make tribal children more sensitive to local contexts and sustain them in their respective environments instead of forcing them to move out in search of another life.

In Karnataka a textbook for class I & II has been developed and introduced for *Soliga* language. A handbook has been developed for sensitisation of teachers towards social and cultural specificities of tribal societies. In Maharashtra tribal language dictionaries have been developed. Language resource groups have been set up for Bhili, Pawara, Madia, Gondi, etc. Bridge material has been developed in Dhule district. Kerala has developed bilingual language materials at district level in Kasarkode, Waynad, Malappuram and Palakkad.

Orissa took the initiative to develop a comprehensive strategy for education of tribal children as early as 1997. The state has initiated a number of activities for addressing the quality improvement of tribal education.

Andhra Pradesh has developed bilingual dictionaries and teacher training has been organised in Warangal and Vizianegarem districts. Research studies have also been undertaken on the issue of language and maths learning by tribal children. It has been decided to use the multi-level kits developed for tribal areas in Vishakapatnam district and also in other tribal areas.

Gujarat has developed dictionaries in Dangi and Bhili dialects. A local word glossary in Dangi has been prepared and distributed in schools for class I-IV in Dang district. Similarly a local word glossary in Adivasi dialect has been prepared for class I-IV in Banaskantha district and distributed in schools. The Vidyasahayaks were given training on the use of these dictionaries. Gujarat has also initiated extensive work for preparation of TLM in tribal languages. The TLM developed include flash cards for different languages and also cards for mathematics. These have been supplied to all schools in tribal areas. A Bridge Language Inventory has also been introduced in Ho and Mundari languages in Ranchi district of Bihar.

Use of Local Teachers

The acceptance of teachers by the community as one of them is critical for increasing schooling participation in tribal areas. An understanding of and respect for tribal cultures and practices and some amount of familiarity with the local language are important for teachers to gain this acceptance:

The presence of tribal teachers, especially from the same community, has shown and improved school participation of ST children. Coming from the same community, it is believed that the teachers would understand and respect the culture and the ethos with much greater sensitivity. Studies suggest that teacher motivation contributes more to teaching – learning process than teacher competence (Vaidyanathan and Nair, 2001).

Realising the importance of having teachers from the local community, many states have appointed community teachers or para teachers as they are popularly referred to. The deployment of community teachers was first experimented in the late Seventies in NFE and later in the formal school with the Volunteer Teacher Scheme of Himachal Pradesh (1984). Nineties saw spurt in the appointment of community teachers, who are from the local community and appointed by the gram panchayat or Village Education Committees. Different states have different schemes for appointing community teachers – Shiksha Karmi Scheme (Madhya Pradesh and Rajasthan), Shiksha Mitra Yojna (Uttar Pradesh), Lok Shikshak (Bihar), Andariki– Vidya Volunteer Scheme (Andhra Pradesh). Vidya Upasak Yojana (Himachal Pradesh), Shikshan Sevak (Maharashtra), Guruji (under EGS in Madhya Pradesh) Shikshak (under Basti Shala Scheme in Maharashtra) etc. It is estimated that there are about 220,000 para teachers engaged in full time schools in the country.

The issues relating to classroom transactions are difficult as they deal with well entrenched attitudes and prejudices of teachers as well as seemingly intractable problems of the huge difference between home and school languages. Attempts have been made to address the first issue through training programmes for teachers.

However, more emphasis on attitudinal training of teachers on the lines of Orissa is required in most of the states. The second issue has been addressed mainly through the BLIs and primers in tribal languages. There may be a problem of acceptance of the tribal language as a medium of instruction in the tribal communities, therefore, adequate dialogue with tribal communities and their leaders is required to prepare them on this issue. The discussion presented above gives us two important lessons. One is that the cognitive qualities of tribal children have to be viewed and evaluated taking into consideration their ecological and cultural contexts that place very different demands on day-to-day life. Because of differences in the demands of tribal ecology, the patterning of their cognitive abilities shows considerable variation from those of other groups. A related and more important lesson is that tribal children are neither culturally inferior nor cognitively less competent than the children of other groups. Instead many of their skills and abilities are highly developed and extremely sophisticated.

The implications of these findings for schooling of tribal children are clear. A programme of schooling, which does not pay attention to the ecological, cultural and psychological characteristics of tribal children is highly unlikely to make any significant impact. The educational system of the dominant non-tribal population is of very limited value in the tribal cultural milieu because it does not match with the lifestyle of individuals and the needs of the tribal community. Linking school education with life in general and the needs of the tribal communities in particular is a most important step that requires serious attention.

The evidences suggests that tribal children do possess the basic cognitive abilities and psychological dispositions necessary for successful participation in school. Yet tribal children have very low levels of participation and success in school education programmes. This points to our failure to develop a sensitive model of education that is rooted in the psychological strengths of tribal children. Studies indicate that, in comparison to other groups, hunters and gatherers possess a high level of visual and tactual differentiation; they demonstrate capacity for fine judgment of shape and size of stimuli as well as spatial relations and they produce fine categorization of an array of objects (Mishra et al

1996). These abilities are required for success in science, art, music, dance, athletic activities, and vocations like carpentry, tailoring, wood and stone crafts. These skills need to be utilized not only for education of tribal children in schools, but also in the broader economic spheres of tribal life. Such attempts will be helpful in generating and promoting the sense of competence, self-efficacy, selfrespect and positive self-image among tribal children in general.

Such attempts are also highly likely to provide tribal children with a culturally meaningful, ecologically valid and economically viable alternative to life by reinforcing the dignity of their culture and identity. Ever increasing contact of tribals with the outside world over the years has introduced several changes in their culture and life. These changes are reflected in their psychological characteristics also. Studies indicate that their ways of perceiving the world, categorizing objects, interpreting pictures, and strategies of learning and memory become more similar to those with whom they interact and negotiate their life in these changed circumstances. This suggests that tribal children can acquire all those skills that the members of other groups of the society possess. What is important on our part is to develop a positive frame of mind about tribal children.

This is possible only through sensitivity to tribal culture and life, recognition of the cognitive strengths of tribal children, and appreciation of their personality qualities. Efforts in these directions will be very helpful in organizing the programme of tribal education as well as promoting economic and other aspects of tribal development.

Similarly a clear policy for language use in schools has to be developed. Research evidence suggests that significantly fewer students drop out of schools in which the language of tribal groups is used for instruction at the primary level. Development of primers in the tribal dialect involving content from the local context will go a long way in ensuring children's active participation in the learning process in school.

While there is a general need for improvement in physical facilities in all schools in remote tribal regions, change in perceptions and outlooks of teachers about tribal children are equally important. Teachers must be sensitized to the cultural and behavioural strengths of tribal children and motivated to do their best for them in schools. Incentives should be initiated to attract effective teachers to work in tribal schools and to retain them there. Only such motivated teachers are likely to generate interest among tribal children towards schools education by attempting to link the contents of the curriculum with the existing realities of tribal communities through the use of innovative technologies.

TRIBAL EDUCATION EMPOWERMENT AND ACTION: LAYA'S WORK IN TRIBAL EDUCATION

'Learning for empowerment' is a phrase so often quoted in literacy programme reports that we may no longer stop to think what it really means. This case study from India however takes us into what 'empowerment' means to young women and men living in tribal communities in Andhra Pradesh. Through a first-hand account of the activities initiated by the organisation, Laya, we are introduced to an unusually holistic approach to adult education, based on the philosophy that "major learning in the tribal context takes place through struggles on issues focusing on human rights of tribal communities". The word 'empowerment' is not used in a rhetorical sense here, but becomes the guiding principle behind the educational processes developed: whether in terms of setting up appropriate organisational structures, identifying and responding to specific needs of different groups of tribal women and men, or developing new training approaches.

'Laya' represents 'rhythm' and belief in 'the wisdom of the "rhythm" underlying tribal societies' which drew together the team of people who began working to empower tribal communities in the East Godavari District of Andhra Pradesh, back in 1985. In this area of India, tribal groups were increasingly affected by the adverse effects of development – deforestation meant that many people were displaced and government attempts to integrate tribal communities into the mainstream brought their whole culture and way of life under threat. Though the government aimed to increase access to education for tribal communities, only poor quality schooling was offered, with a curriculum which neither met their needs nor recognised their traditional knowledge and value systems. Laya's alternative educational approach grew out of experiences with young tribal people who were campaigning against government land reform in 1989 – although they were acting on this specific issue, it became clear that they did not "demonstrate a broader vision of tribal rights". Since then, Laya has developed training programmes for the young tribal people to gain a deeper understanding of the macro and micro level context within which they act, as well as the skills to tackle injustices within their communities. This case study describes in detail the innovative training curriculum and methods used in a variety of programmes, such as mock courts where trainees can practise their legal skills and health courses where traditional medicine is promoted through trainees growing medicinal herbs in their gardens.

Over time, Laya recognised that women were not participating fully in the training programmes, partly because of their limited mobility and domestic pressures. In response to the realisation that development had actually had greater negative effects on tribal women, Laya initiated a separate programme for women addressing the specific issues they faced, including domestic violence and lack of property rights. We read here about the opportunities that arose when women came together as a group, not just to share their similar experiences but to learn from each others' differences: for example, in relation to whether dowry was still an oppressive tradition within each community.

What is striking in this case study is that literacy is not identified as a major issue or constraint: training methods were developed to enable both literate and non-literate women to participate. This is in contrast to the common viewpoint of literacy as the entry point to women's empowerment. The many examples of people successfully challenging injustices and initiating reform illustrate the effectiveness of a process that started with the simple step of outsiders joining a tribal community campaign, "asking provocative questions, supporting some of their activities and creating an environment for deliberation and reflection".

THE TRIBAL COMMUNITY CONTEXT IN INDIA

The total number of tribal communities recognized by the government as Scheduled Tribes is 572 in number. Scheduled Tribes are those tribal communities who have been listed so by the President of India in keeping with Articles 341 and 342 of the Constitution. These tribal communities mainly live in Scheduled

Areas, or those outlying areas, which during the British times did not come under the direct purview of civil, criminal and revenue administration.

REGIONAL CONCENTRATION OF TRIBAL COMMUNITIES IN INDIA

North-Eastern region: In the mountain valleys and other areas of northeastern India, covering the States and Union Territories like Arunachal Pradesh, Assam, Manipur, Meghalaya, Mizoram, Nagaland and Tripura live tribes like the Abor, Garo, Khasi, Kuki, Mismi, Naga, etc., who mostly belong to Mongolian racial stock. Himalayan region: In the sub-Himalayan regions covering parts of North-Bengal, Uttar Pradesh and Himachal Pradesh live tribes like Lepcha, Rabha, etc., mostly belonging to Mongolian racial group.

Central India region: In the older hills and Chotanagpur Plateau, along the dividing lines between peninsular India and the Indo-Gangetic basin, live many tribal communities like the Bhumij, Gond, Ho, Oraon, Munda, Santal, etc., covering the States of Bihar, Orissa, Madhya Pradesh and West Bengal and mostly belonging to Proto-Australoid racial stock. Western India region: Covering the States like Rajasthan, Maharashtra, Gujarat, Goa, Dadra and Nagar Haveli live a number of tribal communities the most important of them being the Bhil racially belonging to the Proto-Australoid group.

Southern India region: Covering the States of Karnataka, Andhra Pradesh, Tamil Nadu and Kerala, in the Nilgiri Hills and converging lines of the Ghats live the Chenchu, Irula, Kadar, Kota, Kurumba, Toda, etc., having Negrito, Caucasoid, Proto-Australoid or mixed physical features.

Island region: Covering Andaman, Nicobar and Lakshadweep Islands live a number of small tribes like the Andamanese, Onge, Sentinelese, etc.

Source: Chaudhuri, Bhddhadeb (Ed). (1992), Tribal Transformation in India Vol. I, New Delhi: Inter-India Publications

Traditional tribal communities are mainly characterized by:

- Relative geographical isolation and thus experiencing political, economic and social discrimination. The mainstream ruling elite treats the homeland of the tribal communities in India as their internal colony.

- Dependence for their survival mainly on natural resources and being spiritually linked to their lands.
- A distinct culture, which is community oriented and valuing the power of nature. They believe no one should take advantage of another's weakness.
- No centralized political institutions and are organized at the level of the community making decisions on a consensus basis.
- A differing worldview, consisting of a custodial and non-materialistic attitude to land and natural resources.
- Women enjoy relative freedom within their society.

However, traditional tribal societies are undergoing a rapid change with the mainstreaming policy of the Indian government. For the tribal communities the process of becoming a part of the mainstream has meant a declining control on their resources and erosion of their cultural heritage. The major issue affecting the tribals in India is displacement: not merely displacement by large projects but resource displacement, thus violating the basic survival rights of tribal communities. Tribal areas reveal a high degree of land alienation. Non-tribals have invaded tribal protected areas. Deforestation, mainly due to exploitation of forests for industrial purposes, is another manifestation of resource displacement. This has resulted in decreasing access to forest resources by tribal communities. With increasing globalization and privatization, the land rights of tribal areas is under even greater threat since these are regions, which have a high natural resource base and has tremendous potential to meet multiple market demands. Added to resource displacement is project displacement where development projects have threatened the livelihood needs of tribal communities. More than 40% of displaced persons of all large development projects are tribals.

More importantly displacement has been accompanied by erosion of the identity of tribal communities, which is being subsumed within the dominant culture. There is a breakdown in their own community institutions, which hitherto safeguarded their resources, traditional practices and values. In the process the richness and wealth of their knowledge systems, identity and survival with integrity is being destroyed.

Although there are protective laws governing tribal areas these laws are being circumvented or not implemented in spirit. For example the Fifth Schedule of the Constitution of India which is a protective legal framework for tribal areas is under threat of being amended due to the mining lobby in India which is keen to exploit the minerals from the habitats of tribal people.

The forest laws and land acquisition laws also run counter to the land rights of tribal communities. The government programmes especially earmarked for tribal areas do not reach the people for whom they are meant due to ineffective implementation systems.

The Context of Laya's Work

The word 'laya' represents 'rhythm'. We believe in the wisdom of the 'rhythm' underlying tribal societies. 'Laya' in mythology implies a cosmic balance of creation and destruction, which to us means retaining what is beneficial and destroying the impediments to the development process.

Our work began in East Godavari District of Andhra Pradesh way back in 1985 mainly in tribal pockets of the district on local issues and programmes. In 1989 Laya was registered as an organization and a Resource Centre for Tribals was initiated at Visakhapatnam with the idea of reaching out to the tribal areas of Andhra Pradesh and linking up with the adjacent tribal region. India IEP Case Study Asian South Pacific Bureau of Adult Education (ASPBAE) Empowerment and Action: Laya's Work in Tribal Education

Our major work objectives in relation to the tribals are:

- To empower tribal communities to secure access and control of their land, forest and water resources;
- To sustain and promote sustainable alternatives for security of livelihood; and
- To ensure self-governance recognizing their cultural identity and value systems

Our programme thrust areas include:

- Legal Assistance and Advocacy

- Sustainable Resource Management: (health, agriculture, micro enterprise)
- Capacity Building of Tribal Youth and People's Institutions
- Empowerment of Tribal Women
- Issues in the Region and Campaign Activities
- Research, Documentation and Dissemination.

We are a team of approximately 30 persons: 15 from varied professional backgrounds relating to social work, management, environment, law and agriculture, 10 are graduates and field based, playing community mobilization functions, and the rest perform support functions. Eight of us in Laya are women. None of our team members belong directly to the communities we work with, as our strategy is to promote and encourage independent, self managed groups or organizations of the target communities.

Our engagement is mainly with the tribal communities residing in the Scheduled Areas of North Andhra region and we network with other tribal regions in India. There are about 33 tribal communities in Andhra Pradesh. Although some of them still retain their own dialects, most of them speak Telugu, the local language of Andhra Pradesh.

9

Indian Tribal and its Corporates

While many reports on the human rights crisis in Chhattisgarh focus on the escalation of violence since the launch of Salwa Judum and the suffering of tribals caught in the crossfire, few probe the causes of the conflict. While condemning the Naxal's violent crimes, some identify the cause of their growth as stemming from their other work, i.e. to raise the daily wages of tendu workers and provide services to neglected areas. But it is not only lack of wages, health and education facilities that has kept this mineral rich region in the throes of dire poverty and starvation.

Apart from the headline-grabbing encounters and operations is a civil war between the state and the armed Maoists over control of resources. Will democratic development and governance serve to eliminate the root causes of the conflict? Is our democracy strong enough to include the voices of the weak, and to probe the role of corporate power and corruption?

Karthik Ranganathan and Tathagata Sengupta, part of AID Chhattisgarh group, have started studying the role of corporations in the conflict over development in Chhattisgarh. The premise: Understanding the corporate scenario today in Chhattisgarh (the corporations that exist, the Government's dealings with them, and their impact on the people's lives and livelihoods) is essential to understanding the current conflict that plagues the state. They have shared their preliminary findings.

CORPORATIONS IN THE CENTRAL INDIAN TRIBAL HEARTLAND

On 25th Feb 2006, Vedanta Resources, a global mining corporation whose current aluminium operations are based in

Chhattisgarh, announced that they are adding another one billion dollars to their Indian budget. This would be aimed at increasing output of copper, zinc and lead, as well as more than doubling its aluminium production. Vedanta had "persuaded" India's Supreme Court to postpone the judgment on its Lanjigarh refinery until July, which was precisely when the plant was due to come on-stream, and this was despite a Supreme Court sub-committee report which damned the project the previous September.

In June 2005, Tata Steel inked a deal with the state government for setting up a five-million tonne per annum plant in mineral rich Bastar, 320 km south of the state capital Raipur, with Rs 10,000 crore initial investment. The State Finance minister Amar Agrawal also said that Tata would get 500 million tonnes of iron ore stocks from Chhattisgarh's Bailadila area in Dantewada district for 50 years besides 2,500 hectare land for the plant. Also, Tata bagged a prospecting license for deposit number 1 that has an estimated stock of 150 million tonnes. Another multi-national company, Essar Steel, is committed to set up a 3.2-mtpa plant in Dantewada with an investment of Rs 7, 000 crore. They have also obtained a prospecting license for deposit number 3, which has stocks of about 100 million tonnes. Bailadila, incidentally, is one of the worst affected areas in terms of Salwa Judum and other state-sponsored atrocities. As early as of March 2006, the Salwa Judum had displaced 644 villages, affecting tens of thousands of people.

ROLLING OUT A RED-CARPET FOR MEGA PROJECTS

In an effort to speed up the economic development of Chhattisgarh to reach the same level as the "developed states" in India, the state government of Chhattisgarh came up with multiple policies and studies earlier this decade. The Chhattisgarh 2010 Vision Document, prepared by the global consultancy firm PricewaterhouseCoopers, in its SWOT (Strengths, Weaknesses, Opportunities, Threats) analysis of the region, considered the extensive dependence of the local population on natural resources a 'threat' to the state's development. This and every other policy that has been formulated since the state's inception, in the context of natural resources in general and water resources in particular, reflects the same trend. The Water Resource Development Policy 2000, the Industrial Policy 2004-09 and even the Environment

Policy of the state point clearly in the direction of water privatisation as the viable and only alternative for water use and management. Three case studies from Chhattisgarh — privatisation of the Sheonath river, insatiable use of water from the Kelu river by the industry, and construction of a private dam on the Kurkut river — clearly illustrate how the political economy is promoting the commodification of water, cornering water for the economic interests of the few at the cost of local communities. The case of Jindal Steel's plant expansion in 2005 is even more enlightening. Independent researcher and current AID Saathi, then with NCAS Pune, Manshi Asher, has shown through her research that as part of the steel plant's expansion to 800,000 TPA (tonnes per annum), for every person who got employed, there were 124 who lost their drinking water supply.

But water privatisation is only the tip of the iceberg. The extent to which the state government has facilitated the establishment of large-scale industrial projects can be best gauged from the fact that the Industrial Policy 2004-2009 has a system of deemed approvals for projects, if the concerned government agencies fail to give the necessary clearances within the specified time limit.

The state govt assures investors special efforts for the supply of uninterrupted and quality power to the industries. The state has also provided incentives for captive power generation. According to the MOU between the state and Tata Steel, the state government would provide 322 MW of power to Tata Steel for the Bastar plant till it sets up its own captive power plant and supply 5 million gallon a day (MGD) water during the plant construction period and 35 MGD when it actually starts production. In contrast, the following facts and figures best describe the electricity and the water situation in the villages in these districts: 68% of the households do not even have electricity connections, 49% of the households do not have access to drinking water in their homes, and only 19% of agricultural lands is irrigated, as per the IPCS (Institute of Peace and Conflict Studies, New Delhi) report.

Chhattisgarh has earned around Rs.7 billion royalty on coal, bauxite and iron ores during the first nine months of fiscal 2007-08. To put things in perspective, the state had earned Rs. 8.32

million royalty revenue in the fiscal year 2006-07, and Rs.7.37. million in fiscal 2005-06.

In these industries, "local employment generation", the phrase that the Government often uses to couch its industrial policy decisions in, turns out to be a bluff. Quoting from the Chhattisgarh Industrial Policy Document 2004-2009,

"Section 4.4.11: Directed incentives (exemptions/concessions) will be available only to those industrial undertakings which employ, in the case of unskilled labour at least 90 percent, in the case of skilled workers at least 50 percent, and in the case administrative posts at least 1/3rd persons domiciled in the State."

According to the same policy document,

"Section 4.4.13 Public sector undertakings of the Government of India or any State Government (except their joint ventures with private companies) will not be entitled to directed incentives (exemptions/concessions) under this policy."

Thus NMDC's joint venture with Tata Steel, having enjoyed "directed incentives", should ensure similar local employment generation. But below are the details of an RTI query filed with the NMDC regarding this issue:

Question: What is the percentage of tribals employed in executive positions of the PSU,NMDC?

Answer: The total number of ST Executives in NMDC was 45 and the percentage is 4.82%, as on 31st Oct 2006.

Question: What is the percentage and number of STs employed directly by the Bailadila projects (BIOP) of NMDC in non-executive positions?

Answer: The percentage of the Tribals employed directly by the BIOP in non-executive positions is 31.41% and the total number of ST's employed directly by BOIP is 935.

The same policy document listed local industries such as ice factories, biscuit and bakery products, manufacturing of sweets, purification of edible salt, grinding of masala and chillies, manufaturing of papad, flour mill, book binding, manufacturing of envelopes, paper bags, manufacturing of bricks, ridges, lime powder, lime chips, dolomite powder, mineral powder, electrical job work, tea blending and packing,photo laboratories, soap and detergent industries, and public undertakings as "negative industries" which will be de-incentivised. Whereas, it lists processing of medicinal, aromatic and dye plants, automobile, auto components, downstream products based on aluminium, food processing industries, pharmaceutical industry, white goods and electronic consumer products, information technology, bio technology and advanced technology industry as "Special Thrust Industries", entitled to receive all sorts of incentives, also listed in the same document. This reflects the Government's centralised and skewed model of "development", where resources are being extorted from community ownership using colonial laws like the Land Acquisition Act 1894, and handed over to a select few, without caring about the lives and livelihoods of people who directly depend on these resources. Although tribal lands are protected under Schedule 5 of the Indian Constitution, the tribal communities have not been able to assert their constitutional rights.

As of Feb 22, 2009, the Chhattisgarh government suffered a revenue loss of over Rs.1.85 billion (Rs.185 crore)) during 2007-08 because of 'undue benefits' provided to various companies, a report by India's audit watchdog said. The Comptroller and Auditor General (CAG) of India in its report on Chhattisgarh said: 'The state government stood to lose revenue of Rs.185.71 crore due to undue benefits to the allottees such as allotment of land at reduced rates.' 'The company (CSIDC) caused a revenue loss of Rs.22.09 crore (Rs.221 million) to the state due to supply of water at less rates, non-revision of usage charges and delay in execution of lease deeds,' it added. Also, the CSIDC did not recover bank guarantee equivalent to concession amount from the mega industrial units, mentioned the report.

Environment and Livelihood

Rules of the game: The Promotion of Industrial Development Act (2002), the Chhattisgarh Industrial Policy (2004-2009) and the Special Economic Zones Act (2005) provide for incentives to the corporates, including provisions such as mandatory automatic approval if the government fails to make a decision within the rigid dates that have been set. After the Promotion of Industrial Investment Act was implemented, 55 MoUs were signed for steel, power and sponge iron plants, and for mines and aluminum smelters across the state.

Another law related to the acquisition process is the Provisions of the Panchayats (Extension to the Scheduled Areas) Act, or PESA. PESA was passed in 1996 to protect the interests of tribal communities. The act mandates that the local panchayat be involved in the land acquisition process, but the extent to which the panchayat's word is eventually upheld remains a matter of debate. Section 4 of PESA has several clauses about land acquisition, such as clause (i), which provides for a participatory role for the gram sabha.It reads,

"...the Gram Sabha or the Panchayat at the appropriate level shall be consulted before making the acquisition of land in the Scheduled Area for development projects and before resettling or rehabilitating persons affected by such project in the Scheduled Areas."

Clause (m)(iii) provides further ammunition to prevent loss of tribal land:

"...a State Legislature shall ensure that the Panchayats at the appropriate level and the Gram Sabha are endowed specially with the power to prevent alienation of land in the Scheduled Areas and to take appropriate action to restore any unlawfully alienated land of a Scheduled Tribe."

Clause (d) articulates the right of the gram sabha to protect community resources:

"...every Gram Sabha shall be competent to safeguard and preserve the traditions and customs of the people, their cultural identity, community resources and the customary mode of dispute resolution."

But on most occasions, the Government managed to find its ways around this law, by holding *Gram Sabha* hearings when the villagers were away, by forging the resolution minutes, and of course by sheer use of power when nothing else worked.

Essar Steel

Dhurli and Bhansi, two tribal villages located in Dantewada district, speak of a distressing story. Essar, after signing a MoU with the government in July 2005, has been attempting to acquire these very lands from the villages to set up a 3.2 million tonne steel plant. The company hopes to obtain 1,254 hectares of land from the two villages; 280 hectares belong to farmers in Bhansi, 109.5 hectares to Dhurli villagers and 865 hectares to the government. According to Vijay Kranti, Essar, the project will directly affect 149 out of the 280 families in both the villages. Physical removal of people is definitely one element. But the second important thing is access to resources. Far more people are dependent on the resources that the plant will eventually hold.

For instance, lets consider the amount of water that the steel plant will need on a day-to-day basis. Water consumption is very high in the steel industry. As a 3.2 million tonne steel plant, the proposed Essar project will require at least 80,000 meters cubed of water per day. This will not only jeopardise the water supply to villages in the plant's immediate vicinity, but it will also affect those living downstream from the plant. The average amount of water consumed per person in rural India is 100 litres per day. Going by that rate, the Essar plant's usage will equal the water needs of 80,000 people.

Bharat Aluminium Company Limited (BALCO)

On July 2, 1992, around 639.169 hectares of land in Mainpat was leased to BALCO, a public undertaking, for 20 years, for bauxite excavation. At that time, Mainpat was a part of Madhya Pradesh. 325 acres of the land that was leased to BALCO belonged to the Manjhi-Manjhwar tribes of Mainpat. BALCO gave some of the displaced compensation calculated @ Rs 12,000 per acre of land though the government-set rate of land in the area was Rs 50,000 per acre. Many people were not lucky enough to receive even this meagre amount. In 1992, around 112 people lost their land but only 50 received compensation. When Chhattisgarh was carved out of Madhya Pradesh on November 1, 2000, the tribals and Dalits hoped that their grievances would now reach the new state government. But a few days later, BALCO was sold to a private company — the Sterlite group, which denied all the responsibilities it should have inherited from its predecessor.

The livelihoods of people have taken a toll in ways more than one. Along with the agricultural areas, the crops also disappeared. The quantum of paddy produce reaching local cooperative societies for sale reduced rapidly. While the government could purchase thousands of tonnes of paddy from cooperative societies in every development block in Surguja district, not even a single kilo of paddy reached the cooperative society at Mainpat for sale. Deep-hole blasting done for excavating bauxite has a violent impact on the whole area. It creates cracks in the farmland, and farming cannot be done on cracked surfaces. The blasting has also caused an increase in health problems among the residents, with people suffering mainly from ophthalmic and otologic infections. Manoj Pingua, the then Surguja collector who was recently transferred to the post of director (tribal welfare), pointed out that the company had ignored all the rules and regulations while excavating bauxite. When the lease was initially inked with BALCO, over 9,000 sal trees stood on the land. When Pingua surveyed the area, he found that Sterlite had cut down 4,000 trees illegally, including sal and other trees. As of 12th Feb 2009, the Chhattisgarh government had served notices to 37 industrial units in two years, including BALCO (now controlled by Vedanta), for violating industrial pollution norms.

Tata Steel

Tata Steel selected 10 villages in Lohandiguda, Bastar, an area of 5,300 acres of land, for setting up a five-million tonne steel plant. It's worth mentioning here that Tata needed only 2,500 acres of land for its six-million tonne steel plant at Kalinga Nagar, Orissa. Essar said it needed 2,500 acres of land in the MoU, but ultimately zeroed in on 3,097 acres in Dhurli and Bhansi villages, 20 km from Dantewada. The story of the Bhilai Steel Plant, set up in 1955 is relevant here. A large number of people were displaced when it was originally set up, but by 1972, it became clear that the plant didn't need that much land after all. The steel plant returned nearly 50% of the land to the government, from whom businessmen purchased the land at low rates.

Tata and Essar claim that they will use the extra land to acquire loans from banks. One of the most unfortunate parts of Tata's acquisition plans is that the land it intends to acquire includes area under cultivation. Out of the 3,906,000 hectares of land in Bastar, only 27.5% is suitable for farming. In Jagdalpur, 56% of the population comprises farmers whose land holdings are a mere acre or less. Lohaniguda itself has more agricultural land than any other village. Out of the 2,161 hectares of land that

Tata wants to acquire for the steel plant, 1,861 hectares comprise agricultural land.

National Mineral Development Corporation (NMDC)

NMDC authorities themselves put the percentage of tribals holding executive posts at 4.82, in itself an unimpressive figure. But the matter goes beyond the question of employment. The lease of NMDC's mines ended in 1995, and in the interim, a report on NMDC's activities, prepared by the Science and Technology Cell of the Indian government, was published. The cell conducted a survey of the area and concluded that NMDC's continuous extraction of iron ore had adversely affected the environment in an area up to 35,000 hectares surrounding the mines; the region had been deforested, and its biodiversity and ecological wealth had been destroyed as also the people's farming land.

Nagarnar is a village 40 km from the district headquarters of Jagdalpur. When NMDC announced its plans to set up a steel plant here in May 2001, the corporation assured tribals that 40,000 people would be given employment, and that they would be given land in exchange for land acquired by the corporation. The government tried to force people to give up their land. On October 24, 2001, when tribals resisted the acquisition, the police beat up and fired on innocent people. Over 50 were badly injured, many of them women. Despite this, the tribals decided in their *Gram Sabha* on March 2, 2002, that the land acquisition, whenever it was done, would have to be carried out according to the laws of the land. They decided that the displaced tribals would have to be rehabilitated, and given land to make up for what they would lose. The police started beating up people late in the night, broke the doors of houses and attacked even the sleeping villagers. They imprisoned 300 people, including women.

HOLCIM, Switzerland

Another international company, HOLCIM, based in Switzerland, recently took over the Indian cement giants ACC and Ambuja Cement. Here are some points, among others, raised in a letter written by the Tribal Welfare Society to HOLCIM regarding the ACC and Ambuja Cement plants at Rawan and Jamul:

- almost 50% of the families losing land have not got employment even for one member, even as contract labour.
- the land had been acquired forcibly at extremely low rates, even below the prevailing market rates. For example an owner of 0.568 hectares of land has been paid Rs. 6862.50.
- HOLCIM is liable to providing employment as had been assured by its predecessors.
- the workmen are being paid only Rs. 60/-to Rs. 80/-per day. i.e. US$ 1.30-1.70 a day. Thus they are not even being paid the statutory minimum wages (Rs. 107/-per day)
- the workers are being paid only single pay even when they work for twelve hours.
- the management forced them to do overtime on the threat that their refusal would result in being denied work,
- the hazardous working conditions a worker is exposed to in a cement industry, for instance-exposure to high temperature; exposure to dust of slag, silica, limestone, gypsum, coal and cement;
- A small drainage type canal has also been constructed for free flow of water from the stop dam to the village pond. The water flowing from the small open canal overflows onto the farm land and destroys the crop on the lands on which it flows.
- The dust discharged from the chimneys of the plant spreads across the land and destroys crops by forming a layer on the same. Despite potential health hazards for people living on the periphery of the plant, the company has never bothered to investigate.
- Burnt oil is thrown into the rivulet (*nala*) that flows through the company premises, resulting in the complete loss of farm produce on which such polluted water flows. The polluted water also flows to a few village ponds where the fishes in the ponds also die and it adversely affects those persons who are used to take bath in those ponds.
- The villagers are facing severe water shortages. But despite exploiting natural water bodies within the plant area by tube wells, the company also procures about 400 tankers of water from the private tube wells of the farmers. This

continuous unchecked, uncontrolled exploitation of underground water has resulted in water level going down from open wells as well as ponds going dry.

- ACC Jamul, on occasion usually late at night, has a practice of releasing polluting effluent without any notice to the near by villagers.

Jindal Steel and Power Ltd (JSPL)

The Government of Chhattisgarh moved a proposal for forest clearance of 1.517 ha *chhote bade jhad ke jangal* (scrub forests) to lay a water pipeline from the village of Rabo to the Tamnar thermal power plant belonging to M/s Jindal Power Ltd, in Raigarh district. The total length of the pipeline is 23 km. The proposal claims that no trees will be felled in the course of laying the pipeline. The pipeline is centrally linked to another project with two other components, which were challenged before the CEC. The linked components were a 1,000 MW thermal power plant at Tamnar and an 18-metre-high dam to be constructed near Rabo village on the Kurkut river. The environment clearance letter for the thermal power plant clearly mentions the need for a dam that necessitates diversion of forest land. It also states that construction cannot begin without the forest clearance in place.

Despite this, construction at both Tamnar and Rabo ("preliminary work", as the project proponent admitted before the CEC) began before forest clearance for the diversion of 177.542 ha was granted. When the Ministry of Environment and Forests (MoEF) carried out a revalidation of environment clearance, it was on the grounds that construction activity had begun. Legally there should have been no construction there, as forest clearance for the project was not yet in place. But nothing could be done as, by the time the matter came up for hearing, forest clearance for the dam had come in: three years after environment clearance for the thermal power plant was revalidated. Now, the same company, through the state forest department, was seeking additional forest clearance for the third linked component — the pipeline.

JSPL also set up a sponge-iron plant of 650,000 TPA capacity in Raigarh town, following a treaty with the CG Government. Ramesh Agarwal, a resident of Raigarh and also an activist with

Jan Chetana, said that 50 sponge iron plants exist within a radius of 15 kilometres of Raigarh town. 17 units of JSPL, against which cases were filed in 2005, under Environmental Protection Act and other pollution control and prevention acts by Chattisgarh State Pollution Control Board for which primary hearing is still pending. In 2007, SPCB again filed cases against the same units. But the SPCB functions under pressure from the Sponge Iron companies due to which they couldn't take any regulatory action against these SIUs. Filing the case in the court, denies fast and just actions for most of the cases, which keeps the industries running for indefinite period without any regulatory action.

Mr. Agarwal cited another example of a subsidiary unit of JSPL in Raigarh, which had been granted clearance. The unit in order to withdraw water had submitted a letter to the Ministry. The permission was granted to withdraw with one of the condition stating ground water survey by CGWA. The catch was that, the ground water survey was not in the jurisdiction of CGWA. At present no records exists for this case.

Unrest due to the pollution caused by these plants has grown in the town as well as rural areas over the past year. In an effort to express this protest, about 10000 people mobilized for the Environmental Public hearing held for expansion of the Jindal Steel sponge iron plant in the district. People expressed disappointment with use of judicial processes and mechanisms for recognition of their environment and livelihood rights.

The struggle of Chauranga, a village near Raipur, the state capital managed to instill inspiration. Rama Shankar Chauhan, of Chauranga, narrated how their village managed to stop a sponge iron plant from coming up in their area. Said Chauhan "Almost 90% of the construction work was complete when we started realizing that this plant might not be good for our village. We had the experience of the neighbouring village where such a plant had affected grazing grounds and agriculture produce and fields. We had daily meetings and made a strategy for stopping the work. While the administration did not support us, after consistent opposition, the company owner realized that he would not be able to run the factory and decided to withdraw."

What about water supply? As part of the steel plant's expansion to 800,000 TPA, which received clearance as recently as August 10, 2005, again amidst strong local protests, the company plans to draw 2,000 cubic metre/hr of water from the Mahanadi river. An estimation of withdrawal of 2,000 cu. m/hr of water from the river, over a 24-hour daily cycle, totals 77,328,000 litres of water per day (lpd). If an average rural household were to be provided 500 lpd, that would equal the daily consumption of 154,656 households, or a population of 850,608.

It is worthwhile juxtaposing this figure with the figures given in the project's Environmental Impact Assessment (EIA) report, to get a clear picture. The report states that, every year, the expansion would generate additional permanent employment to the tune of 1,250; even the total number of beneficiaries from the project, according to the report, is a mere 6,875. The ratio works out to 1:124. That is, for every one person getting employment there will be 124 who will lose their drinking water supply.

Here is an excerpt from the risk appraisal study on Sponge iron plants, Raigarh District conducted by Jan Chetana, Raigarh and National Centre for Advocacy Studies, Pune:

1. Jindal Steel and Power Ltd (JSPL) is located in Patrapali village, about 8 km North-west of Raigarh town. The area around Raigarh town appeared to be recently cleared forest to make way for industry. Solid wastes were visible along the sides of the roads leading to the sponge iron plants and the entire area was very dusty. Plants and leaves in the area were coated with an unusual amount of dust. Leaf burn is visible close to the plant sites.
2. Iron ore handling at Raigarh station and its storage in open yards close to schools in Raigarh town was also causing air pollution. Ash, apparently from the JSPL ash pond, was being dumped in an open area as fill up an area that is later to become a bus stand. Besides the air pollutants contributed by the sponge iron plants, the above activities also entrained significant quantities of suspended particulate matter into the air. Iron ore, coal and ash are known to contain heavy metals and are released to air.
3. Significant air pollution from stacks and as fugitive emissions from area sources (solid waste dumps)
4. Heavy metals released to air from the sponge iron plants are highly toxic. Some of them, eg, chromium (as Cr+6),

cadmium, nickel, are human carcinogens. The toxic effects of heavy metals are varied and may often manifest after a prolonged period, sometimes several years, as in the case of cancer.

5. Sponge iron plants also emit oxides of sulphur and nitrogen and hydrocarbons. These air pollutants are likely to increase the incidence of respiratory tract ailments, eg, cough, phlegm, chronic bronchitis and also exacerbate asthmatic conditions

A population of 1.9 lakhs in 75 villages in a 10 km radius around the JSPL plant is at significant cancer risk, and elevated non-cancer toxic risk. A population of 1.8 lakhs in 231 villages in the area between 11-25 km radii around the JSPL plant may be at an elevated cancer risk. The total population that may be at cancer and non-cancer toxic risk in a 25 km radius around the JSPL plant is about 3.75 lakhs. The greatest impact of air pollution on plants occurs close to emission sources. Sulphur dioxide (SO_2), nitrogen dioxide (NO_2) and particulate matter are primary pollutants, whereas ozone is a secondary pollutant formed by photochemical reactions involving nitrogen oxides (NO_x) and hydrocarbons. Results of field studies have been used for risk assessment to estimate crop loss due to air pollution close to various power plants. Individual farmers may have suffered losses in the range of 13-59%, which for a small or marginal farmer is unbearable.

Chhattisgarh today lives in a regime of systemic plundering of resources, a regime of robbing people of their dignity, lives and livelihood, suffocating the environment to death, a regime of playing games with basic human rights like the right to live, a regime where neither the administration, nor the legislative, nor the judiciary... none of the State organs are ready to lend an ear to the appeals and protests, a regime where guilt and ethics have been hierarchized, a system where the rules of the game are decided by a select few, and the rest are supposed to follow sheepishly, a system where disagreement is not an alternative. And all of this have become synonymous with what some call "Development".

In the current context of Government military measures to "sanitize" the area of Maoists, the State has played out its cards.

It has portrayed the conflict as a clash between armed red guerrilas and the common people who took up arms in retaliation under the banner of Salwa Judum. The Government has claimed that "development" will follow once the Maoists have been deleted.

Not even going into the "collateral damage" of murder of innocent civilians and giving the Government the benefit of the doubt that it will only selectively kill the "Maoists" and no one else, also, not getting into the question of who is a "Maoist" and who is "not a Maoist", how will the situation change once this operation ends? How has the situation changed in Jammu and Kashmir and North-East India over the last 50 years of armed occupation? What are the exact detailed "development" plans that the State has in mind? How does it plan to implement them? What happens to the Tatas, the Essars, the Jindals who are the current feudal lords in the state? That the Government claims to have heard the voices of its people who are calling for a "Naxal-free" Chhattisgarh, is definitely a start. But has it also heard the voices who are demanding their right to live with dignity, a life free of corporate threats and regular structural violence? If yes, what are the policies the State is drafting for their redressal? If no, how long will it take for the State to listen to these people?

10

SCs and STs and OBCs in India

Scheduled Castes ("SC"s) and Scheduled Tribes ("ST"s) are Indian population groupings that are explicitly recognized by the Constitution of India, previously called the "depressed classes" by the British. SCs/STs together comprise over 24% of India's population, with SC at over 16% and ST over 8% as per the 2001 Census. The proportion of Scheduled Castes and Scheduled Tribes in the population of India has steadily risen since independence in 1947. Some Scheduled Castes in India are also known as Dalits Some Scheduled Tribe people are also referred to as Adivasis.

Post Independence Scheduled Castes are benefited by reservation policy. With Reservation in India The Constitution laid down 15% and 7.5% of vacancies to government aided educational institutes and for jobs in the government/public sector, as reserved quota for the SC and ST candidates respectively for a period of five years, after which the situation was to be reviewed. This period was routinely extended by the succeeding governments.

Scheduled castes and scheduled tribes in 2010 Many SC/STs were successful in adapting to post-independence India, becoming civil servants, bureaucrats and lawyers. Scheduled Castes are now considered as a progressive caste. In 2010 most of the sub-castes of scheduled castes have become economically well off and Rich. They have acquired technical and management education as well. Scheduled Castes and Tribes are now working as successful Doctors, Engineers, Architects, Lawyers, Managers, IT professionals and Entrepreneurs. Further,they are now also working as scientists in India's most prestigious research organization like Indian Space Research Organisation, Bhabha Atomic Research Centre, DRDO.

History

From the 1850s these communities were loosely referred to as the "Depressed Classes". The early part of the 20th century saw a flurry of activity in the British Raj to assess the feasibility of responsible self-government for India. The Morley-Minto Reforms Report, Montagu-Chelmsford Reforms Report, and the Simon Commission were some of the initiatives that happened in this context. One of the hotly contested issues in the proposed reforms was the topic of reservation of seats for the "Depressed" Classes in provincial and central legislatures.

In 1935 the British passed The Government of India Act 1935, designed to give Indian provinces greater self-rule and set up a national federal structure. Reservation of seats for the Depressed Classes was incorporated into the act, which came into force in 1937. The Act brought the term "Scheduled Castes" into use, and defined the group as including "such castes, races or tribes or parts of groups within castes, races or tribes, which appear to His Majesty in Council to correspond to the classes of persons formerly known as the 'Depressed Classes', as His Majesty in Council may prefer." This discretionary definition was clarified in *The Government of India (Scheduled Castes) Order, 1936* which contained a list, or Schedule, of castes throughout the British administered provinces.

After independence, the Constituent Assembly continued the prevailing definition of Scheduled Castes and Tribes, and gave (via articles 341, 342) the President of India and Governors of states responsibility to compile a full listing of castes and tribes, and also the power to edit it later as required. The actual complete listing of castes and tribes was made via two orders *The Constitution (Scheduled Castes) Order, 1950*, and *The Constitution (Scheduled Tribes) Order, 1950* respectively.

Constitutional Framework for Safeguarding of Interests

The Constitution provides a framework with a three pronged strategy to improve the situation of SCs and STs.

1. Protective Arrangements-Such measures as are required to enforce equality, to provide punitive measures for transgressions, to eliminate established practices that perpetuate inequities, etc. A number of laws were enacted

to operationalize the provisions in the Constitution. Examples of such laws include The Untouchability Practices Act, 1955, Scheduled Caste and Scheduled Tribe (Prevention of Atrocities) Act, 1989, The Employment of Manual scavengers and Construction of Dry Latrines (Prohibition) Act, 1993, etc.

2. Compensatory Discrimination-provide positive preferential treatment in allotment of jobs and access to higher education, as a means to accelerate the integration of the SCs and STs with mainstream society. Compensatory discrimination is also popularly referred to as Reservation.
3. Development-Provide for resources and benefits to bridge the wide gap in social and economic condition between the SCs/STs and other communities.
4. SC means Sonar Chaand, ST means Sonar Tukro.

National Commissions

To effectively implement the various safeguards built into the Constitution and other legislations, the Constitution, under Articles 338 and 338A, provides for two statutory commissions-the National Commission for Scheduled Castes, and National Commission for Scheduled Tribes.

History

In the original Constitution, Article 338 provided for a Special Officer, called the Commissioner for SCs and STs, to have the responsibility of monitoring the effective implementation of various safeguards for SCs/STs in the Constitution as well as other related legislations and to report to the President. To enable efficient discharge of duties, 17 regional offices of the Commissioner were set up all over the country.

In the meanwhile there was persistent representation for a replacement of the Commissioner with a multi-member committee. It was proposed that the 48th Amendment to the Constitution be made to alter Article 338 to enable said proposal. While the amendment was being debated, the Ministry of Welfare issued an administrative decision to establish the Commission for SCs/STs as a multi-member committee to discharge the same functions as that of the Commissioner of SCs/STs. The first commission came into being in August 1978. The functions of the commission were modified in September 1987 to advise Government on broad policy issues and levels of development of SCs/STs.

In 1990 that the Article 338 was amended to give birth to the statutory National Commission for SCs and STs via the *Constitution (Sixty fifth Amendment) Bill, 1990*. The first Commission under the 65th Amendment was constituted in March 1992 replacing the Commissioner for Scheduled Castes and Scheduled Tribes and the Commission set up under the Ministry of Welfare's Resolution of 1987.

In 2002, the Constitution was again amended to split the National Commission for Scheduled Castes and Scheduled Tribes into two separate commissions-the National Commission for Scheduled Castes and the National Commission for Scheduled Tribes

Distribution

Sachar Committee report of 2006 revealed that scheduled castes and tribes of India are not limited to the religion of Hinduism. The 61st Round Survey of the NSSO found that almost nine-tenths of the Buddhists and one-third of the Sikh's in India belonged to the notified scheduled castes of the Constitution while one-third of the Christians belonged to the notified scheduled tribes of the Constitution.

Religion	Scheduled Caste	Scheduled Tribe
Buddhism	89.50%	7.40%
Christianity	9.00%	32.80%
Sikhism	37.0%	0.90%
Hinduism	22.20%	9.10%
Zoroastrianism	-	15.90%
Jainism	-	2.60%
Islam	0.80%	0.50%

Sikh Light Infantry is the Regiment of Indian Army. The Sikh Light Infantry comprises the Mazhabi (dalit) and Ramdasia Sikh soldiers.It is well known for their dountless daring, loyalty courage, and tenacity,it is one of the oldest Regiments of the Indian Army.

Scheduled Caste Sub-Plan (SCSP)

The strategy of Scheduled Castes Sub-Plan (SCSP) which was evolved in 1979 is one of the most important interventions through the planning process for social, economic and educational development of Scheduled Castes and for improvement in their working and living conditions. It is an umbrella strategy to ensure flow of targeted financial and physical benefits from all the general sectors of development for the benefit of Scheduled Castes. Under this strategy, population. It entails targeted flow of funds and associated benefits from the annual plan of States/Union Territories (UTs) at least in proportion to the SC population i.e. 16 % in the total population of the country/the particular state. Presently, 27 States/UTs having sizeable SC populations are implementing Scheduled Castes Sub-Plan. Although the Scheduled Castes population, according to 2001 Census, was 16.66 crores constituting 16.23% of the total population of India, the allocations made through SCSP in recent years have been much lower than the population proportion. Table below provides the details of total State Plan Outlay, flow to Scheduled Castes Sub-Plan (SCSP) as reported by the State/UT Governments for the last few years especially since the present UPA government is in power at the Information in respect of 14 States/UTs only and as on 31-12-2007.

2004-2005	108788.9	17656	2065.38	11.06	68.3	5591
2005-2006	136234.5	22111	16422.63	12.05	74.3	5688
2006-2007	152088	24684	21461.12	14.11	86.9	3223
2007-2008	155013.2	25159	22939.99	14.80	91.2	2219

Source: Network for Social Accountability (NSA) http://nsa.org.in

Prominent menmebrs of SC/STs

- B. R. Ambedkar, also known as Babasaheb, was an Indian jurist, political leader, Buddhist activist, thinker, philosopher, historian, anthropologist, orator, prolific writer, economist, editor, scholar, revolutionary and the revivalist of Buddhism in India. He was also the chief architect of the Indian Constitution.
- Dr. Faguni Ram, Ph.D(3-Time Member of Parliament and Ex-Minister of State)
- Prem Singh (MLA)

- Kashi Ram, Founder of Bahujan Samaj Party
- Lala Ram Ken, Member of Parliament(7th and 8th), India
- Divya Bharti, Late Bollywood actress
- Babu Jagjivan Ram, Former Deputy Prime Minister of India.
- Mayavati, Chief Minister of Uttar Pradesh.
- Sushilkumar Shinde, Cabinet Minister for Power in the Manmohan Singh government
- K. R. Narayanan, tenth President of India
- Shibu Soren, current Chief Minister of Jharkhand state in India
- Ajit Jogi, first chief minister of the state of Chhattisgarh, India
- Bangaru Laxman, former President of Bharatiya Janata Party (BJP)
- Birsa Munda, freedom fighters in the Indian struggle for independence against British colonialism
- Jyotirao Phule, was an activist, thinker, social reformer, writer, philosopher, theologist, scholar, editor and revolutionary from Maharashtra, India in the nineteenth century
- Damodaram Sanjivayya (1921-1972) (First dalit Chief Minister of a state in India and first dalit President of Indian National Congress party)
- G. M.C. Balayogi (1951-2002) (First dalit speaker, Lok Sabha, India)
- K. S. R.Murthy IAS, Retired, Former MP, Lok Sabha
- Ram Vilas Paswan, the president of the Lok Janshakti Party, political party
- Meira Kumar, is an Indian politician and a five time Member of Parliament. She was elected unopposed as the first woman Speaker of Lok Sabha on 3 June 2009

POVERTY AND UNDER-NUTRITION AMONG SCHEDULED TRIBES IN INDIA

The main objective of this paper is to document the poverty and under-nutrition among the districts in India that are inhabited largely by indigenous population groups, referred to as Scheduled Tribes (STs) or Adivasis. It is fairly well documented that the well being of social groups in India differs. Recent researches have tried to quantify the disparities in level of living of various population groups. As a population group, Scheduled Tribes (STs) are at the bottom on a range of development indicators including consumption and poverty (de Haan and Dubey (2005); GOI (2007); Newman and Thorat (2009)).

A large part of this literature relies on complex Indian social structure, the Hindu Varna System, for explaining the disparities. It is argued that the Hindu Verna System evolved into a social structure and process that has traditionally excluded, discriminated, and isolated groups of population on the basis of their caste, ethnicity and religion. There are several such groups identified on the basis of their caste, the untouchables or scheduled castes (SCs). The other group is recognized on the basis of their ethnicity, the STs. The SCs are larger group between the two, accounting for nearly 17 percent of Indian population. It is argued that their exclusion is a direct consequence of the Hindu social order. The caste system as a form of social structure is based on the division of people into a distinct social group, or caste with unequal rights. That got institutionalized and is said to be the cause of multiple exclusions that have severe consequence on their deprivation and poverty.

This rigid structure remained in place despite influences brought about by other religions, especially Islam and Christianity which were introduced by outsiders and a few indigenous religious groups, notably Sikhism, Buddhism and Neo-Buddhism. Within each one of these groups, caste structure remains relatively rigid even though some of these religious denominations tried to shun the caste and advocated equality.

In this paper the focus is on deprivations, especially in consumption, it would suffice to note that the four broad categories that emerge by identifiable social groups are STs, SCs, Other Backward Classes (OBCs) and a residual group identified as Others (OTH) (comprising of mostly the so called Forward Castes). Among the Hindus, the last three, i.e. SCs, OBCs and OTH, are considered directly as consequence of Hindu Varna System. The available welfare indicators for these three groups show that, on an average,

SCs are worse off group and OBCs lie within SCs and OTH.

The other excluded group mentioned above, the STs (also called Adivasis or Tribals) appear to have been excluded from detailed analysis. While most of the STs have remained outside the purview of rigid Hindu hierarchal social structure, in terms of the welfare indicators, they are, on the average lower than even the SCs.

Though scattered over the geographical domain of India, there are regions where STs have very high to moderate concentration. Their exclusion is a consequence of geographical isolation as these groups inhabit hills and forest areas that have been considered remote and not easily accessible. However, unlike SCs, there are thousands such groups scattered across the length and breadth of India with a diverse socio-cultural and economic organization.

During the post independence period, though, STs were provided with the Constitutional safeguards including reservation in the government jobs besides a separate administrative structure that is still evolving.

For example, the draft National Tribal Policy document is under circulation and being debated (GOI, 2006). One of the key safeguards in governance of the STs is provided in the Fifth and the Sixth Schedule of Indian Constitution. Under the Sixth Schedule, entire state has different set of governance provisions provided that state is inhabited predominantly by STs. The fifth schedule, on the other hand, is applicable at the district level. This provides for administration and control of Scheduled Areas (falling under Schedule V) and gives powers to the Governors to make regulations for the peace and good governance of the schedule areas inhabited by the STs.

In this paper I have identified the districts that have sizeable ST population and calculated the level of living, poverty and undernutrition. The rest of the paper is organised in the following fashion. In the next section, a brief description of the data used and distribution of ST population is discussed. This is followed by the level of living and poverty incidence among STs vis-à-vis other (OTH) population groups at aggregate level in section 3. In section four, the analysis is repeated at the district level. Findings of the paper and policy issues are summarised in section five.

DATA RELATED ISSUES

The quantitative assessment of deprivations and disparities requires a set of comparable data across different social groups. In this paper we have used household level data collected by the National Sample Survey Organisation (NSSO) to investigate the disparities in consumption, poverty incidence and malnutrition among the STs. The consumption expenditure data has been collected during two recent and comparable surveys conducted by the NSSO. The reference periods are July 1993 to June 1994, and July 2004 to June 2005. These are also referred to as the 50th and 61st round quinquennial surveys, respectively.

The households in these surveys are identified using a two stage stratified sampling design. Therefore, weights or multipliers are an integral part of the data. The quinquennial rounds of NSSO surveys cover almost the entire territory of India except some inaccessible areas that are less than 0.01 percent of the Indian Territory and even lower proportion of population. The consumption expenditure data is used in conjunction with the employment and unemployment surveys which has the same reference period. In addition, we have also used some information from Indian census but it is limited to the study of the distribution of ST population across districts in India.

ST population across districts in India taken from 1991 census. There are about 21% districts (94 out of 453 districts in 1991 census) without a single ST household. Another 36% districts have less than 5% of ST population and only 51 districts (just over 12% of the total districts) have 50% or more ST population with only about 30 districts with 75% or more ST population. In this last category, out of 30 districts, only one district, Jhabua in Madhya Pradesh, has about 86% ST population and located in central part of India. Thus, unlike SCs which have on an average 18-20 percent share in population in most of the districts in plains or major states (there are about 70 districts in India which have less than 5% SC population but these districts are located in northeastern states and other smaller states union territories).

The point that emerges from the distribution of ST population across districts is that unlike the distribution of SCs among the districts in most part of India, ST population is concentrated only in a few, just about 50-60 districts. Also, unlike SCs who have no numerical majority in any of the districts, STs have in over 50 districts. Recent literature points out towards the caste dominance as one of the leading factors in determining the participation in growth. As SCs could never have such dominance given their distribution pattern in the population, their limited participation in growth and in the share of the cake is understandable. In case of STs, this issue has not figured in the discourses.

SAMPLE SIZE AND MEASURES OF DEPRIVATION

Recall that we are using household level consumption expenditure data to measure poverty and malnutrition at the disaggregated level. Given that the households in NSSO surveys are selected through a stratified sampling design, the probability of the ST households being in the NSS sample in a large number of districts is very small. Therefore, the analysis in this paper is restricted to only selected number of districts that have substantial (50% or more) ST population.

Though there are a few studies in recent time that estimate the district level consumption and poverty incidence (Bhandari and Dubey, 2009; Chadhuri and Gupta, 2009), there are some words of caution here. First, districts in India have been undergoing constant reorganisation. As a result, the number of districts in the data during the two quinquennial rounds of surveys is vastly different. Moreover, given the NSSO sampling strategy, there are substantial number of districts where sample sizes are too small (e.g. there are 64 districts in 61st round survey that have a total of less than 100 hundred household selected for survey). In order to have comparable geographical areas to be designated as districts, therefore, we have resorted to combining the districts. As a result we could get about 280 comparable districts for tabulation that have reasonable sample size and reasonably reliable estimates of characteristics under investigation. Secondly, we have restricted reporting of the poverty measures and other indicators to the districts where the number of ST households in the NSS CES surveys is more than 100. There are about 43 „districts 4 for which the results are reported in this paper.

For the measurement of poverty, there are two indispensable requirements, welfare profile of the population and poverty norm. In this paper household consumption expenditure data, arguably the best suited for measuring level of living and poverty, collected by the NSSO is being used. The other requirement is a suitable poverty norm. The issue of a suitable poverty norm is contentious. Several aspects of poverty norm— its specification, spatial variation, adjustment for temporal change and spatial variation in prices has been hotly debated in the literature. We have kept away from these issues and adopted the poverty norm used by the Planning Commission, Government of India for calculating poverty incidence for 1993-94 and 2004-05.6

Another matter of detail is the comparison of the consumption expenditure over the two time points in this paper. NSSO collects consumption expenditure data in nominal rupees. For comparison over time or across states, one needs to convert the nominal expenditure at constant prices. One can use several alternative deflators here, for example, implicit price deflator from GDP at the all India level or from net state domestic product (NSDP) or from aggregate private final consumption expenditure. The main limitation of these deflators is that these are available for state as a whole. Since there are significant differences in rural and urban prices, we need a deflator separately for the two sectors.

We have converted the nominal PCTEs at constant (1993-94) prices. The price deflator that we used to covert the household expenditure at constant prices is implicit price deflator derived from the state-wise poverty line for two sectors separately. This is equivalent to deriving a deflator using state and sector-wise CPIs. In this paper the incidence of poverty in the two sectors and among different social groups is captured using only one measure, Head Count Ratio (HCR).

In addition to measurement of consumption expenditure and poverty incidence, in this paper the incidence of malnutrition is also discussed. Malnutrition is a situation where a person is not able to consume enough food which provides the normatively food energy for metabolic process in the body, measured in calories. In CES surveys, NSSO collects information on quantity as well as value of various food items consumed by the households. While it is straight forward to calculate the calorie consumption from quantity of food consumed by the household, the normative requirement is contentious. I have used the methodology for calculating normative calorie requirement at the individual level from the Task Force report (GOI, 1979) but modified it substantially by taking into account the age-sex-activity pattern at two-digit NCO classification along with consumer units in 1993-94 and 2004-05 separately from NSSO EUS data. The main reason for modifying the Task Force methodology is differential occupational structure across place of residence and social groups.

CONSUMPTION AND POVERTY INCIDENCE: AGGREGATE LEVEL

As pointed out in the last section, unlike the SCs, the ST population is unevenly distributed across districts in India. Based on the population share in the districts, I have created six groups of districts. Group 0 are the districts which have no ST population whereas group 1 has less than two percent ST population.

The hierarchy in mean consumption expenditure discussed above. Mean consumption of STs as a group is less than 64% of the OTH group comprising of non-SC and non-ST population. Compared to STs, SCs are marginally better off at about 72% of OTH mean consumption expenditure. When we look at the mean expenditure of STs by the share in the population, with lower share of population (groups 1, 2 and 3), STs are marginally better of than the average and in group 4, where STs have numerical majority, the mean consumption of STs is about 20% higher than the OTH group. Curious result is in case of less than majority population (group 5) where mean consumption of STs is lowest at 54%. If the population group dominance argument is used to scrutinize these results, then until a group has majority in the population, its participation in the income earning and growth is severely hindered. The other surprising result is the level of inequality as captured by the Gini coefficient. The distribution is most equitable where STs are dominant group and it is the most unequal where there is substantial but less than majority ST presence.

Poverty incidence (head count ratio) is reported. Going by the disparities in mean consumption and inequality, HCRs mirror similar pattern and inter-group difference. In 2004-05, the ST-OTH difference in HCR is 21 percentage points at the aggregate level. Going by the share of ST population among the districts, for less than majority population of STs in the districts, the poverty ratios are higher with largest gap (over 28 percentage points) between the two groups is for the districts which have less than majority population and are located in the so called major states. Another key observation is the substantially lower incidence of poverty among the districts that have STs as the largest population group. This appears to be the direct consequence of higher mean per capita consumption among these districts coupled with lower level of inequality.

The temporal change in poverty incidence in 61st round over 50th round is consistent with changes in the mean consumption expenditure and inequality. The disparities in poverty incidence between STs and OTH have increased marginally over the rounds. This is driven largely by the increase poverty incidence in the group five districts as all other groups have experienced reduction in poverty. While poverty has declined for all the groups except five, it is the ST dominated group of districts which has benefited most from the growth.

Invariably, the average calorie requirements are marginally higher for the STs compared to OTH which could be due to occupational patterns among the ST population— a larger proportion is engaged in primary sector activities. Compared to the normative requirement, the mean food energy consumption is consistently higher for OTH group across all the groups except group 4. When these two indicators are combined to check the incidence of malnutrition, results are not surprising at all. Among the STs, incidence of malnutrition is over 15 percentage points more than the OTH. It may, however, be noted that the normative calorie requirement is another debatable issue and is beyond the scope of this paper.

Consumption, Poverty Incidence and Malnutrition: Districts

As pointed out earlier, there are only 43 districts for which the district level calculations are reported. These 43 districts have been created from a total 126 districts that account for over 21% of total districts in India. These 126 districts (43 after merging contiguous districts) account for over 12% of total population but have 54% of total ST population. Thus, the calculations in this section cover about 12% of total population and over 54% of total population of India. The mean per capita consumption expenditure is reported for STs and OTH for the 50th and 61st rounds. There seven districts in which mean consumption of STs either at par or higher than OTH. Compared to these, there six districts with substantial ST population that have highest ST-OTH disparities.

Firstly, the location of the districts is quite distinct. Most of the districts where ST-OTH gap is favoring STs are located in northeastern region. These are smaller states that fall under VI Schedule or the dominant tribal population among the districts makes them fall under the Vth Schedule. One of the specific provisions of VI Schedule states is incidence of direct taxes where indigenous population is exempted from paying individual direct taxes. Secondly, the districts with largest ST-OTH gap in mean consumption are located in major states, Gujarat, Madhya Pradesh, Maharashtra, Orissa and Rajasthan. Thirdly, out of the major states which have the largest ST-OTH consumption differences, Gujarat, Maharashtra and Rajasthan have benefited most from the recent episode of liberalization and economic growth. Clearly, the participation of STs in growth is not happening even in the fastest growing states.

The differences in consumption could persist between population groups for some more time even if different groups get equitable share from the surging economic growth. In these six districts (with highest ST-OTH consumption gap), the ST-OTH gap has increased during 1993-94 and 2004-05. The annual average change in mean real consumption expenditure over the two time points suggests that the largest increase in APCTE (over 10 percent per annum) is recorded among the OTH groups in the six districts that have largest ST-OTH mean APCTE difference. Compared to this, the annual average increase in the real mean consumption among the STs in the districts that have favourable gap (ST-OTH) in mean consumption has experienced highest growth though substantially lower than the OTH group in the districts that have largest ST-OTH gap. In fact, there is perceptible decline in mean consumption of OTH groups that have dominant ST population group and located in northeastern region.

The patterns observed in the mean consumption expenditure and changes therein are reflected in the incidence of poverty and mean calorie consumption. Given that districts located in northeastern region have experienced significant growth in mean consumption and ST-OTH difference favouring STs in these districts, the level of poverty in these districts is substantially lower compared to the districts with sizeable ST population but located in major states. For example, among 16 districts that have less than 10% HCR, all are located in northeast with three districts reporting no poverty at all.

On the other hand, the highest incidence of poverty (over 84%) is recorded in xxx district located in Orissa. In fact out of seven districts that have more than 70% incidence of poverty, four districts are in Orissa, two in Chhattisgarh and one in Madhya Pradesh. Additional ten districts have poverty incidence in the range of 50-70 percent and these are located in Chhatishgarh, Gujarat, Jharkhand, Madhya Pradesh, Maharashtra, Orissa and Rajasthan. One, there is substantial STOTH disparity in poverty incidence too (as observed earlier in mean real consumption). Secondly, there is some kind of inertia in the poverty incidence, as the high level of poverty incidence in some of the districts continues to be there despite impressive economic growth path that the Indian economy is on for over last 15 years.

Conclusion and Policy Issues

In this paper levels and changes of mean consumption expenditure and poverty incidence is reported for two time points, 1993-94 and 2004-05 at the district level. The focus of the analysis has been the level and change in consumption and poverty among STs and the disparities in these two indicators STs and other population groups (OTH).

The analysis in this paper reaffirms the existence of large disparities in mean consumption and poverty incidence between ST and OTH population groups. At the aggregate levels, the worrying factor is the rise in the ST-OTH disparities on both the indicators. Average annual change in mean consumption of STs is substantially lower than the growth experienced by the OTH group which is fostering the disparities. Clearly, the post-1991 economic growth has not been inclusive.

The small proportion of STs who have benefited during this period are located in the areas that have majority ST population and enjoy various constitutional privileges including governance. Though detailed sectoral growth data is not available at the district level, location of these districts (where STs are dominant population group) in Schedule V and VI areas seems to have helped. In most of these Scheduled areas, the service sector led growth has benefited the STs. The deprivation levels of STs residing in major states and with less than majority ST population appear to be the most vulnerable groups among all STs. Incidence of poverty in excess of 50% among the districts with substantial ST population and located in the states that are recognised as the most investor friendly and have been fastest growing, Gujarat and Maharashtra, suggests non-participation of STs in current episode of economic growth. The analysis also indicates that that some of these districts do not fall in economically stagnating regions and benefits of growth is concentrating among the majority OTH and fostering inequality. Clearly, a lot more is desired than "inclusive growth" approach adopted in the current Five Year plan.

SCHEDULED CASTE AND SCHEDULED TRIBE (PREVENTION OF ATROCITIES) ACT, 1989

The Scheduled Castes and Tribes (Prevention of Atrocities) Act, 1989 was enacted by the Parliament of India, in order to prevent atrocities against Scheduled castes and scheduled tribes. The purpose of the Act was to help the social inclusion of Dalits into Indian society, but the Act has failed to live up to its expectations.

Special Court

Special Court Justice Ramaswamy observed in the case of State of Karnataka v. Ingale that more than seventy-five percent of the cases brought under the SC/ST Act end in acquittal at all levels. The situation has not improved much since 1992 according to the figures given by the 2002 Annual Report dealing with SC/ST Act (of the Ministry of Social Justice and Empowerment) Of the total cases filed in 2002 only 21.72% were disposed of, and, of those, a mere 2.31% ended in conviction. The number of acquittals is 6 times more than the number of convictions and more than 70 percent of the cases are still pending.

Speedy trial

The framers of the SC/ST Act kept this aspect (the increasing number of cases pending in the judiciary) in mind and provided for the setting up of a Special Court for speedy trial of offences committed under this Act.

Implementation of Law

They failed, however, to give any real powers to Special Courts for the admission of complaints. This is evident from the provision relating to setting up of Special Courts which gives a false impression that a case of atrocity can be directly filed with the Special Courts. Various State Governments have notified the Special Courts, in accordance with the provision of the Act, but these courts cannot take cognizance of any complaint directly. The Supreme Court, in the case of Gangula Ashok v. State of AP, clarified that Special Courts can take cognizance of an offence only when a case is committed to it by a magistrate in accordance with provisions of Section 193 of Criminal Procedure Code (Cr.P.C). This means that a charge sheet cannot be directly filed before a Special Court. When a Session Court is constituted as a Special Court, it cannot take cognizance of an offence without such a case being committed to it by magistrate unless it is expressly provided so in the Act. Neither in the Cr.P.C. nor in the SC/ST Act is there any provision which grants the power to Special Court to take cognizance of the offences as an original jurisdiction without the case being committed to it by a magistrate. Hence, it is mandatory to go through the course established under the Cr.P.C.

Biases

Going through the normal judicial system is self degrading for any dalit. This is because of the still existing biases of the court judges. One example is the conduct of an Allahabad High Court judge who had his chambers "purified" with water from the 'ganga jal' because a dalit judge had previously sat in that chamber before him. Another example is the case of *State of Karnataka v. Ingale*. The State of Karnataka had charged five individuals with violating the SC/ST Act. At trial, four witnesses testified that the defendants had threatened dalits with a gun in order to stop them from taking water from a well. The defendants told the dalits that they had no right to take water, because they were untouchables. The trial judge convicted all of the defendants. On appeal, the Additional Sessions judge confirmed the conviction of three defendants but acquitted two. On further appeal to the High

Court, the judge acquitted all the defendants after rejecting the testimony of the four dalit witnesses. The dalits finally got relief from the Supreme Court.

Contradictions

The legal regime is fraught with contradictions. While the legal text is explicit in seeking remedies, the implementation of the text appears to evade actual performance. Laws and legal processes are not self executing; they depend on the administrative structure and the judiciary with the anticipation that the social attitudes are driven by notions of equity, social justice and fair play. However, the increasingly indifferent responses of those involved in the implementation of laws protecting the weak, the oppressed and the socially disadvantaged have persisted over the years and the system has failed to provide for self-correction. What needs to be appreciated is that victims of attrocites suffer not only bodily and mental pain but also feelings of insecurity and socialavoidance which is not present for the victims of other crimes. If the judge delegated to protect them shows indifference, it further aggravates their already vulnerable position.

Investigation

Section 23 of the Prevention of Atrocities Act authorises the Central Government to frame rules for carrying out the purpose of the Act. It was the drawing power from this section that the Scheduled Castes and the Scheduled Tribes (Prevention of Atrocities) Rules of 1995 were framed. According to Rule 7(1) investigation of an offence committed under the SC/ST Act cannot be investigated by an officer not below the rank of Deputy Superintendent of Police (DSP). Various High Courts have vitiated the trail based on the above rule and have improperly set aside the order of conviction.

RANK OF INVESTIGATING OFFICER

The Andhra Pradesh High Court, in *D. Ramlinga Reddy v. State of AP*, took the position that provisions of Rule 7 are mandatory and held that investigation under the SC/St Act has to be carried out by only an officer not below the rank of DSP. An investigation carried out and charge sheet filed by an incompetent officer is more than likely to be quashed. Similarly, the Madras High Court in *M. Kathiresam v. State of Tamil Nadu* held that investigation conducted by an officer other than a DSP is improper and bad in law and proceedings based on such an investigation are required to be quashed. The Courts without taking into consideration the inadequacies of the State, have been punishing SC/STs for the same. Shri Pravin Rashtrapal, Member of Parliament rightly pointed out that ther are insufficient officers at that level. His statement is supported by the Annul Report of 2005-2006 of Ministry of Home Affairs. Of the total posts sanctioned by the government under Indian Police Service (IPS) more than 15 percent of the posts are vacant. This basically means that there is one IPS officer for 77,000 SC/STs.

Rehabilitation

According to the preamble of the SC/ST Act, it is an Act to prevent the commission of offences of atrocities against SC/STs, to provide for Special Courts for the trial of such offences and for the relief and rehabilitation of the victims of such offences. The Madhya Pradesh High Court also had the same view and observed in the case of Dr. Ram Krishna Balothia v. Union of India that the entire scheme of the SC/ST Act is to provide protection to the members of the scheduled castes and scheduled tribes and to provide for Special Court and speedy trial of the offences. The Act contains affirmative measures to weed out the root cause of atrocities, which has denied SC/STs basic civil rights. The Act has addressed the problem the regarding the dispensation of justice, but what the failed to deal with is the problem of 'rehabilitation'. There is mention of rehabilitation under Section 21(2)(iii), but there are no provision addressing the same. As it has been stated earlier that victims of atrocities are on a different level when compared to victims of other crimes, hence there should be special provision for the same. According to the report submitted by the National Commission for Review and Working of the Constitution victims of atrocities and their families should be provided with full financial and any other support in order to make them economically self-reliant without their having to seek wage employment from their very oppressors or classes of oppressors. Also it would be the duty of the State to immediately take over the educational needs of the children of such victims and provide for the cost of their food and maintenance. SC/STs constitute 68 percent of the total rural population. According to the 1991 Agricultural census a large number of SC/STs are marginal farmers compared to the other sections of the society and because of this the number of cultivators are going down. In other words the landlessness is increasing at a faster rate among SC/STs. At the same time the number of SC/ST workers as agricultural labourer is increasing at a faster rate when compared to other sections of the society. This basically implies that after losing their land holdings SC/ST cultivators are becoming agriculture labourers. Loss of land, on the one hand, is caused by atrocities making the more vulnerable. This in turn fuels and promotes continuance of atrocities and untouchability. Marginalisation is one of the worst forms of oppression. It expelles a whole category of people from useful participation in the society and therefore potentially subjected to material depravation and this could even lead to extermination. Moreover, this leads to the state of powerlessness which perhaps is best described negatively; the powerless lack authority, status and a sense of self. Moreover, every right has three types of duties:

- Duties to avoid deprivation.
- Duties to protect from deprivation
- Duties to aid the deprived.

Though the SC/ST Act does cover the first two duties but totally ignores the third one; duty to aid the deprived. Hence, it is necessary to make the SC/STs self dependent.

Migration

Under constitutional provisions, a caste or tribe is notified with reference to a State or Union territory. Hence a person born in state/UT gets certificate of SC/ST if his/her father belongs to specified caste/tribe in that state as SC/ST. If he/she migrates to another state, he/she lose status for affirmative actions, i.e. benefit of admission in educational institutes, reservation in government employment etc. But he/she does not lose protection as guaranteed by constitution like PoA & other Acts in any other state. In brief once a person is notified as SC/ST in any one state/UT, he gets protection under SC ST (Prevention of Atrocities) Act, 1989 throughout the country, irrespective that caste or tribe is notified in the state/UT where offence is occurred.

Suggestions

The statement of object and reason of the SC/ST Act clearly reveals that the Act, in its letter and spirit, desires that dalits lead a dignified life. However, even after 16 years of its existence in the statute book, it has not shown its desired effect. The majority of the beneficiaries of this Act are unaware of the legitimate claims of leading a dignified way of life or are unwilling to enforce it intensively. Even the Police, prosecutors and judicial officers are unaware of this Act as was pointed out by Calcutta High Court in the case of *M.C. Prasannan v. State of West Bengal*. What further aggravates the problem is the misapplication of the Act by police as well as by the courts which ultimately leads to acquittals.

Rural atrocities which are not covered under this Act

Social and economic boycott and blackmail are widespread. In view of the fact that the main perpetrators of the crime sometimes co-opt a few SC/STs with them and take advantage of local differences among the SC/STs and sometimes they promote and engineer crimes but get them executed by some members of SC/STs, the Act should be suitably amended to bring such crimes and atrocities within the purview of the definition of atrocities under the Act. Likewise, the Special Courts established under Section 14 of the Act are required to follow the committal procedure under Cr.P.C. Such an interpretation prevents the speedy trail envisaged under the Act. Further the absence of the adequate number of special courts has also resulted in slow disposal of atrocity cases and a huge back log.

OTHER BACKWARD CLASS

The Central Government of India classifies some of its citizens based on their social and economic condition as Scheduled Caste, Scheduled Tribe and Other Backward Class (OBC). The OBC list presented by the commission is dynamic (castes and communities can be added or removed) and will change from time to time depending on Social, Educational and Economic factors. For example, the OBCs are entitled to 27% reservations in public sector employment and higher education. In the constitution, OBCs are described as "socially and educationally backward classes", and government is enjoined to ensure their social and educational development.

OBC list includes castes and communities that belong to all four varnas (Brahmin, Kshatriya, Vaishya and Shudra) that are deemed to be socially and educationally backward.

Until 1985, the affairs of Backward Classes were looked after by the Backward Classes Cell (BCC) in the Ministry of Home Affairs. With the creation of a separate Ministry of Welfare in 1985 (renamed as Ministry of Social Justice and Empowerment on 25 May 1998) the matters relating to Scheduled Castes, Scheduled Tribes, Other Backward Classes (OBCs) and Minorities were transferred to the new Ministry.

The Backward Classes Division in the Ministry looks after the policy, planning and implementation of programmes relating to social and economic empowerment of OBCs. It also looks after matters relating to two institutions set up for the welfare of OBCs: National Backward Classes Finance and Development Corporation (NBCFDC) and the National Commission for Backward Classes (NCBC).

Obligation of the government

Under Article 340 of the Indian Constitution, it is obligatory for the government to promote the welfare of the Other Backward Classes (OBC). Article 340(1) states, " The president may by order appoint a commission, consisting of such persons as he thinks, fit to investigate the conditions of socially and educationally backward classes within the territory of India and the difficulties under which they labour and to make recommendations as to the steps that should be taken by the union or any state to remove such difficulties and as to improve 'their condition and as to the grants that should be made, and the order appointing such commission shall define the procedure to be followed by the commission."

Article 340(2) states, "A commission so appointed shall investigate the matters referred to them and present to the president a report setting out the facts as found by them and making such recommendations as they think proper."

COMMISSIONS

First Backward Classes Commission

The First Backward Classes Commission was set up by a presidential order on January 29, 1953 under the chairmanship of

Kaka Kalelkar. The commission submitted its report on March 30, 1955. It had prepared a list of 2,399 backward castes or communities for the entire country and of which 837 had been classified as the "most backward". Some of the most notable recommendations of the commission were:

1. Undertaking caste-wise enumeration of population in the census of 1961;
2. Relating social backwardness of a class to its low position in the traditional caste hierarchy of Indian society;
3. Treating all women as a class as "backward";
4. Reservation of 70 per cent seats in all technical and professional institutions for qualified students of backward classes.
5. Reservation of vacancies in all government services and local bodies for other backward classes.

The commission in its final report recommended "caste as the criteria" to determine backwardness. But this report was not accepted by the government as it feared that the backward classes excluded from the caste and communities selected by the commission may not be considered and the really needy would be swamped by the multitude and would hardly receive special attention.

Mandal Commission

The decision to set up a second backward classes commission was made official by the president on January 1, 1979. The commission popularly known as the Mandal Commission, its chairman being B. P. Mandal. It submitted the report in December 1980.The recommendations of the commission were: The population of OBCs which includes both Hindus and non-Hindus is around 52 per cent of the total population according to the Mandal Commission.

However, this finding was criticized as based on "fictitious data." The National Sample Survey puts the figure at 32%. There is substantial debate over the exact number of OBC's in India, with census data compromised by partisan politics. It is generally estimated to be sizable, but lower than the figures quoted by either the Mandal Commission or and National Sample Survey.

27 per cent of reservation was recommended owing to the legal constraint that the total quantum of reservation should not exceed 50 percent. States which have already introduced reservation for OBC exceeding 27 per cent will not be affected by this recommendation. With this general recommendation the commission proposed the following over-all scheme of reservation for OBC:

1. Candidates belonging to OBC recruited on the basis of merit in an open competition should not be adjusted against their reservation quota of 27 per cent.
2. The above reservation should also be made applicable to promotion quota at all levels.
3. Reserved quota remaining unfilled should be carried forward for a period of three years and de-reserved thereafter.
4. Relaxation in the upper age limit for direct recruitment should be extended to the candidates of OBC in the same manner as done in the case of SCs and STs.
5. A roster system for each category of posts should be adopted by the concerned authorities in the same manner as presently done in respect of SC and ST candidates.

These recommendations in total are applicable to all recruitment to public sector undertakings both under the central and state governments, as also to nationalised banks. All private sector undertakings which have received financial assistance from the government in one form or other should also be obliged to recruit personnel on the aforesaid basis. All universities and affiliated colleges should also be covered by the above scheme of reservation. Although education is considered an important factor to bring a desired social change, "educational reform" was not within the terms of reference of this commission. To promote literacy the following measures were suggested:

1. An intensive time-bound programme for adult education should be launched in selected pockets with high concentration of OBC population;
2. Residential schools should be set up in these areas for backward class students to provide a climate specially conducive to serious studies. All facilities in these schools

including board and lodging should be provided free of cost to attract students from poor and backward homes;

3. Separate hostels for OBC students with above facilities will have to be provided;
4. Vocational training was considered imperative.
5. It was recommended that seats should be reserved for OBC students in all scientific, technical and professional institutions run by the central as well as state governments. The quantum of reservation should be the same as in the government services, i e, 27 per cent.

Backward class people is a collective term, used by the Government of India, for castes which are economically and socially disadvantaged and face, or may have faced discrimination on account of birth. Most of them do not have any land ownership or economic independence and are dependent on Forward Castes for employment, mostly as farm hands or menial labour; or derive income from self employment on caste-dependent skills assignment. They typically include the Dalits, the Scheduled castes, and the Other Backward Classes (OBCs). They live mainly in rural India and perform hard physical labour such as agriculture and janitorial work. Backward Castes constitute around 50% of the Indian population. Even though they have a rich culture, many live below the poverty line. According to estimates from the Indian government's National Sample Survey, in 1999-2000 44% of Scheduled Tribes and 35% of Scheduled Castes lived in poverty.. Their plight is regarded as a serious issue in Indian society.

Political parties in India have attempted to use these communities as votebanks. In contrast, some politicians like Ambedkar, D. Devaraj Urs, V.P. Singh have tried to self-empower the Backward Castes. As a result, there are now many opinion leaders, including Bangarappa, Siddaramaiah, Narendra Modi, Uma Bharathi, Ramachandra Veerappa, Laloo Prasad Yadav, and Mulayam Singh Yadav, in these communities.

Supreme Court Interim Stay

On 29 March 2007, the Supreme Court of India, as an interim measure, stayed the law providing for 27 percent reservation for Other Backward Classes in educational institutions like IITs and IIMs. This was done in response to a public interest litigation —

Ashoka Kumar Thakur vs. Union of India. The Court held that the 1931 census could not be a determinative factor for identifying the OBCs for the purpose of providing reservation. The court also observed, "Reservation cannot be permanent and appear to perpetuate backwardness".

Supreme Court Verdict

The Supreme Court of India on April 10, 2008, upheld the Government's move for initiating 27% OBC quotas in Government funded institutions. The Court has categorically reiterated its prior stand that "Creamy layer" should be excluded from the ambit of reservation policy and private institutions are also not to be included in. The verdict produced mixed reactions from supporting and opposing quarters. Several criteria to identify creamy layer has been recommended, which are as follows:

Those with family income above Rs 250,000 a year (Now Rs 450,000 a year) should be in creamy layer, and excluded from the reservation quota. Also, children of doctors, engineers, chartered accountants, actors, consultants, media professionals, writers, bureaucrats, defence officers of colonel and equivalent rank or higher, high court and Supreme Court judges, all central and state government Class A and B officials. The court has requested Parliament to exclude MPs' and MLAs' children, too.

ASHOKA KUMAR THAKUR VS. UNION OF INDIA

1. The Constitution (Ninety-Third Amendment) Act, 2005 does not violate the "basic structure" of the Constitution so far as it relates to the state maintained institutions and aided educational institutions. Question whether the Constitution (Ninety-Third Amendment) Act, 2005 would be constitutionally valid or not so far as "private unaided" educational institutions are concerned, is left open to be decided in an appropriate case.
2. "Creamy layer" principle is one of the parameters to identify backward classes. Therefore, principally, the "Creamy layer" principle cannot be applied to STs and SCs, as SCs and STs are separate classes by themselves.
3. Preferably there should be a review after ten years to take note of the change of circumstances.

4. A mere graduation (not technical graduation) or professional deemed to be educationally forward.
5. Principle of exclusion of Creamy layer applicable to OBC's.
6. The Central Government shall examine as to the desirability of fixing a cut off marks in respect of the candidates belonging to the Other Backward Classes (OBCs)to balance reservation with other societal interests and to maintain standards of excellence. This would ensure quality and merit would not suffer. If any seats remain vacant after adopting such norms they shall be filled up by candidates from general categories.
7. So far as determination of backward classes is concerned, a Notification should be issued by the Union of India. This can be done only after exclusion of the creamy layer for which necessary data must be obtained by the Central Government from the State Governments and Union Territories. Such Notification is open to challenge on the ground of wrongful exclusion or inclusion. Norms must be fixed keeping in view the peculiar features in different States and Union Territories. There has to be proper identification of Other Backward Classes (OBCs.). For identifying backward classes, the Commission set up pursuant to the directions of this Court in Indra Sawhney 1 has to work more effectively and not merely decide applications for inclusion or exclusion of castes.
8. The Parliament should fix a deadline by which time free and compulsory education will have reached every child. This must be done within six months, as the right to free and compulsory education is perhaps the most important of all the fundamental rights (Art.21 A). For without education, it becomes extremely difficult to exercise other fundamental rights.
9. If material is shown to the Central Government that the Institution deserves to be included in the Schedule (institutes which are excluded from reservations) of The Central Educational Institutions (Reservation in Admission) Act, 2006 (No. 5 of 2007), the Central Government must take an appropriate decision on the basis of materials placed and on examining the concerned

issues as to whether Institution deserves to be included in the Schedule of the said act as provided in Sec 4 of the said act.

10. Held that the determination of SEBCs is done not solely based on caste and hence, the identification of SEBCs is not violative of Article 15(1) of the Constitution.

NATIONAL COMMISSION FOR SCHEDULED TRIBES

The objectives of the National Commission for Scheduled Tribes are to act as an independent agency that will investigate, monitor and record any violation of the Constitutional rights of the Scheduled Tribes, suggest measures for their development and in general act on their behalf. This report focuses on the extent to which the Commission performs its role and how effectively it does so. It does not touch upon the wider issues pertaining to the Scheduled Tribes, except insofar as they are addressed or not addressed by the Commission. The study involved interviews with the Chairman and staff at all levels, a study of the various reports prepared by the Commission, a detailed perusal of several petitions filed in the Commission under different heads, as well as interviews with petitioners to assess their impression of the Commission.

A BRIEF HISTORY OF THE NATIONAL COMMISSION FOR SCHEDULED TRIBES

The National Commission for Scheduled Tribes was set up in February 2004, replacing the National Commission for Scheduled Castes and Scheduled Tribes.1 This Commission, in turn, replaced a series of offices/Commissions, which had their origin in the Special Officer for the Scheduled Castes, and Scheduled Tribes as laid down in Article 338 of the Constitution. As such, the scope of this study is both too short and too long – since the current National Commission for Scheduled Tribes has been functioning only for two years, and the functions or powers as such have existed in one form or another since 1950.

Initially, in 1950, the Special Officer was designated the Commissioner for Scheduled Castes and Scheduled Tribes, and was responsible for investigating the 'safeguards' provided by the Constitution and other laws, and reporting to the President.

In 1978, a multi-member (non-statutory) Commission for SC & ST was set up, with a Chairperson and four members, of which one was to be the Special Officer. For a while, the statutory office of the Commissioner for SC & ST co-existed with the non-statutory Commission for SC and ST. From 1981-85, the statutory office of the Commissioner remained unfilled. In 1987, the functions of the two offices were separated – the Special Officer/Commissioner was to submit reports to Parliament, while the National Commission was to conduct studies on the socioeconomic situation of SC & STs, and submit them in project mode to the Government.

In 1990, by a Constitutional Amendment, the Special Officer (Office of the Commissioner) for SC & ST was replaced by a National Commission for SC & ST (NCSC&ST). However, the first National Commission following this was set up only in 1992. Since then there have been four Commissions for SC & ST.

Increasingly, however, functions related to Scheduled Tribes began to be separated from the functions relating to Scheduled Castes. This was reflected in the creation of a separate Tribal Development Division in the Ministry of Home Affairs, and in 1999, the creation of a new Ministry of Tribal Affairs. The National SC & ST Finance Development Corporation was also bifurcated to create a separate National ST Finance Development Corporation in 2001.

In 2004, by amendment of Article 338 and the insertion of Article 338 A, the NCSC&ST was divided into the National Commission for Scheduled Castes and the National Commission for Scheduled Tribes. Since the bifurcation there have been two National Commissions for ST.

The Commissioner for SC and ST initially had 17 regional offices, but in 1967 these were re-grouped into five zonal offices and placed under the control of a newly created Directorate General of Backward Classes Welfare in the Department of Social Welfare, which was then under the Home Ministry. In 1978, however, they were brought back under the control of the Commission. In the bifurcation of the SC & ST Commision, the NCST retained six regional offices. These are located in Bhopal, Bhubaneswar, Jaipur, Raipur, Ranchi and Shillong.

Apart from the annual reports prepared by the Commissioner for SC & ST, and later, the NCSC & ST, there have been two

Commissions appointed under article 339 of the Constitution to look into the administration of scheduled areas and the welfare of scheduled tribes. The first was the 1960 UN Dhebar Commission, which yielded the tribal sub-plan strategy, and the second was the Dilip Singh Bhuria Commission (appointed 2002, report submitted 2004).

The history of the various shifts that the NCST has undergone reveals three striking issues:

1. Right from the beginning, the Office of the Commissioner was envisaged in paternalist mode, and the provisions of the Constitution relating to Scheduled Tribes seen as 'safeguards' (to be taken away when they were deemed to be no longer required) rather than rights (such as the right to non-alienation of land, or the right to an alternative form of governance and different laws from those that govern the rest of the country).
2. The long periods when the statutory office of the Commission remained unfilled, the initial creation of a non-statutory commission which would merely give reports to the government in project-mode, the way in which the office has been periodically reorganised suggests that it is seen merely as one more department of the government, rather than an independent body with Constitutional powers, intended to provide a corrective to the functioning of the government when required. There is a regrettable lack of seriousness with which the office has been treated. Its current uneasy co-existence with the Ministry of Tribal Affairs underlines the continuing nature of this problem.
3. The running down of the regional offices is another trend that has continued till the present, when there are only six regional offices to deal with Scheduled Tribes across the country. These are severely understaffed to deal with the areas they are meant to cover. In general, they are little recognised and complaints are generally made directly to the National Commission. The Commission has asked for four additional offices in AP, Maharashtra, HP and Gujarat, but failing that, there is a feeling among some officers that it would be better to consolidate all the offices in Delhi,

rather than spreading itself thin. However, this would fundamentally defeat the purpose of the Commission. To expect adivasis to have the resources to come to Delhi or even the state capital to pursue their cases is clearly unrealistic.

4. While some of the Commissioners for SC & ST were people who were extremely knowledgeable and concerned about the Scheduled Tribes, such as the anthropologist NK Bose and the former administrator Dr. B.D. Sharma, subsequent appointments of Chairpersons and members have been political sinecures for those ST representatives of the ruling party whom it needs to satisfy. They have displayed little vision or imagination in addressing the issues of Scheduled Tribes, and been unwilling to take up issues that are uncomfortable for their party.

FUNCTIONS AND POWERS

The functions, duties and powers of the Commission include:

1. to investigate and monitor all constitutional and legal safeguards for Scheduled Tribes, and make recommendations on these
2. to enquire into specific complaints regarding the violation of these safeguards and rights
3. to participate and advise on the planning process regarding the socioeconomic development of Scheduled Tribes, and evaluate their progress
4. to discharge any other functions related to the protection, welfare and development of Scheduled Tribes which the President, subject to Parliament may specify (clause 5f).

In pursuance of these objectives, the Commission is both required and empowered to:

1. Report to the President annually on the working of safeguards, and make recommendations. The Government (Centre or State, depending on whether a particular report concerns a State Government) is required to table these in the concerned legislature along with an Action Taken Report.

2. Act as a civil court to investigate all complaints, including the power to summon attendance, requisition documents etc. However, it does not have the power to issue injunctions against anyone on the basis of its investigations.
3. The Union and State governments are required to consult the Commission on all major policy matters affecting Scheduled Tribes.

In 2004, the Ministry of Tribal Affairs (MOTA) also assigned the NCST additional functions to carry out studies and hold workshops on specific subjects. While initially reluctant to accept the added burden, in the light of limited funds, the NCST eventually gave in and included the work in its Rules of Procedure (as part of clause 5 f of Article 338). It also requested MOTA to sanction additional funds under the head of 'Other Administrative Expenses' to meet the cost of workshops and studies on these issues.

The issues that MOTA specified are:

1. Measures that need to be taken to confer ownership rights over NTFPs to STs living in forest areas
2. Measures to be taken to safeguard rights of tribal communities over mineral, water and other resources as per law
3. Measures to be taken for the development of tribals and to work for more viable livelihood strategies
4. Measures to be taken to improve the efficacy of relief and rehabilitation measures for tribal groups displaced by development projects
5. Measures to be taken to prevent alienation of tribal people from land and to effectively rehabilitate such people in whose case alienation has already taken place
6. Measures to be taken to elicit maximum cooperation and involvement of tribal communities for protecting forests and undertaking social afforestation
7. Measures to be taken to ensure full implementation of the provisions of Panchayat (Extension to Scheduled Areas) Act 1996 (40 of 1996)
8. Measures to be taken to reduce and ultimately eliminate the practice of shifting cultivation by tribals that lead to

their continuous disempowerment and degradation of land and the environment.

Relation between MOTA and NCST: This manner of handing over responsibility for such studies to the NCST and the list of issues themselves betray government's attitude towards the rights of Scheduled Tribes. First, MOTA seems to be assuming the right to give instructions to the NCST, thus establishing a relation of superiority over NCST. This is contrary to the spirit of Article 338, which envisages the NCST as an independent body capable of giving advice and directions to the government. The NCST has the powers to regulate its own procedures (clause 4). When asked the Chairperson of the NCST said that MOTA was the nodal ministry for NCST in terms of funding and the provision of infrastructure, but otherwise the two were independent. He also said that NCST reviews the work of MOTA and the Tribal Sub-Plan, but the NSCT is responsible only to the President.2 While this is no doubt the official line, the reality of the relation between the two entities appears to be somewhat different. Control over funding and infrastructure effectively means control over an organisation.

Second, the list of issues is itself biased – it assumes displacement is inevitable, that it is shifting cultivation which is responsible for forest and land degradation rather than diversion of forest land for industrial and development projects or the forest department's own production forestry, that it is the government which needs to elicit people's cooperation in protecting forests and so on.

One of the points to be covered in this report is whether a citizens charter has been developed in consultation with the stakeholders. Adivasi communities and organisations have repeatedly made their views known, and have framed resolutions on their demands. These have included the right to land titles, the right not to be displaced, the right to protect their forests on their own without government interference and so on. These demands are mostly met with repression by agencies of the government, like the police and the district administrations. However, for the

Ministry of Tribal Affairs to come up with such a list of measures which already presuppose what should be studied, and which is at variance with what adivasi communities have repeatedly expressed and demanded, shows that it is far from developing a citizens charter. It also shows that the paternalist view of 'government knows best for the backward ST' continues to dominate government thinking.

Finally, it is not clear how these are further responsibilities placed upon the Commission, since all these issues were previously taken up by the Commissioner SC and ST in the past. An assertive Commission should have been looking into these issues anyway, since they centrally concern the planning process regarding the development of tribes.

While Article 338 (9) clearly states that "the Union and every state government shall consult the Commission on all major policy matters affecting Scheduled Castes and Scheduled Tribes", this does not seem to be happening. For instance, the Commission complained that it was not consulted by the Ministry of Tribal Affairs while framing the Scheduled Tribes (Recognition of Forest Rights) Act; it does not seem to have much of a role in suggesting rules for PESA and so on. Similarly, when it comes to framing the industrial or mining policy of the country, the Ministry of Tribal Affairs or even the NCST does not appear to be involved, even though this centrally concerns many ST populations.

Parliament. Not only does this deprive the public of valuable information, but it is a serious abdication of government responsibility. Commission Members and Officers attribute this failure to the delay in tabling the ATR alongside, and recommend that the two be delinked, and that the Report be tabled within 3 months and the ATR within six months of the report being given to the President. It is the Ministry of Tribal Affairs which is responsible for preparing the ATR (previously it was tasked to the Ministry of Social Justice), and its failure to do this is once again a reflection of the fact that it appears to be MOTA which controls NCST because it controls funding, infrastructure and the ATR, rather than the other way around.

In short, while Article 338 of the Constitution envisages the Commission as an independent body empowered to give advice to the government, the Government and the Ministry of Tribal Affairs treat the NCST as an appendage of its normal activities. The Commission, in turn, has not cared to exercise or be vocal about its independence. Thus it is unable to play the balancing, watchdog function it is meant to. On the other hand, even in Article 338, the powers of the Commission are limited to reporting and investigating. The fact that it has no independent powers to sanction officials who have committed atrocities against Scheduled Tribes makes it somewhat of a paper tiger.

Organisational Structure

The organisational structure of the Commission consists of the Chairperson at the top, followed by a Vice-Chairperson and three members. The senior administrative staff comprise of a Secretary to the Commission assisted by a Joint Secretary, two

Directors, and an under-secretary, Finally there are the principle investigators of the different units, as well as their 'dealing hands' or assistants.

Work of the Members: In a section on the approach and methodology of the Commission, we are told of the number of meetings held by the Commission. These are largely on the issue of reservations, inclusion of communities in the list of STs, delimitation of constituencies, the report of the Commission and its internal functioning. In other words, issues of identity and reservation – which affect a small portion of the overall ST population of the country. However, a look at the field visits of the Chairman reveals quite an interesting range of issues covered: medical treatment of children in Orissa, rehabilitation of Kadana dam oustees in Gujarat, conflicts between STs and the Army in J& K, visits to Sikkim and Jharkhand to talk to local people and state officials about their problems, visit to the Andaman and Nicobar islands to assess the schemes taken up by the administration and review post-Tsunami work, visit to Sardar Sarovar and Kalinganagar to investigate rehabilitation, meetings with SC/ST employees of nationalised banks and PSUs like NTPC and so on. Some members tend to tour their own areas, whereas others tour more widely. One Chairman is said to have spent the last few months of his tenure visiting all the *swamis* and *peeths* in the country.

Senior Staff of the Commission: While the members of the Commission change with every new Commission that is appointed the Commission has been fortunate to have some continuity in the form of some senior staff, who have been with the Commission in its various avatars from the 1970s. It is they who are largely responsible for the Report of the Commission, which is an extremely useful and comprehensive document, but which, as mentioned before, has not been tabled in Parliament.

Principle Investigators assigned to each research unit: It is this level which is most crucial for the bulk of cases handled by the Commission, and the impact felt by the public in everyday matters (which do not require major policy or political interventions). These units are severely understaffed, and fresh recruitment appears to be a serious problem, especially of the kind of graduates who are either from Scheduled Tribe communities themselves, or knowledgeable and concerned about them. Turnover is said to be high – recently PhDs were hired as investigators but they were leaving for better jobs. The number of staff to officers is also skewed with 1 dealing hand and research officer to 7 officers above him/her. The gender and caste composition of the Commission also bears attention. The representation or lack thereof of STs within the Commission manifests itself in subterranean tensions.

At this level, the staff is divided into four wings:

1. Administration/Establishment and Coordination Wing
2. Economic and Social Development Wing
3. Service Safeguards
4. Atrocities wing

While the administrative wing looks after all internal establishment and administrative matters of the Commission, the Services Safeguards wing deals with service issues. The issues it takes up include the implementation of reservation policies within the government, cases relating to false community certificates and the inclusion (and very rarely exclusion) of various communities in the list of Scheduled Tribes. The Atrocities wing deals with cases as defined by the Scheduled Castes and Scheduled Tribes (Prevention of Atrocities) Act 1989, the Bonded Labour system (Abolition) Act, the Minimum Wages Act etc. The main complaint under this head is the non-registering of cases under the Atrocities act. The Economic and Social Development Wing is intended to monitor government schemes. A list of policy matters dealt with under this theme include: matters relating to land and rehabilitation, education/scholarships, health, drinking water and nutrition, matters relating to financial institutions – banks/corporations, matters relating to scheduled areas and tribal areas, matters relating to forest and excise policy for tribals, tribal policy, matters relating to distributive agencies like petrol pumps, LPG etc., matters relating to central ministries, the Tribal Sub-Plan, and the Planning Commission. While the index page of the register carried all these items, the register itself was rather empty.

From July 2006 onwards, this structure was replaced with a regional division of labour where each of the four research units deals with all issues, region wise. Research Unit I deals with the northern and western states, Research Unit II covers the north-east, Research Unit III covers the central states as well as the Andamans, while Research Unit IV covers the southern states. In addition, since the bulk of the Commission's work is to do with the activities of different ministries and government departments, especially service matters, each research unit has been assigned specific ministries/departments.

The rationale given for this by the senior officers was that it prevented over-specialisation and the problems that occurred when a specialist in one field was away. The staff handling the cases, however, felt that the issues required that kind of specialised knowledge across regions. Further, by clubbing all regional issues together, services matters got more attention than the others by sheer weight of numbers. Having separate wings for atrocities and economic and social development ensured that they had their own space. This remains an issue of discussion within the Commission.

There are three or four ways in which the Commission takes up cases. The first is the routine way, whereby petitions are received and attended to by the principle investigators and their dealing hands. Sometimes the petitions are forwarded by MPs, which ensures that they get attended to. The other route is for the Chairperson or members to take up issues/complaints they encounter on their field visits and pass them on to the staff for further action. Inevitably, they are more interested in their own states than elsewhere, and the number of petitions from a state is also higher if one of the members comes from there. For example, in 2006, the highest number of atrocities complaints came from

MP, and although MP is the state with the highest number of atrocities against ST even according to the National Crime Records bureau, the representation of the other states in terms of complaints to the NCST was disproportionately low. The third route is for the Commission to take suo moto cognisance of an issue from newspaper reports. Earlier the librarian used to make clippings of cases relevant to STs, but now the system seems more haphazard.

There are two problems regarding the handling of cases by the Commission. The first is the low number of cases handled, compared to the large number of cases that occur in the country. For instance, in 2005-6, a mere 204 new cases were recorded by the atrocities wing, 461 cases by the economic and social development wing, and 489 by the services wing.

The number of atrocities cases in the country runs into thousands. According to the National Bureau of Crime Statistics, there were 6217 cases of atrocities against ST in 2001, 6774 in 2002 and 5889 in 2003.[7] The Chairperson, however, claimed that since the NCSC&ST was bifurcated, the number of cases has gone up as the NCST is able to devote more attention to STs alone. The fact that there are now 5 members specifically focussing on issues related to STs as against the 2 on the joint Commission for SCs & STs has also helped. The problem of lack of cases in certain areas may also have to do with the inability of this particular section of society which is affected by atrocities – STs – to access institutions like the Commission.

Unfortunately, even all the petitions that the Commission gets are not recorded. I am personally aware of petitions submitted to the Commission following a meeting with the Chairperson, but which do not figure in the records of the relevant research unit.

The mismatch between the atrocities that take place and the cases that the Commission deals with could be due to at least three reasons: 1.) not all cases which are registered require the intervention of the Commission, 2.) lack of staff to deal with the volume of cases that come in (each research unit gets about 4-500 letters on average per month) 3.) a tendency among staff to concentrate on the more easily manageable service cases where the petitioners are more organised and hence more vocal, and thus neglect the atrocities cases. The shortage of staff is quite severe, and appears to be half of the sanctioned strength.

The second issue is the pendency of cases. Here again, it is not clear whether the problem is primarily a.) shortage of staff, b.) the nature of the files where explanations are called for and letters go back and forth. The usual procedure is for the Commission to write letters to the concerned Secretary/Chairperson of the organisation from which the complaint originated, or with which the complaint is concerned and ask for an explanation. In cases where they do not get an answer they can issue summons to the officer to appear in person before the Commission and explain. However, this is rare, and from March 2004-2007, summons have been issued in only two cases.

This procedure – of asking for clarification and explanation from the concerned officials – assumes a situation where governments respond honestly. As one staff member said, in the course of interviews, "where rules are knowingly violated by the administration, the tendency is to cover up the matter." In such cases, the Commission is helpless. This procedure is especially problematic for STs, since a large part of the atrocities committed on them are by agencies of the government like the police and the forest staff. Of course, in a few cases, especially service matters, where the law is complicated, organisations do respond and the problem is resolved. In rare cases, the organisation is actually grateful for the intervention by the Commission and the clarification on law it offers. The point, however, is that while not every case can be independently investigated by the Commission and letters asking for an explanation do constitute some form of pressure, this mode of functioning as the dominant norm needs to be seriously rethought. Apart from visits by the members, the existing independent investigating machinery in the Commission needs to be strengthened.

This mode of functioning also saps the interest of the staff. One person said that when he joined the Commission it was with the expectation of doing research and giving policy suggestions on development. Now, however, the Commission had become a 'petition cell' and the work had become routinised.

Issues Taken Up by the Commission

The Commission has divided the issues that come before it into the following categories:

1. Constitutional Provisions for protection and development of STs
2. Socioeconomic development of STs (land alienation, rights over MFP, housing, education etc.)
3. Resettlement and Rehabilitation of displaced tribals
4. Education
5. Service Safeguards
6. The problem of authenticating ST certificates
7. Crimes and atrocities against ST

This listing of issues before the adivasis of the country is fairly exhaustive (although it does not deal with important issues such as the growing militarisation of tribal areas). The report of the Commission also deals quite exhaustively with the statistics and overall situation under all these sections, and makes broad recommendations to the Ministry of Tribal Affairs and other departments of the government, such as the need to 'expedite the passage of the Forest Rights Bill', the need to 'preserve the cultural heritage of the tribal people' with respect to their places of worship, arts and crafts, the need for states to implement PESA effectively etc. It also recommends that "the Dept. of Mines should introduce a bill to give effect to the recommendations of the Bhuria Committee 1995 to the effect that in all industrial enterprises set up in the Scheduled Areas (other than small ventures) the community should be deemed to be the owner with 50% shares in its favour by virtue of its allowing the industry to use local resources and get established.". Having made this recommendation, however, the Commission is unable to back it up with sufficient voice when actual cases of acquisition of adivasi land for industrial purposes takes place. Even on Kalinganagar, when 12 adivasis were killed by the police for protesting against land acquisition, while the Commission visited the area, and called for a report from the state government, the Government set up its own enquiry commission, thus sidestepping the Commission. In cases like the Narmada dam or the Polavaram dam, where large number of adivasis are to be displaced, the Commission writes to the concerned engineers and government officials, but is unable to make much difference.

In terms of the everyday cases handled (as against policy recommendations), it is clear both from the volume of cases disposed of and conversations with the staff that the bulk of the cases before the Commission are individual service matters pertaining to employment by government, including the banking and insurance sector, and other nationalised bodies. Scheduled Tribes are rarely employed in the organised private sector. The focus on service matters is in part because government staff are the people most able to make use of a grievance redressal mechanism, and to follow up with the Commission staff in person, a factor which the staff admitted was of help in pushing a case forward. In part it is also because the other issues confronting adivasis are so vast and so difficult for a single Commission to address in the face of the overwhelming power of other ministries keen on pushing a certain model of development that marginalizes adivasis, that Commission staff themselves feel that only these cases yield tangible results for them. In effect however, this means that the Service Safeguards wing acts as an internal branch of the government, ensuring better service conditions for the scheduled tribe employees of the government.

This is by itself an important service considering that the vast majority of ST government staff belong to classes III and IV, and are relatively powerless within the system. For example, a petition by the All India General Insurance SC/ST employees federation states that there is a serious need for compassionate appointments for SC/ST staff, since their statistics showed that 80% of class IV staff had died while in service, particularly the safai karamcharis. Other charges against management are that they tend to promote only those SC/ST employees who were subservient, that more vigilance cases are filed against SCs/STs than against the general category employees (borne out by the figures), that SC/ST employees are posted to more difficult places, that reservations are being filled only at the lowest levels and not in managerial jobs, that the post-based reservation roster (instead of a vacancy based one) has destroyed whatever little reservation is available, since over time at least 15% SCs and 8% STs have been appointed in the organisation. In some cases, these ST staff are also the sole members of their community and thus have a model effect. One example comes from a case concerning the recruitment of one Major Sugathan who belongs to the Ulladan ST community of Kottayam district, a very small community and who is the first and lone commissioned officer from this community.

On the other hand, these cases are trivial in the light of the enormity of problems faced by the adivasis of this country, the majority of whom are in agriculture or unorganised sector work. The Commission is unable to seriously address their concerns in any concrete sense.

Among the communities served by the commission, dominant communities like the Meenas from Rajasthan have the maximum number of cases, in part because they are the best represented in the services. There are relatively few petitions from the North east. A look at the registers indicates that some organisations, especially PSU employees federations or unions are relatively frequent petitioners, and therefore more likely to get heard.

In the following sections, I will take up some examples of cases which have come before the Commission, starting with those cases where the Commission has been successful.

Several of the complaints described as 'successful' in the first report, under the heading of Economic and Social Development, deal with complaints by students who were not given admission into courses in engineering, or were not given attendance and so on. In all these cases, the Commission intervened with the university authorities and succeeded in getting the students grievances redressed. There is also a listing under different heads, like the provision of drinking water, a health centre, electricity and land pattas to villages in West Bengal, following a visit by the Chairman to West Medinipur district, in WB. There is little to distinguish these cases from the 'successful cases' handled under the service safeguards wing which also deal with individual service related grievances, such as denial of promotion, the refusal of an organisation to return original marksheets to the petitioner when he changed jobs, non-payment of pension and so on..

A look at the cases reported under the atrocities section of the report reveals far less success in handling these cases. To begin with, the reach of people who undergo atrocities of this nature is more limited, and they are unable to take their complaints directly to the Commission. Many of these cases have been taken up by the Commission following newspaper reports. To give one example:

"A case of abduction and gang rape of a Scheduled Tribe woman in Chindwada, Madhya Pradesh was reported in the newspaper 'Dainik Bhaskar' dated 21.8.04. The Commission suo moto took up the case with the District Superintendent of Police Chindwada. The SP reported that a case under Sections 366, 376 (2) and 506-B IPC and Section 3 (1) (xii) of the SCs and STs (POA) Act 1989 had been registered and chargesheet submitted in the Court and that an interim relief of financial assistance of Rs. 25,000/-had been paid to the victim as per the SC and ST (POA) Rules, 1995. Since an offence under Sec 376 (2) of IPC is punishable with an imprisonment for a term of 10 years or more, the Dist. Superintendent of Police, Chindwada has been advised by the Commission to submit supplementary chargesheet taking cognizance of Section 3 (2) (v) of the SCs/STs (POA) Act 1989 in place of Section 3 (1) (xii).

Moreover, all these cases are of individual atrocities and the Commission seems unwilling to take up the widespread atrocities on adivasis that are going on in the name of militarization and internal security, both in the north-east and central India, including the gang rapes and widespread murders by the Salwa Judum in

Chhattisgarh, or by the armed forces in the northeast despite these having been brought to its notice.

The Commission also gets a significant number of cases pertaining to false ST certificates or demands from particular communities to be included in the ST list, such as the Sarania Kachari or the ex tea-garden tribes in the list for Assam, the Gujjars for Rajasthan and so on. For a community to be included in the scheduled list, its claims have to be agreed to by the concerned state government, the Registrar General and the National Commission for Scheduled Tribes. While the Commission does list some cases of this kind that it settled, such as the claim of the Maleru tribe in Karnataka to be recognised as Primitive Tribal Groups (PTG), in general it is doubtful whether it commands the kind of expertise on such subjects that is required. The petitions that are sent usually contain gazetteer style ethnographic information on the claims of their own communities over others. One petition signed by a number of Delhi University students from different ST communities of the North east asks the Commission to take action against the appointment of Baruas in teaching posts reserved for STs since they were really Bengali Buddhists and not STs.12 While the Commission has written to the Governments of West Bengal and Meghalaya asking for the facts, it is clear that such cases are really beyond the capacity of the Commission except to push paper back and forth.

Public Perceptions of the Commission

Several adivasi organisations fighting on land and forest issues do approach the Commission, but mainly in terms of routinely covering all bases, and not because they expect any serious help from the Commission. Many of them do not bother, since it is evidently more time-effective to approach the concerned authorities directly like the state government, or the various ministries, or file cases in court.

One would have thought that regular petitioners of the Commission in service matters would find greater uses, but a long interview with an SC/ST insurance employees federation revealed rather negative perceptions of the Commission. They called both the ST and SC Commission 'tigers without teeth' and the members of the Commission 'political people working for their own survival'. One chairman was even accused of being purchased by the management.

The personnel manager of the company, on the other hand, was more positive about the Commission. In the last two years his office had got 3-4 references per month from the Commission (for an overall SC staff of 4549 and ST staff of 1062) but, he said, the exchange is 'positive and fruitful. Once they are convinced there is no case of discrimination they stop the case.'

OVERALL IMPACT OF THE COMMISSION

The overall impact of the Commission will have to be judged by two criterion:

1. Factors within the Commission's Control, such as its political courage in defending the rights of the STs and acting as a watchdog body on other ministries and government organisations, or its overall sensitivity to adivasi issues. In the case of R&R issues, for example, despite a strong constitutional mandate the Commission has not been able to exercise much influence. Certain issues have not been taken up by the Commission at all despite petitions – e.g. militarisation.

2. Factors outside the Commission's Control, such as funding, staff, and the overall policy of the government regarding investment in tribal areas, and subsequent displacement. Increasingly, the Commission is at best a palliative, as market forces have increasingly come to usurp the space in tribal areas, and decisions about scheduled areas are made not in the Commission or even the Ministry of Tribal Affairs but by the various ministries dealing with forests, water, mining etc., as well as by the WTO and other international agencies. The NCST, like other institutions such as the NHRC is useful as an instrument to tell the international community that India is serious about its STs, and therefore does not require any outside intervention but such a stance is of little help to the adivasis of India.

The following recommendations are therefore rather limited, keeping in mind the overall political economy in which the Commission functions. None of the institutions envisaged by the Constitution to protect the rights of the STs are working – whether it is the Tribes Advisory Councils or the office of the Governor. The standard and shocking response by the MOTA or the Home Ministry whenever complaints are made to it of gross violations is that x or y is a state subject, despite the fact that the 5th Schedule empowers the Union to give directions to the states on the administration of scheduled areas.

The issue for scheduled areas and scheduled tribes is not simply one of the failure of government to provide essential services like health and education, but a deliberate policy to disenfranchise people and deprive them of their resources.

Recommendations

The primary recommendation in this report is that the Government follow the Constitution in the spirit it was envisaged, among other things, by strengthening the role of the Commission as a truly independent watchdog body with punitive powers.

The composition of the Commission needs to be examined, in particular, the implications of a commission composed entirely of political appointments by the ruling party. The qualifications of the Chairperson and Members should be publicly available, and there should be an effort to involve people from different professions concerned with Scheduled Tribes.

The overlap with the Ministry of Tribal Affairs needs to be examined, and the independence of the Commission vis-à-vis MOTA asserted.

The Commission is short staffed, as well as underfunded and therefore unable to deal satisfactorily with the volume of cases. The Regional offices need to be strengthened, along with an independent investigating mechanism. This should replace the standard procedure of asking for clarification as the dominant mode of functioning.

11

Land Alienation and Tribal People's Rights in India

Tribal people's rights being a part of the broad human rights phenomena has acquired significance in recent times. As human beings the people who live in tribal lands acquire a similar set of rights like others. Being citizens of the country they are entitled to a number of privileges as well. From time immemorial there have been violations of their fundamental rights. In contemporary society the state comes to their rescue to some extent. The increasing awareness of the concept of human rights under the aegis of the UNO, world media, NGOs etc. proves beneficial to the victims.

Human rights are those conditions which are inherent to nature and without which one can not live as a human being. These rights and fundamental freedoms allow one to develop fully and use one's human qualities, intelligence, talents and conscience to satisfy one's spiritual, physical, social and other needs. They are based on human kind's increasing demand for life in which the inherent dignity and worth of each human being will receive respect and protection.

Human rights constitute a variable category as is adequately demonstrated by the history of the last few centuries. The list of human rights has been modified and continues to be modified in changing historical circumstances. Thus rights may not be fundamental by nature. That which appears to be fundamental in a given historical era or civilization is not fundamental in other era or civilization. Since the time of Hobbes and Locke, liberal political theorists have made it their primary purpose to explore relationships between the individual and the State.

It is not enough to think in terms of two level relationship, the individual at one level and the State at another nor is it enough if the nation is added. Considering the heterogeneity of mankind and of the population of virtually every existing State it is also necessary to think of ethnic communities and certain other kinds of groups, and to include them among the kinds of rights and duties bearing units whose inter relationships are to be explored. Rights that belong to individuals may go the them either as human beings or as members of a group. The Universal Declaration of Human Rights enumerates rights of the first sort; they go to, "everyone.... without distinction of any kind, such as race, colour, sex, language, religion, political or other opinion, national or social origin, property, birth or other status".

With regard to the legal rights of groups, ethnic communities are sometimes treated as political units within countries, both through territorial delimitations and through the use of separate electoral rolls. Ethnic communities in many countries are differently treated with respect to rights of property and residence; it is not only a question of territorial reservation for the indigenous but also a question of special measures designed to make it possible for the communities to preserve their distinctive identify. In case of less advanced groups that have suffered discrimination, it is now not uncommon to give them a right to expect special measures (affirmative action) designed to promote their quality, e.g. in the educational and economic realms.

Human rights are often held to be inter-related and mutually complementary. According to this view the 'first generation,' civil and political rights form the bedrock of 'second generation' economic, social and cultural rights, while collective and solidarity rights, such as the evolving indigenous rights constitute a 'third generation' of human rights. Further human rights are often said to be compatible with the rule of law and representative democracy. As per Stig Toft. Madsen's (State, society and Human rights in South Asia) hypothesis, "some instances of human rights do not form an integrated whole but are rights in intergenerational conflicts."

The conflict according to Madsen is between the presently dominant 'first generation', civil and political rights professed and guaranteed by a liberal State accepting the ideals of democracy and rule of law and the rights of legal and political, cultural and economic autonomy enjoyed by tribal groups. The outcomes of the conflict between the two incongrous orders of rights has been a working understanding or compromise. While this compromise has guaranteed the survival of tribal cultures, it has also meant that the tribal in question have been denied many of the rights enjoyed by others. So the question is how the tribal autonomy or collective right to autonomy including legal autonomy have circumscribed first generation rights, democracy and the rule of law.

The recent international thinking on indigenous rights is exemplified by the draft of Universal Declaration on the rights of indigenous peoples. According to this draft, "indigenous people have the right to participate fully in the political, economic, social and cultural life of the state while maintaining their distinct political, economic social and cultural characteristics". The Rio de Janerio Declaration on Environment and Development, adopted on 14th June, 1992 by the United Nations conference proclaims that states should recognize and duly support indigenous peoples' identity, culture and interest and enable their participation in the achievement of sustainable development.

Indigenous people and their communities have an historical relationship with their lands and are generally descendants of the original inhabitants of such lands. They have developed over many generations a holistic traditional knowledge of their lands, natural resources and environment. According to the Rio Declaration, they shall enjoy the full measures of human rights and fundamental freedoms without hindrance or discrimination. Their ability to participate fully in sustainable development practices on their lands have tended to be limited as a result of factors of an economic, social and historical nature.

The International Labour Organisation also in its convention No. 169, year 1989, on "Indigenous and Tribal Peoples", suggested that governments must consult with indigenous and tribal peoples within their countries on development projects and other activities effecting them. It provided for respect for their land rights. This right include protection of their lands and right to refuse displacement form their lands except in exceptional circumstances and against compensation.

TRIBAL RIGHTS IN INDIA

At the time of independence the Indian Government inherited a large tribal population. The Govt. of India has made a number of plans to protect the rights of the tribals and to integrate them into national developmental planning. The Minority Commission, the National Human Rights Commission etc., are there to prevent atrocities against them and to bring their plight to national lime light. Above all, in the Constitution of India the rights of the tribals were explicitly recognized and clauses were included to permit positive discrimination in their favour.

But the evaluation reports have pointed out that these special provisions have so far failed to bring about any positive gains to the tribal population. As per the Planning Commission Document 1973, "Reviewing the policies and programmes of the proceeding Five Year Plans we are of the opinion that the efforts so far made for social and economic development of the scheduled tribes have not brought an appreciable change in their condition." There can be a number of explanations for the failure of the governmental programmes for tribal development. However, the oppression and appropriation of the tribal people by the economically and politically more powerful groups have led to tribal movements or tribal unrest. For instance, the Santal rebellion, the revolt by Birsa Bhagwan, the Praja Mandal Movement, the Tana Bhagat Movement, the Naxalbari Movement, the Jharkhand Movement etc., are all attempts by the tribal people to shake off the yoke of exploitation.

In recent times the traditional territories of the tribal people have been subjected to incursions. Their lands are taken away in the name of economic advancement of the country. But in return they receive landlessness, impoverishment and long term degradation of the environment on which they totally depend. For almost two centuries now, tribal communities, like many other non-tribal peasants and forest dwellers, have been witness to the collapse of their multiple relationship with the land, the forest and among themselves. The basis of their cultural ethos, their systems of meaning have faced the collective unslaught of outsider exploiters, the disruptive impact of proselytizing Christianity, and of foreign models of economic betterment which have been conceived without their participation and implemented without their consent. Laws like Land Acquisition Act and the Indian Forest Act legitimise the continuing decline in access and control over forest resources that are the basis of their subsistence economy.

Initiatives from the Bharat-Jan-Andolan, Shosit Jan Andolan, the Indian Council of Indigenous and Tribal Peoples, Adivasi Sangamams in South India, PUCL, PUDR etc., are indicative of these modest attempts to raise-fundamental issues and define an alternative political agenda that frontally challenges the institutions and structures of our bourgeois democracy.

STATE POLICY AND THE TRIBALS

The edifice of colonial forestry was inherited by the Government of Independent India and immediately put to work in the service of the State's primary goals of repaid industrialization. The National Forest Policy 1952 underlies continuity of the colonial policy. It reinforced the claim of the State to exclusive control over forest protection and production. Significantly this policy identifies shifting cultivation as one of the main threats to State forestry. But in turn this affects the basic rights of the tribals to be dependent on forest resources. Hence, many tribal groups mounted a sustained challenge to the continuing denial of their rights. The Khanwar tribes of Madhya Pradesh protested in 1957 against revenue collection and called upon the people to defy forest laws which violated their customary rights. Their slogan, "Jangal Zamin Azad Hai", (forest and land are free gifts of nature) succinctly expressed the opposition to external control and commercial use. Another concept of conflict is the 'Contractor System' which is the modus operandi of forest working in India. The State's unwillingness to replace the contractor system has given rise to militant movements. Naxalite movement is one of the results of this type of exploitation.

Process of Depeasantization and Land Alienation

An overwhelming majority of the tribals are agriculturists. They owned the land in their own rights. Their entire life process was centred and built upon two major means of production i.e., the forest and the land. To understand the dynamics of land problem in the totality, one needs an understanding of the logic of the underlying forces that govern its ownership pattern. The specific economic form in which unpaid surplus labour is pumped out of the direct producers, determines the relation of the rulers and the ruled. Hence land problem of a particular area has to be understood from its historical perspective. Historical evidences are ample which proves the conception of depeasantization as a net result of the uneven structural changes that have taken place from time to time due to the commoditization of the tribal economy in which land plays a critical and predominant role.

Land Alienation as a Concept

As per Marx, in a Capitalist society an alienated man lives in an alienated nature and he performs estranged labour and the product of his labour becomes alien to him. Alienation as a concept is used by many social scientists in India, merely as a sociological phenomenon. Since land alienation is the crux of the depeasantization of the tribals, the concept assumes utmost importance in the analysis of tribal rights as a part of human rights discourse. The problem of land alienation is a much deeply connected phenomenon with full of contradictions related to the existing socioeconomic order. The separation of land from the tribal communities can be understood in a more scientific way with the assistance of the theoretical formulations of the concept of alienation.

Alienation was defined by Hegel and was used by Marx to describe and criticise a social condition in which man far from being the active initiation of the social world seemed more a passive object of determinate external processes. Marx says, alienation is fundamentally a particular relation of property, involving involuntary surrender to autagonistic 'other'. Alienation is inherent in exploitative relations of production and its nature varies with that of exploitation. Hence alienation's manifestations also differs among societies based on slavery, serfdom and capitalism etc. Thus the concept of alienation may be interpreted to understand a specific problem of the tribals where land becomes the primordial source of exploitation and results in the creation of a society where exploitative production relations exit.

Violation of Land Rights

The question of land is not just result of the existing situation but its origin may be traced to the periods of deprivation of tribal lands or to periods of the withdrawal of their rights to exploit forest. Gradually, due to various structural changes within and outside the tribal systems, the more advanced groups forced the tribals either to retreat to the nearest jungles or to become landless labourers. Though land is the only source of their livelihood, as their other assets being extremely meagre, tribals were severally deprived. Basically, moneylenders, traders, the feudal lords, or the rich peasants exploit the tribals most. It is an established fact that there is a large scale alienation of lands which belong to the tribes and grabbers invariably in all cases are the non-tribes. This phenomenon has further been ruined by the emergence of new forces of production. Commenting on this, the National Commission on Backward-Areas Development (1980) says, "In a number of areas new industrial and mining complexes, many major irrigation projects were located in the tribal areas resulting in the submergence of extensive lands, belonging to the tribals".

Also in the operations of denudation of forest on a massive scale tribal labour had been used to a great extent to clear off the forest area which was a method of the land lords to alienate the tribals from the forests. This further widened the gap between the tribal landless and landed gentry of the non-tribal communities.

Commenting on the problem of land alienation in tribal areas, the Committee on Plan Projects, Planning Commission, presented a report on the Tribal Development Programmes in 1969. The committee noticed that tribal lands in many areas passed into the hands of non-tribals, the legal prohibitions against such transfers notwithstanding. Sample studies in Andhra Pradesh, Orissa and some other States have shown that transfers have taken place on large scale without the permission of the collector or other competent authorities as required by law. The loopholes were exploited by the money lenders and others and they continue to circumvent the legal provisions by entering into 'benami' or other clandestine transactions with the native tribals. The impotency of legislation to arrest this growing menace to the economic advancement of the tribal in such a situation is thus obvious.

FORMS OF LAND ALIENATION

The first and foremost is the manipulation of land records. The unsatisfactory state of land records contributed a lot to the problem of land alienation. The tribals were never legally recognized as owners of the lands which they cultivated. The second form of land alienation is reported to have taken place due to 'benami' transfers. The report of the study team of the Union Home Ministry (May 1975) pointed out that large scale transfers of ownership of the Adivasis' lands are being allowed to go out of hands through illegal and benami transactions, collusive civil proceedings etc., in which land remains to be in the names of the original owners who are reduced to the level of share croppers.

Another form of land alienation is related to the leasing or mortgaging of the land. To raise loans for various needs the tribals have to give their land as mortgage to the local moneylenders or to the rich farmers. Encroachment is another form of dispossessing the tribals of their lands and this is done by the new entrants in all the places where there were no proper land records. Bribing the local Patwari for manipulating the date of settlement of land disputes, ante-dating etc., are resorted to claim the tribal lands.

Concubinage or marital alliance is another form to circumvent the law and grab tribal lands at no cost at all.

Fictitious adoption of the non-tribals by the tribal families is also another method to snatch the lands of the tribals.

Also the slackness in the implementation of the restrictive provisions encourages the non-tribals to occupy the tribal lands. Lands alienation which takes place in various ways has assumed alarming proportion threatening the right to life of the tribal population. Though the problem lies elsewhere, it is being unfortunately always interpreted as the handiwork of certain individuals like the moneylender, traders, land lords, etc, without understanding the class connection of these individuals. The unsystematic land records of the pre-colonial and colonial periods was followed by the present State. There was collection of 'taxes- (a strange phenomenon for the natives and it was the beginning process of alienation) in the tribal areas.

In the name of protecting the interest of the tribals stringent laws were enacted by the government but the non-tribals found the loopholes to their advantage. This double edged nature of State policy in one of the facets of the existing contradictions in the Indian Tribal Society. The process of land alienation is not an accidental one, but it has arisen because of the concerted efforts of the antagonistic class interest that are operating in the tribal areas. This is not just migration of the non-tribals into tribal areas rather there is a history behind this migration and the State has supported the migrant non-tribals to the settle down in the tribal lands.

However, being the natural owners of forests and its adjoining lands the tribals are being deprived of their rights to own them. They have been relegated from their earlier 'self-reliant' status to a 'dependent' one. Coupled with the exploitation by the non-tribals, the State legislations also proved detrimental to their interests. Therefore to understand the root causes of the land alienation process of the tribal communities its relationship with the changes in the socioeconomic structures have to be understood properly.

Case Study of Mayurbhanj District in Orissa

Orissa occupies a special position in the tribal map of India. In the State the Scheduled Tribes Constitute 22.21%. There are 62 different types of tribes in the State. Mayurbhanj is one of the most tribally dominated districts, lying at the Northern border of Orissa. This district was formed in 1949 out of the ex-State of Mayurbhanj. The percentage of Scheduled Tribes in the district in nearly 58.56%. The district is extremely important from anthropological point of view. It is inhabited by almost all the important tribes found in the eastern region of India through it is a fact that only a few of them have a concentrated settlement here e.g. the Santals, Hos, Bhunyas, Bhumijas, Bathuris and Gonds etc. The basic tribal population of the district is therefore formed by these six principal tribes.

As it has happened in other tribal parts of this country, the tribals of Mayurbhanj are also not spared off. Land alienation is rampart here. Due to poor economic conditions and illiteracy the tribes have not been able to understand the vicious circle thrown by their non-tribal exploiters. The Tribal Research Bureau conducted surveys and studies to analyze the relationship between the tribals and non-tribals who settled down in tribal areas e.g. an untouchable caste, Dom and Pano, the first non-tribals to settle down on the hills, live in intimate relationship with the Kandhas and Saoras of South Orissa. Similarly milkmen oilman and others live with the Juangs and Paudi Bhunyas of North Orissa. Many researchers put this relationship of the tribals with the non-tribals as parasitism but sometimes a symbiotic relationship is also found between them. Indebtedness among the tribals is a chronic malady. Schemes by the State Government have been bogged down in bureaucratic red-tapism. According to the Tribal Research Bureau the original purpose of these schemes is lost sight of. The two major steps by the Govt. of Orissa to prevent land alienation of the tribals are,

- Orissa Scheduled Areas Transfer of Immovable Property (by STs) Regulation, 1956, provides for the control and check of the transfers made by the scheduled tribes to the non-scheduled tribes in the Scheduled Areas.
- Also outside the Scheduled Areas, alienation of land of the scheduled tribes has been restricted under Orissa Land Reformed Act, 1960.

Though Mayurbhanj possesses enormous forest wealth, the tribal people have no freedom to enjoy its benefits. Even for making agricultural implements they have to seek permission of the authorities. Permission to cut fire wood is available on payment of a stipulated amount. Sardari system of collection of land revenue gave enough scope for the feudal practices to survive. In the Colonial revenue administration Sardars, Tehsildars and Lakrajdars were the intermediaries. Notwithstanding various welfare measures introduced by the Colonial Government, there seemed to be a deep-seated unrest among the peasants of Mayurbhanj which provided congenial atmosphere for the growth of Prajamandal Movement during 1930s and 40s.

The tribal composition of Mayurbhanj is another important aspect of its history. The tension between the tribals and non-tribals often resulted in violent outburst leading to direct intervention by the Govt. The Kol insurrection and the Bamanghaty disturbances were instances which speak of tribal's refusal to accept a alien system.

However, in order to understand the present tribal problem of land alienation in Mayurbhanj a general background of the land structure of the district is to be analyzed starting from the pre-colonial phase. Also an analysis is to be made to understand the changing pattern of the land structure in Orissa's plains and its effect over the neighboring forest regions that lead to the fast depeasantisation of the tribal communities. As this depeasantisation has emerged as a criteria of the class antagonisms, its effects are to be examined in the district. Above all, the failures of State Govt.'s policy and the result of such failures are to be found out.

However, there is an imperative to project the land alienation of the tribals as human rights violation and to bring to attention of the government as well as non-government agencies. Nowadays the awareness of human rights brings about a certain awakening and often generates courage of tribals to stand up for their own rights. As far as the concept of tribal rights are concerned the challenges are to make the tribals aware of judicial systems, prepare them for political participation, create opportunity for equality, prepare them for self-governance to guarantee rights to traditional natural resources, provide them land rights etc.

TRIBAL AND INDIAN LAND

Definitions of common terminology related to tribal and Indian land ownership.

The application of laws and regulations to energy development activities may depend on where the activity takes place. It is important to determine the status of all impacted land ownership before applying Federal, Tribal and State laws and regulations.

Individually owned lands are of two kinds:

- Trust land-The federal government holds legal title but the beneficial interest remains with the Individual Indian
- Restricted fee land-An individual Indian holds legal title but with legal restrictions against alienation or encumbrance

Tribally owned lands are of three kinds:

- Trust land-The federal government holds legal title but the beneficial interest remains with the tribe
- Restricted fee land-The tribe holds legal title but with legal restrictions against alienation or encumbrance
- Fee land purchased by tribes-The tribe acquires legal title under specific statutory authority. Fee land owned by a tribe outside the boundaries of a reservation is not subject

to legal restrictions against alienation or encumbrance, absent any special circumstances. The law is not clear whether such restrictions apply to fee land within the boundaries of a reservation.

Under the statute establishing the Indian Energy Resource Program, the term "Indian land" means –

1. Any land located within the boundaries of an Indian reservation, pueblo or Rancheria;
2. Any land not located within the boundaries of an Indian reservation, pueblo or Rancheria, the title to which is held –
   - In trust by the United States for benefit of an Indian tribe or an individual Indian;
   - By an Indian tribe or an individual Indian, subject to restriction against alienation under laws of the United States; or
   - By a dependent Indian community; and
3. Land that is owned by an Indian tribe and was conveyed by the United States to a Native Corporation pursuant to the Alaska Native Claims Settlement Act (43 U.S.C. 1601 et seq.) or that was conveyed by the United States to a Native Corporation in exchange for such land.

Under the regulations established for Tribal Energy Resource Agreements, "Tribal land" means any land or interests in land owned by a tribe or tribes, title to which is held in trust by the United States, or is subject to a restriction against alienation under the laws of the United States. For the purposes of TERAs, tribal land includes land taken into trust or subject to restrictions on alienation under the laws of the United States after the effective date of the TERA. (25 CFR 224.30)

The statute and regulations concerning leasing of Indian land for public, religious, educational, recreational, residential, or business purposes (which would include most renewable energy projects) apply to trust or restricted land, defined in the regulations as "any tract, or interest therein, that the United States holds in trust status for the benefit of a tribe or individual Indian" and "land the title to which is held by an individual Indian or a tribe and which can only be alienated or encumbered by the owner with the approval of the Secretary because of limitations contained in the conveyance instrument pursuant to federal law", respectively. (25 U.S.C. 415; 25 C.F.R. 162.101) For BIA mineral and mining regulations the term "Indian lands" means any lands or interest in lands owned by any individual Indian or Alaska Native, Indian tribe, band, nation, pueblo, community, rancheria, colony or other group, the title to which is held in trust by the United States or is subject to a restriction against alienation imposed by the United States. For rights-of-way, the regulations define tribal land as "land or any interest therein, title to which is held by the United States in trust for a tribe, or title to which is held by any tribe subject to Federal restrictions against alienation or encumbrance, and includes such land reserved for Indian Bureau administrative purposes. The term also includes lands held by the United States in trust for an Indian corporation chartered under section 17 of the Act of June 18, 1934 (48 Stat. 988; 25 U.S.C. 477)." and Individually owned land as "land or any interest therein held in trust by the United States for the benefit of individual Indians and land or any interest therein held by individual Indians subject to Federal restrictions against alienation or encumbrance." (25 C.F.R. 169.1) Under the statute that establishes Department of the Interior jurisdiction for granting approval for some other contracts and agreements with Indian tribes, "Indian lands" means lands the title to which is held by the United States in trust for an Indian tribe or lands the title to which is held by an Indian tribe subject to a restriction by the United States against alienation. (25 U.S.C. 81)

Reference to "Indian country" is sometimes used for other federal regulations. "Indian country" means (a) all land within the limits of any Indian reservation under the jurisdiction of the United States Government, notwithstanding the issuance of any patent, and, including rights-of-way running through the reservation, (b) all dependent Indian communities within the borders of the United States whether within the original or subsequently acquired territory thereof, and whether within or without the limits of a state, and (c) all Indian allotments, the Indian titles to which have not been extinguished, including rights-of-way running through the same. (18 United States Code [U.S.C.] 1151) While Section 1151 is a criminal law statute, its definition of Indian country applies in the civil context as well.

For certain environmental regulations, the term "Federal Indian reservation" is used and means all land within the limits of any Indian reservation under the jurisdiction of the United States Government, notwithstanding the issuance of any patent, and including rights-of-way running through the reservation. (33 U.S. C. 1377(h)).

However, even in the case of a statutory or regulatory definition there have been interpretation issues. For instance, for the EPA definition of Federal Indian reservation, the EPA has had to interpret the law in light of Supreme Court case law, including Oklahoma Tax Comm'n v. Citizen Band Potawatomi Indian Tribe of Oklahoma, 111 S.Ct. 905, 910 (1991) that a "reservation," also includes trust lands that have been validly set apart for a tribe's use even though the land has not been formally designated as a reservation (59 Fed.Reg. at 43960; 56 Fed.Reg. at 64881). In applying this precedent to the term "reservation," the Agency recognizes two categories of lands: Pueblos and tribal trust lands. The EPA must consider on a case-by-case basis whether other types of lands may be considered "reservations" under federal Indian law even though they may not be formally designated as such.

TRIBAL POLICY-ISOLATION, ASSIMILATION AND INTEGRATION

The coexistence of fundamentally different culture patterns and styles of living has always been a characteristic feature of the Indian stage. Unlike most parts of the world, in India, the arrival of new immigrants and the spread of their way of life did not necessarily cause the disappearance of earlier and materially less advanced ethnic groups.

The old and the new co-existed. Such a consequence was partly due to the great size of the sub-continent and dearth of communications. More important than this was an attitude basic to Indian ideology, which accepted variety of cultural forms as natural and immutable, and did not consider their assimilation to one dominant pattern in any way desirable. This does not mean, however, that none of the tribes ever became incorporated in the systems of hierarchically ranked castes. Wherever economic necessity or encroachment of their habitant by advanced communities led to continued inter-action between tribes and

Hindus, cultural distinctions were blurred, and what had once been self-contained and more or less independent tribes gradually acquired the status of castes.

In many cases they entered caste systems at the lowest rung of the ladder. Some untouchable castes of Southern India, such as the Cherumans and the Panyers of Kerala, were undoubtedly at one time independent tribes, and in their physical characteristics they still resemble neighboring tribal groups, which have remained outside the Hindu society. There are some exceptions, such as the Meitheis of Assam who achieved a position comparable to that of Kshatriyas. Tribes who retained their tribal identity and resisted inclusion within the Hindu fold fared on the whole better than the assimilated groups and were not treated as untouchables, even if they indulged in such low-caste practices as eating beef. Thus the Raj Gond princes sacrificed and ate cows without thereby debasing their status in the eyes of their Hindu neighbors, who recognized their social and cultural separateness and did not insist on conformity to Hindu patterns of behavior.

This respect for the tribal way of life prevailed as long as contacts between tribes and Hindu populations of open plains were of a casual nature. The tribal people, though considered strange and dangerous, were taken for granted as part of the world of hills and forests, and a more or less frictionless co-existence was possible, because there was no population pressure and the advanced communities did not feel any urge to impose their own values on people placed clearly outside the spheres of Hindu civilization.

This position remained unchanged during the Muslim period. Now and then a military campaign extending for a short spell into the wilds of tribal country would bring the inhabitants temporarily to the notice of princes and chroniclers, but for long period the hill men and forest-dwellers were left to themselves. Under British rule, however, a new situation arose. The extension of a centralized administration over areas, which previously were outside the effective control of princely rulers, deprived many aboriginal tribes of their autonomy. Though British administrators had no intention of interfering with tribesmen's rights and traditional manner of living, the very process of establishment of law and order in outlying areas exposed the tribes to the pressure of more advanced populations. Thus in areas which had previously been virtually un-administered and hence unsafe for outsiders who did not enjoy the confidence and goodwill of the tribal inhabitants, traders and money-lenders could now establish themselves under the protection of the British administration and in many cases they were followed by settlers who succeeded in acquiring large stretches of tribes' land.

Administrative officers who did not understand tribal system of land tenure introduced uniform methods of revenue collection. But these had the un-intended effect of facilitating the alienation of tribal land to members of advanced populations. Though it is unlikely that British officials actively favored the latter at the expense of primitive tribesmen, little was done to stem the rapid erosion of tribal rights to land.

In many areas tribals unable to resist the gradual alienation of their ancestral land, either withdrew further into hills and tracts of marginal land, or accepted the economic status of tenants or agricultural labourers on the land their forefathers had owned. There were some tribes, however, who rebelled against an administration, which allowed outsiders to deprive them of their land.

In the Chhota Nagpur and the Santhal pargansas such rebellions of desperate tribesmen recurred throughout the nineteenth century, and there were minor risings in the Agency tracts of Madras and in some of the districts of Bombay inhabited by Bhils. Thus the Santhals are believed to have lost about 10,000 men in their rebellion of 1855.

None of these insurrections were aimed primarily at the British administration, but they were a reaction to their exploitation and oppression by Hindu landlords and money-lenders who had established themselves in tribal areas and were sheltered by a Government which had instituted a system of land settlement and administration of justice favoring the advanced communities at the expense of simple and illiterate tribes. In some cases these rebellions led to official inquiries and to legislative enactments aimed at protecting tribes' right to their land. Seen in historical perspective it appears that land alienation laws had, on the whole, only a palliative effect. In most areas encroachment on land held by tribes continued even in the face of protective legislation.

Assimilation of Tribals

Acceptance or denial of the necessity for assimilation with Hindu society is ultimately a question of values. In the past, Hindu society had been tolerant of groups that would not conform to the standards set by the higher castes. True, such groups were denied equal ritual status; but no efforts were made to deflect them from their chosen style of living. In recent years this attitude has changed. Perhaps it is the influence of the Western belief in universal values which has encouraged a spirit of intolerance vis-a-vis cultural and social divergences. Yet India is not only a multilingual and multiracial country, but is also multi-cultural. And as long as Muslims, Christians, and Parsis are free to follow their traditional way of life, it would seem only fair that the culture and the social order of tribes however distinct from that of the majority community should also be respected. Assimilation, of course, will occur automatically and inevitably where small tribal groups are enclosed within numerically stronger Hindu populations. In other areas, however, and particularly all along India's northern and northeastern frontier live vigorous tribal populations which resist assimilation as well as inclusion within Hindu caste system.

DEMOCRATIC DECENTRALIZATION AND TRIBALS

With the introduction of a system of democratic decentralization to take the place of paternalism characteristic of traditional form of Indian government, a new element has entered the relations between tribes and the more advanced majority communities. The ability to vote in general elections for the Parliament in Delhi and the Legislative Assembly of their respective States did not make much difference to tribals, because they did not understand the implication of the franchise, but the local elections aroused their interest to a much greater extent. The very fact, that some of the most powerful people of the district approached the poorest villagers for their votes and tried to gain their confidence, convinced them of a fundamental change. The very idea that they could choose their representatives was novel. At first, tribals only voted, for non-tribals, for very few were sufficiently educated to stand for election. Even in areas with a preponderance of tribals, the elected representatives were often non-tribes and abused their powers by exploiting those who had voted for them. But as time passed and the tribes gained experience, they have become shrewder in the choice of their representatives.

The Government of India has adopted a policy of integration of tribals with the mainstream aiming at developing a creative adjustment between the tribes and non tribes leading to a responsible partnership. By adopting the policy of integration or progressive acculturation the Government has laid the foundation for the uninhibited march of the tribals towards equality, upward mobility, and economic viability and assured proximity to the national mainstream. The constitution has committed the nation to two courses of action in respect of scheduled tribes,viz

- Giving protection to their distinctive way of life
- Protecting them from social injustice and all forms of exploitation and discrimination and bringing them at par with the rest of the nation so that they may be integrated with the national life.

Thus by the Constitution Order 1950 issued by the President of India in exercise of powers conferred by Clause9 (i) of Article 342 of the Constitution of India 255 tribes in 17 states were declared to be scheduled tribes. Besides enjoying the rights that all citizens and minorities have the member of the Scheduled Tribes have been provided with special safeguards as follows:

Protective Safeguards

- Educational safeguards-Article 15(4) and 29
- Safeguards for employment-Articles 16(4), 320(4) and 333
- Economic safeguards-Article 19
- Abolition of bonded labour-Article 23
- Protection from social injustice and all forms of exploitation-Article 46

Political Safeguards

- Reservation of seats for ST in LokSabha and Assemblies-Article 330,332,164
- Appointment of Minister in charge of Tribal welfare
- Special provisions in respect of Nagaland, Assam and Manipur-Articles-371(A), 371(B) and 371

Developmental Safeguards

- Promoting the educational and economic interests of the Scheduled Tribes-Articles 46
- Grants from Central Government to the states for welfare of Scheduled Tribes and raising the level of administration of Scheduled Areas-Article 75.

Following the reorganization of states, the list of STs was modified by the Scheduled Castes and Tribes List (Modification) order, 1956 on the recommendations of the Backward Classes Commission. In the revised list 414 tribes were declared STs. Since the revision of the list in 1956 there have been several proposals for fresh inclusions and deletion from the lists of the SC and STs

12

Adivasi: A Contentious Term to denote Tribes as Indigenous Peoples of India

In India the term 'Adivasi' has gained immense popularity in the last few decades to identify the tribes. This term is more commonly brought to use by the NGO circles and activists of the 'mainstream' or 'mainland' India. The term has also gained currency amongst the tribes mainly belonging to central India. In Kerala too the tribes of late prefer to be identified as 'Adivasi'. In Hindi the term 'Adivasi' means original settlers.

The term Adivasi is not portrayed just for literary reasons. It has a political underpinning. It has often been used to convey the position of exclusion of the tribes (Kumar: 2001: 4052-4054) and their subaltern status (Ekka: 2000-2001: 4610-4612) The term Adivasi has been even used to focus the tribal rights (Dietrich: 2000), their resistance (Pati: 2001), protests (Viswanath: 1997), assertions (Hardiman: 1988, Rahul: 1998), struggles (Raman: 2002) and movements. The term in a way conveys a sense of 'empowerment' of the tribes. This empowerment is being asserted by linking with the global indigenous people's movement.

Bijoy (2003) Writes

The 67.7 million people belonging to 'Scheduled Tribe' in India are generally considered to be 'Adivasi', literally meaning 'Indigenous People' or original inhabitants, though the term 'Scheduled Tribe' (ST) is not coterminous with the term 'Adivasi'. Scheduled Tribe is an administrative term used for the purpose of 'administering' certain specific constitutional privileges, protection and benefits for specific section of peoples historically considered disadvantaged and 'backward'. However, this administrative term does not exactly match all the peoples called 'Adivasi'. Out of the 5653 distinct communities in India, 635 are considered to be 'tribes' or 'Adivasis'. In comparison, one finds that estimated number of STs varies from 250 to 593.

It must, however, be stated that the Indian Constitution does not use the term 'Adivasi' and instead refers to the STs as 'Anusuchit Jana Jati'. Traditionally 'Jana' was the more popular term to refer to the tribes in the Hindi heartland. (Ray: 1972)

One of the prime factors for claiming aboriginal or indigenous status for the tribes is to enable them to gain territorial, land rights and control over natural resources. There are, however, vicious forces in the country who are overtly active in not conceding these rights. The Hindutva forces term the tribes as 'Vanvasi'. This term not only conveys a sense of primitiveness but also tries to deny the territorial rights. The Gandhians too were not very far from it and they considered the tribes more from a culturological position and referred to them as 'Vanyajati'.

It is disconcerting that most of the anthropologists and sociologists have either remained indifferent to such developments or have passively supported the 'Adivasi' terminology and thus jeopardised the legitimate rights and interests of the tribes dwelling in the regions beyond the Hindi heartland. At the outset it needs to be realised that a nation-state like India is not a cultural but political entity which was borne due to a quirk of history. Imposing Hindi as a national and official State language over all the regions is not a very civilised act—it smacks of North Indian chauvinism. Secondly, it is also not true that the tribes in all quarters of the country are aboriginals of the regions where they inhabit at present. While the famous historian Kosambi (1956) viewed that the tribes had migrated to the plain areas at a much later date only after the vegetation had thinned out and wild animals became less numerous—making the area less dangerous for human habitation and fit for settled cultivation, Archana Prasad (2003), the young scholar from Jamia Millia Islamia, Delhi, feels that the tribes practising settled cultivation in the plains were pushed to the hills and forests by the profligate Aryan invaders and later Hindu settled cultivators and the outside traders. Either way the tribes are not autochthons of the spaces occupied by them at present. In 1980s Andre Betteille` had similarly expressed about the inapplicability of the concept of aborigine to the tribesmen in India. (Personal communication)

The autochthon status of the tribes in their present habitats in different parts of the country can be easily contested. The Kukis in Manipur or the Luseis of Mizoram have migrated to their present areas of dominance from South China and Chin Hills only a couple of centuries back. The Kukis were settled by the British in the Naga predominant areas so as to create a buffer between the Nagas and the Vaishnavite Meiteis. The Sailo chiefs belonging to the Lusei tribe were encouraged by the British to operate as labour contractors for constructing roads in the remote areas of Mizoram. The aboriginal tribes of the State who were pushed to the western borders along Tripura are now known as Tuikuk. In Tripura the tribal king had as a policy invited many Reangs and Chakmas to settle in the State so as to augment the production of cotton through jhum cultivation and ensure forward linkage to the cotton mills. Even the Bodos, believed to be a secondary formation, had migrated in waves from the Bhutan hills to settle in their present domains in Assam. The Toto tribe of Totopara on the borders of North Bengal and Bhutan is too a secondary formation as it evolved as a constellation out of a number of migrant criminal clans who were pushed out by the Bhutan kingdom. The matrilineal Khasis of Meghalaya who belong to the Mon-Khmer linguistic group are believed to have migrated from the Kampuchea region. The Denzong Bhutias, the royal Sikkimese tribe, too on record have migrated from Tibet, in the historical past. The Santhals of Rajmahal Hills or Santhal Parganas in Jharkhand had similarly migrated from the plains of Birbhum and Midnapur, West Bengal, in historical times.

Thirdly, it is important to note that the tribes in India are not the only group to claim indigenous status. Even many of the Dalit intellectuals have made similar assertions. Next, the Government of India itself refuses to grant indigenous status to the tribes. One of the important reasons for this is that a few Brahmin and Rajput communities like the Jaunsari in Uttarakhand or the Kanaura in Himachal Pradesh have been enlisted as Scheduled Tribe. More importantly, the term 'Adivasi' is popularly used in North Bengal,

Sikkim, Arunachal Pradesh, Assam, Meghalaya, Nagaland and Tripura to refer to the tea plantation labourers—the tribes like Santhal, Munda, Oraon and Ho who had migrated to the region during the British colonial period. The local tribes in these States find it humiliating to identify themselves as 'Adivasi'. The indigenous Rabha, Mech and Rajbansi tribes/ethnic groups in North Bengal prefer to identify themselves by their own names and not as 'Adivasi'. The Sikkimese tribesmen too identify the migrant plantation labourers from Chotanagpur as 'Adivasi' and not by their specific tribal names. The Santhal, Oraon, Munda and Ho migrant tribes in the Sunderbans of West Bengal, working as agricultural labourers or cultivating small farms, are collectively referred to as 'Adivasi' by the local Bengali settlers, a majority of whom are Scheduled Castes. The term 'Adivasi' therefore, remains a generic name in East and North-East India for identifying the migrant tribal labourers and small peasants from central India.

In most places in North Bengal and North-East India, the adivasis are considered to be encroachers or intruders. During the Naxalite uprisal at Naxalbari in the late 1960s the Rajbansis en-block resisted the onslaught of the adivasi landgrabbers. Ethnic clashes between the indigenous Bodos and adivasi encroachers in the Bodoland Territorial Council areas are endemic. In one such clash a few years back hundreds of Santhals were killed by the Bodo militants. The Bodo Territorial Council (BTC) is contemplating to move the Supreme Court against the recommendations of the 2006 Tribes and Forest Dwellers Act, which stipulates regularising lands encroached in government forests prior to December 13, 2005. Almost 40 per cent of the forests in the Bodo areas have been encroached upon and majority of the encroachers is outside migrants (many of them are adivasis). The interests of the Bodos and adivasis do not match at all and the former had infact, opposed the formation of autonomus Bodo Territorial Council. They had even led several rallies in Guwahati, the State capital of Assam.

The tribes of Arunachal Pradesh are extremely peeved by the presence of Chakma refugees who claim an indigenous status in the international forums. The tribal students of the state led a protracted movement against the Chakmas. The All Assam Tribal Sangha (AATS) comprising of various tribal organisations, including Bodo, Karbi, Dimasa and Tiwa student organisations are opposing the Adivasi demand for ST status, alleging if granted, it would affect the interests of tribals of Assam. According to AATS, the Adivasis did not fulfil the requisite criteria of their inclusion in the ST list as they are not originally from Assam. (Internet: Indopia)

It needs to be reiterated that it would be a gross mistake to consider the term 'Adivasi' to be equivalent to the term 'Tribe' in India. This could only reinforce the anti-Indian feelings among many of the tribes inhabiting, North Bengal, Sikkim and other North-Eastern States. The term will be considered pejorative and humiliating to most of them. It must be realised that the term tribe itself is a colonial construct and 'aboriginal' 'autochthon' percepts are outcome of colonial conquests. The so-called 'friends of tribes' in India have been amateurishly trying to romanticise the term in the name of radical empowerment. The tribal situation in India is extremely heterogeneous and a unified approach may not do justice to all the communities. It must also be understood that the definition of 'Indigenous Peoples' as projected by the UN Working Group for Indigenous Peoples has an European bias as it states,

Indigenous peoples and nations are those which, having a historical continuity with their pre-invasion and pre-colonial societies that developed on their territories, consider themselves distinct from other sectors of societies, now prevailing in those territories or parts of them. They form at present non-dominant sectors of society and are determined to preserve, develop and transmit to future generation their ancestral territories and their ethnic identity as the basis of their continuous existence as peoples in accordance with their own cultural patterns, social institutions and legal system.

The tribes residing in territories not externally colonised are not deemed to be indigenous as a consequence. This leaves out the scope of around 120 tribal communities in Europe from being declared as indigenous peoples (Griggs: 1993). Their rights of self-determination too are denied as a result. The Basques of Spain and Portugal, Skanians in Sweden, Cornish, Welsh and Shetlanders in the UK are consequently denied of several rights and privileges enjoyed by indigenous people in other parts of the world. It is similarly feared that the use of the term 'Adivasi' in an unqualified manner may fail to ensure legitimate rights of many of the authentic indigenous tribes/peoples in India. In the name of 'Adivasi' pressures are put on the Indian government by the western sources to ensure all types of rights for them. In India some of the tribal NGOs linked to Jharkhand, Chhattisgarh and Delhi which have intimate links with the European Indigenous People's Movement groups are mainly responsible for trying to popularise the 'Adivasi' concept in the last few decades. They too are trying prop up the 'Adivasi' movements in North-East India. In many areas this is leading to serious ethnic conflicts with the indigenous tribes.

Kar and Sharma (1990) have elaborated the imminent dangers of this: Most local tribes are opposed to the adivasis being included in the list of Scheduled Tribe. They are estimated to be around 20 per cent of the Assam population, that is, more than 40 lakhs, while the Bodos are a little over 27 lakhs. The total number of tribes in the northeast being a little over 80 lakhs, if the adivasis are included in the schedule, the number of tribals in the northeast will rise by 50 per cent and they would be a third of the total. Many tribal groups are afraid that it will lead to competition for the few jobs available and for the depleted natural resources. As a result, most tribal of the region oppose their inclusion. Moreover, the adivasis are considered outsiders since they were brought by the British from Jharkhand as plantation labourers. The British appropriated the land of the local populations through unjust means. Since the adivasis worked on this land as indentured labour, the resentment of the local people at losing their land to the colonialist (partners) is not surprising.

To conclude, the term 'indigenous peoples' itself appears to be contentious in the Indian context as there are many claimants to it; these include the Dalits (claiming their Dravidian antecedence), the Vaishnavite Meiteis of Manipur and the caste Hindus of Assam. It will perhaps be always better to avoid using the popular NGO nomenclature 'Advisai' in the tenors of serious academic discourse when dealing with the notion of indigenous groups in the Indian context.

ADIVASIS OF INDIA

The Adivasis (original inhabitants) is the collective name used for the many tribal peoples of India. Officially they are termed

"Scheduled Tribes" but this is a legal and constitutional term which differs from state to state and area to area and therefore excludes some groups who might be considered tribal. Adivasis are not an homogenous group — with over 200 tribes speaking over 100 languages, which vary greatly in ethnicity, culture and language; however there are similarities in their way of life and generally perceived inferior position within Indian society. There are over 50 million Adivasis constituting 7.5% of the Indian population, thus making it the largest tribal population in the world.

Adivasis are found throughout India but are primarily based in the mountain and hill areas, away from the fertile plains. The greatest concentration is in the central states of India, notably Madhya Pradesh, Orissa, southern Bihar, the western *ghats* (hills) of Gujarat and Maharastra and northern Andhra Pradesh; where over 85% of the Tribal population is to be found. However in no peninsula state does the Tribal population reach more than one quarter of the population. There are smaller groups in the mountain areas of the south, notably in Kerala, Tamil Nadu and Karnataka. The other concentration is found in the northeastern states, the "seven sisters" (Assam, Manipur, Nagaland, Mizoram, Tripura, Megalaya and Arunchal Pradesh) but here the situation is significantly different as in most of these states (the exceptions are Assam and Tripura) Adivasis are a majority and are likely to remain so since regulations restrict settlement by outsiders.

The Indian government has a special programme for the welfare of tribes it classes as "primitive" tribes. These are Adivasis engaged in pre-agricultural technology and shifting cultivation with either a static or declining population. In 1988 there were 73 such tribes totalling over one million people.

BACKGROUND AND HISTORY

Adivasis are some of the earliest inhabitants of the sub-continent and once inhabited much greater areas than at present. However little is known of their history although it appears that many were pushed into the hill areas after the invasions of the Indo-Aryan tribes 3,000 years ago. Tribals were not integrated into Hindu caste society; they stood outside it but nevertheless there were many points of contact. Tribal religious beliefs contain many aspects of Hinduism (and vice-versa); Tribals traded with settled villages on the plains and sometimes paid tribute to Hindu rulers. In turn some Tribal rulers conquered and ruled over non-tribals and some Tribals permanently settled and entered caste society.

It was not until the unifying political rule of the British from the late eighteenth century that government made substantial inroads into Adivasi society. British rule brought money, government officials and moneylenders into tribal areas, beginning the process of encroachment of Adivasi land by outsiders. As a result there were tribal revolts from the mid-nineteenth century in several parts of eastern India and this forced the administration to recognize the vulnerable position of Tribals and pass laws to protect their lands from outsiders. These laws (some of which are still on the Statute Book) completely barred the sale of Tribal lands to non-Tribals and made provisions to restore alienated land. However in practice most of these laws were widely disregarded and unscrupulous merchants and money-lenders found ways to circumvent them. These problems still face Adivasis today although their opponents are as likely to be large companies and state corporations as small traders and moneylenders. Christian missions began to proselytize in some tribal areas where (in contrast to Hindu and Muslim areas) they achieved a degree of success and also, most notably in the northeast, began the process of education and political awareness. Tribal peoples played little role in the run-up to independence and it was only in the northeast that they had enough political consciousness to make demands for separation or autonomy.

Constitution and Law

Under the constitution of the Republic of India of 1950, Tribal peoples along with so-called "Untouchables" became subject to special protective provisions. The vast majority of tribes were classified as "Scheduled Tribes". Article 341 authorizes the President of India to specify "castes, races or tribes which shall for the purposes of this constitution be deemed to be Scheduled Tribes". The first amendment to the Constitution passed in 1951 allowed the state to make special provision for the advancement of socially and educationally backward classes of citizens of the Scheduled Castes and Scheduled Tribes. The central Government has a special Commission for Scheduled Castes and Scheduled Tribes which issues an Annual Report. These reports give accounts of illegal actions against Adivasis and makes recommendations to improve their position.

There are reservations for the Scheduled Tribes in legislatures in the central and the state governments. In the two houses of Parliament, the Lok Sabha and the Raiya Sabha, 7% of the seats are reserved for Scheduled Tribe members and similar representation occurs in the state assemblies in proportion to the percentage of Scheduled Tribes in the state's population. However since the "Scheduled Tribe" voters are always a minority (except in the northeastern states where they are a numerical majority) in the reserved constituencies and in the assemblies as a whole, favourable legislation can be blocked by vested interests. Furthermore the system does not encourage Scheduled Tribe organization by separate parties but facilitates organization and representation by the major parties, especially the Congress Party which has been in a dominant position since independence. Governments normally have Scheduled Tribe Ministers and sometimes Cabinet Ministers but to date in peninsula India there has been only one Chief Minister from a Scheduled Tribe (in Gujarat) although in the five predominantly Tribal northeastern states the Chief Minister invariably comes from a Scheduled Tribe.

There have been very few attempts to found distinctive Scheduled Tribe political parties, apart from those in the northeastern states. Perhaps the most notable example in peninsula India has been that in eastern and southern Bihar, where a tribal regionalist movement known as the Jharkhand movement has been a factor since independence. The roots of this movement lie in the Santhal peoples of eastern Bihar and western Bengal, the scene of one of the early tribal revolts against land alienation under British rule. Some of this area also contains India's richest mineral deposits and mining, and subsequent industrialization and deforestation has added to Tribal grievances.

The Jharkhand Party was first formed in 1950 and had as its main demands the formation of a separate state or territory in the traditional Adivasi areas of Santhal Paganas and Chotanagpur and areas in West Bengal, Orissa and Madhya Pradesh. The party went into decline after its leader joined the Congress Party but was revived in 1973 when a new party the *Jharkhand Mukti Mocha* (JMM) was formed, led by a charismatic Santhal leader, who, despite his arrest during the Emergency, later worked closely with and eventually joined the Congress Party. This factionalized the JMM into several smaller groups but in 1987 a new co-ordinating organization the Jharkhand Co-ordinating Committee (JCC) was formed, with over 50 constituent organizations. This group has led a number of *bandhs* (strikes) and mass demonstrations in support of its demands and also tried to set up a parallel government although with little success, and both the central and state governments have consistently refused to consider a Jharkhand state. Were such a state to be granted it would not have a majority of Adivasis although they would probably be the largest single group if the different tribes were totalled together.

LAND AND ECONOMIC FACTORS

Over 95% of Scheduled Tribes still live in rural areas and economic exploitation remains their most acute problem. Less than 10% are shifting hunter-gatherers but more than half depend on forest produce for their livelihood, many in the form of the tendu leaf, used for the production of *bidis* (local cigarettes). From the time of the British administration there have been laws regulating the ownership and use of the forests and today most forest land is effectively nationalized or in the hands of state governments, and large areas are contracted to outside commercial interests. This has progressively deprived Adivasi communities of rights in the land and they can be fined or imprisoned for taking forest produce which has traditionally been theirs.

The ostensible reason for state intervention has been to stop the destruction of forest land which has continued throughout this century. There are a number of reasons for deforestation which is often blamed on Adivasi shifting cultivation practices; one has been the increase in demand for firewood as fuel; another is the impact of commercial, sometimes illegal, cutting down of forests. Although many Adivasis already have a similar lifestyle to small peasant farmers, farming marginal plots of land, they are even less likely to have the traditional agricultural skills to exploit such land, or the knowledge of government to enable them to get the loans and grants to which they may be entitled.

Another threat to Adivasis is large-scale dam building, for irrigation and hydro-electricity. A number of such schemes have been carried out since independence but the largest is the giant World Bank-financed Narmada Valley project which involves 30 major, 135 medium and 3,000 minor dams and which will flood 350,000 hectares of land, including 11% of the forests of the Narmada Valley. Up to 300,000 people, the majority of them Tribals, may be forced to relocate to make way for the dam. Furthermore compensation is limited to landowners (which is difficult for many Adivasis to prove) and is normally given in money rather than land. There have been campaigns by organizations within India and internationally to at least give compensation in the form of an equal amount of land to the displaced but, although these schemes have achieved a limited amount of success in delaying the project and gaining better compensation terms, the dams will still go ahead. Furthermore it is doubtful whether sufficient land for resettlement is available in such a densely populated country, where pressures on land are already high.

Social Developments

As with the Scheduled Castes, members of Scheduled Tribes are beneficiaries of "positive discrimination" provisions laid down in the constitution, reserving places in education, the civil service and nationalized industries. Problems of remoteness, poverty and prejudice mitigate against Adivasis exploiting these provisions however. For example, in Andhra Pradesh the Tribal literacy rate is only 11% against an all-India level of 29% (in the northeast, however, Tribal literacy is considerably higher). Because few Adivasis finish their schooling, few are able to use the reserved places in higher education or the civil service. Nevertheless some Adivasis do manage to achieve positions of responsibility in government and education, although they continue to be under-represented in almost every field.

Some Adivasis have been organized by left-wing groups, known commonly in India as "Naxalites", to press for higher wages and payments for forest produce. As a result Adivasis may become victims of both Naxalite pressures and government counter-insurgency campaigns. More commonly police, forest guards and officials frequently cheat, bully and intimidate Adivasis and large numbers are routinely arrested and jailed, often for petty offences. In such circumstances many Adivasis prefer to bribe officials to escape harassment or flee into the jungles when they appear.

Although Adivasis are not, as a general rule, regarded as "unclean" by caste-Hindus in the same way as Untouchables are, they continue to face prejudice and often violence from society. They are at the lowest point of almost every socioeconomic indicator. The majority of the population regards them as primitive and government programmes aim to "integrate" them with the majority society, rather than to emphasize their distinctiveness. While the larger tribal groups and languages will survive as a result of numbers, the destruction of their economic base and environment poses grave threats to those who are still able to follow the basis of a traditional way of life and may result in the cultural extinction of many of the smaller Adivasi peoples.

ADIVASI AND ITS WORK

Âdivâssi is an umbrella term for a heterogeneous set of ethnic and tribal groups believed to be the aboriginal population of India. They comprise a substantial indigenous minority of the population of India.Adivasi are also commonly known as Tribals.

Adivasi societies are particularly present in the Indian states of Orissa, Madhya Pradesh, Chattisgarh, Rajasthan, Gujarat, Maharashtra, Andhra Pradesh, Bihar, Jharkhand, West Bengal, Mizoram and other northeastern states, and the Andaman and Nicobar Islands. Many smaller tribal groups are quite sensitive to ecological degradation caused by modernization. Both commercial forestry and intensive agriculture have proved destructive to the forests that had endured swidden agriculture for many centuries. Officially recognized by the Indian government as "Scheduled Tribes" in the Fifth Schedule of the Constitution of India, they are often grouped together with scheduled castes in the category "Scheduled Castes and Tribes", which is eligible for certain affirmative action measures.

Connotations of the word 'Adivasi'

Although terms such as *atavika* (Sanskrit for *forest dwellers*), *vanvasi* or *girijan* (*hill people*) are also used for the tribes of India, *adivasi* carries the specific meaning of being the original and autochthonous inhabitants of a given region, and was specifically coined for that purpose in the 1930s. Over a period of time, unlike the terms "aborigines" or "tribes", the word "*adivasi*" has also developed a connotation of past autonomy which was disrupted during the British colonial period in India and has not been restored. Opposition to usage of the term is varied, and it has been argued that the "original inhabitant" contention is based on dubious claims and that the adivasi-non adivasi divide that is created is artificial.

Scheduled Tribes

The Constitution of India, Article 366 (25) defines Scheduled Tribes as "such tribes or tribal communities or part of or groups within such tribes or tribal communities as are deemed under Article 342 to the scheduled Tribes (STs) for the purposes of this Constitution". In Article 342, the procedure to be followed for specification of a scheduled tribe is prescribed. However, it does not contain the criterion for the specification of any community as scheduled tribe. An often used criterion is based on attributes such as:

- Geographical isolation-they live in cloistered, exclusive, remote and inhospitable areas such as hills and forests.
- Backwardness-their livelihood is based on primitive agriculture, a low-value closed economy with a low level of technology that leads to their poverty. They have low levels of literacy and health.
- Distinctive culture, language and religion-communities have developed their own distinctive culture, language and religion.
- Shyness of contact – they have a marginal degree of contact with other cultures and people.

Primitive Tribes

The Scheduled Tribe groups who were identified as more backward communities among the tribal population groups have been categorised as 'Primitive Tribal Groups' (PTGs) by the Government at the Centre in 1975. So far seventy-five tribal communities have been identified as 'primitive tribal groups' in different States of India. These hunting, food-gathering, and some agricultural communities, who have been identified as more backward communities among the tribal population groups need special programmes for their sustainable development. The primitive tribes are awakening and demanding their rights for special reservation quota for them.

Geographical Overview

There is a substantial list of Scheduled Tribes in India recognised as tribal under the Constitution of India. Tribal peoples constitute 8.2% of the nation's total population, over 84 million people according to the 2001 census. One concentration lives in a belt along the Himalayas stretching through Jammu and Kashmir, Himachal Pradesh, and Uttarakhand in the west, to Assam, Meghalaya, Tripura, Arunachal Pradesh, Mizoram, Manipur, and Nagaland in the northeast. In the northeastern states of Arunachal Pradesh, Meghalaya, Mizoram, and Nagaland, more than 90% of the population is tribal. However, in the remaining northeast states of Assam, Manipur, Sikkim, and Tripura, tribal peoples form between 20 and 30% of the population.

Another concentration lives in the hilly areas of central India (Chhattisgarh, Madhya Pradesh, Orissa and, to a lesser extent, Andhra Pradesh); in this belt, which is bounded by the Narmada River to the north and the Godavari River to the southeast, tribal peoples occupy the slopes of the region's mountains. Other tribals, including the Santals, live in Jharkhand and West Bengal. Central Indian states have the country's largest tribes, and, taken as a whole, roughly 75% of the total tribal population live there, although the tribal population there accounts for only around 10% of the region's total population. There are smaller numbers of tribal people in Karnataka, Tamil Nadu, and Kerala in south India; in western India in Gujarat and Rajasthan, and in the union territories of Lakshadweep and the Andaman Islands and Nicobar Islands. About one percent of the populations of Kerala and Tamil Nadu are tribal, whereas about six percent in Andhra Pradesh and Karnataka are members of tribes.

The Peopling of India

The concept of 'original inhabitant' is directly related to the initial peopling of India, which, due to the debate on topics such as the Indo-Aryan migration hypothesis, has been a contentious area of research and discourse. Some anthropologists hypothesize that the region was settled by multiple human migrations over tens of millennia, which makes it even harder to select certain groups as being truly aboriginal. One narrative, largely based on genetic research, describes Negritos, similar to the Andamanese adivasis of today, as the first humans to colonize India, likely 30-65 thousand years before present (kybp). 60% of all Indians share the mtDNA haplogroup M, which is universal among Andamanese islander adivasis and might be a genetic legacy of the postulated first Indians. Some anthropologists theorize that these settlers were displaced by invading Austro-Asiatic-speaking Australoid people (who largely shared skin pigmentation and physiognomy with the Negritos, but had straight rather than kinky hair), and adivasi tribes such as the Irulas trace their origins to that displacement. The Oraon adivasi tribe of eastern India and the Korku tribe of western India are considered to be examples of groups of Australoid origin. Subsequent to the Australoids, some anthropologists and geneticists theorize that Caucasoids (including both Dravidians and Indo-Aryans) and Mongoloids (Sino-Tibetans) immigrated into India: the Dravidians possibly from Iran, the Indo-Aryans possibly from the Central Asian steppes and the Tibeto-Burmans possibly from the Himalayan and northeastern borders of the subcontinent. It should be noted that none of these hypotheses is free from debate and disagreement.

Ethnic origins and linguistic affiliations in India match only inexactly, however: while the Oraon adivasis are classified as an Australoid group, their language, called Kurukh, is Dravidian. Khasis and Nicobarese are considered to be Mongoloid groups and the Munda and Santals are Australoid groups, but all four speak Austro-Asiatic languages. The Bhils and Gonds are frequently classified as Australoid groups, yet Bhil languages are Indo-European and the Gondi language is Dravidian. Also, in post-colonial India, tribal languages suffered huge setbacks with the formation of linguistic states after 1956 under the States Reorganisation Act. For example, under state-sponsored educational pressure, Irula children are being taught Tamil and a sense of shame has begun to be associated with speaking the Irula language among some children and educated adults. Similarly, the Santals are "gradually adopting languages of the areas inhabited, like Oriya in Orissa, Hindi in Bihar and Bengali in West Bengal."

Disruptions during Mughal and Colonial Periods

Although considered uncivilized and primitive, adivasis were usually not held to be intrinsically impure by surrounding (usually, caucasoid-Dravidian or Aryan) caste Hindu populations, unlike Dalits, who were. Thus, the adivasi origins of Maharshi (Sanksrit: *Great Sage*) Valmiki, who composed the Ramayana Hindu religious epic, were acknowledged, as were the origins of adivasi tribes such as the Grasia and Bhilala, which descended from mixed Rajput and Bhil marriages. Unlike the subjugation of the dalits, the adivasis often enjoyed autonomy and, depending on region, evolved mixed hunter-gatherer and farming economies, controlling their lands as a joint patrimony of the tribe. In some areas, securing adivasi approval and support was considered crucial by local rulers, and larger adivasi groups were able to sustain their own kingdoms in central India. The Gond Rajas of Garha-Mandla and Chanda are examples of an adivasi aristocracy that ruled in this region, and were "not only the hereditary leaders of their Gond subjects, but also held sway over substantial communities of non-tribals who recognized them as their feudal lords."

This relative autonomy and collective ownership of adivasi land by adivasis was severely disrupted by the advent of the Mughals in the early 16th century. Similarly, the British beginning in the 18th century added to the consolidation of feudalism in India, first under the jagirdari system and then under the zamindari system. Beginning with the Permanent Settlement imposed by the British in Bengal and Bihar, which later became the template for a deepening of feudalism throughout India, the older social and economic system in the country began to alter radically. Land, both forest areas belonging to adivasis and settled farmland belonging to non-adivasi peasants, was rapidly made the legal property of British-designated zamindars (landlords), who in turn moved to extract the maximum economic benefit possible from their newfound property and subjects without regard to historical tenure or ownership. Adivasi lands sometimes experienced an influx of non-local settlers, often brought from far away (as in the case of Muslims and Sikhs brought to Kol territory) by the zamindars to better exploit local land, forest and labor. Deprived of the forests and resources they traditionally depended on and sometimes coerced to pay taxes, many adivasis were forced to borrow at usurious rates from moneylenders, often the zamindars themselves. When they were unable to pay, that forced them to become bonded labourers for the zamindars. Often, far from paying off the principal of their debt, they were unable even to offset the compounding interest, and this was made the justification for their children working for the zamindar after the death of the initial borrower. In the case of the Andamanese adivasis, long isolated from the outside world in autonomous societies, mere contact with outsiders was often sufficient to set off deadly epidemics in tribal populations, and it is alleged that some sections of the British government directly attempted to destroy some tribes.

Land dispossession and subjugation by British and zamindar interests resulted in a number of adivasi revolts in the late eighteenth and early nineteenth centuries, such as the Santal hul (or Santal revolt) of 1855-56. Although these were suppressed ruthlessly by the governing British authority (the East India Company prior to 1858, and the British government after 1858), partial restoration of privileges to adivasi elites (e.g. to *Mankis*, the leaders of Munda tribes) and some leniency in tax burdens resulted in relative calm, despite continuing and widespread dispossession, from the late nineteenth century onwards. The economic deprivation, in some cases, triggered internal adivasi migrations within India that would continue for another century, including as labor for the emerging tea plantations in Assam.

TRIBAL CLASSIFICATION CRITERIA AND DEMANDS

Population complexities, and the controversies surrounding ethnicity and language in India, sometimes make the official recognition of groups as adivasis (by way of inclusion in the Scheduled Tribes list) political and contentious. However, regardless of their language family affiliations, Australoid and Negrito groups that have survived as distinct forest, mountain or island dwelling tribes in India and are often classified as adivasi. The relatively autonomous Mongoloid tribal groups of Northeastern India (including Khasis, Apatani and Nagas), who are mostly Austro-Asiatic or Tibeto-Burman speakers, are also considered to be adivasis: this area comprises 7.5% of India's land area but 20% of its adivasi population. However, not all autonomous northeastern groups are considered adivasis; for instance, the Tibeto-Burman-speaking Meitei of Manipur were once tribal but, having been settled for many centuries, are caste Hindus.

It is also difficult, for a given social grouping, to definitively decide whether it is a 'caste' or a 'tribe'. A combination of internal social organization, relationship with other groups, self-classification and perception by other groups has to be taken into account to make a categorization, which is at best inexact and open to doubt. These categorizations have been diffuse for thousands of years, and even ancient formulators of caste-discriminatory legal codes (which usually only applied to settled populations, and not adivasis) were unable to come up with clean distinctions.

Demands for Tribal Classification

An additional difficulty in deciding whether a group meets the criteria to be adivasi or not are the aspirational movements created by the federal and state benefits, including job and educational reservations, enjoyed by groups listed as scheduled tribes (STs). In Manipur, Meitei commentators have pointed to the lack of scheduled tribe status as a key economic disadvantage for Meiteis competing for jobs against groups that are classified as scheduled tribes. In Assam, Rajbongshi representatives have demanded scheduled tribe status as well. In Rajasthan, Haryana and other northern states, the Gujjar community has demanded ST status, even blockading the national capital of Delhi to press their demand. In several cases, these claims to tribalhood are disputed by tribes who are already listed in the schedule and fear economic losses if more powerful groups are recognized as scheduled tribes; for instance, the Rajbongshi demand faces resistance from the Bodo tribe, and the Meena tribe has vigorously opposed Gujjar aspirations to be recognized as a scheduled tribe.

Endogamy, Exogamy and Ethnogenesis

Part of the challenge is that the endogamous nature of tribes is also conformed to by the vast majority of Hindu castes. Indeed, many historians and anthropologists believe that caste endogamy reflects the once-tribal origins of the various groups who now constitute the settled Hindu castes. Another defining feature of caste Hindu society, which is often used to contrast them with Muslim and other social groupings, is lineage/clan (or *gotra*) and village exogamy. However, these in-marriage taboos are also held ubiquitously among tribal groups, and do not serve as reliable differentiating markers between caste and tribe. Again, this could be an ancient import from tribal society into settled Hindu castes. Interestingly, tribes such as the Muslim Gujjars of Kashmir and the Kalash of Pakistan observe these exogamous traditions in common with caste Hindus and non-Kashmiri adivasis, though their surrounding Muslim populations do not.

Some anthropologists, however, draw a distinction between tribes who have continued to be tribal and tribes that have been absorbed into caste society in terms of the breakdown of tribal (and therefore caste) boundaries, and the proliferation of new mixed caste groups. In other words, ethnogenesis (the construction of new ethnic identities) in tribes occurs through a fission process (where groups splinter-off as new tribes, which preserves endogamy), whereas with settled castes it usually occurs through intermixture (in violation of strict endogamy).

Bibliography

Bailey, S. F. G.: *Tribe, Caste and Nation: A Study of Political Activity and Political Change in Highland Orissa*, Manchester, England, 1960.

Bland, Celia: *Osceola : Seminole Rebel,* New York : Chelsea House, 1994.

Bullard, Robert D.: *Confronting Environmental Racism: Voices from the Grassroots*, Boston, South End Press, 1993.

Debo, Angie. And Still the Waters Run: *The Betrayal of the Five Civilized Tribes*, Princeton, Princeton University Press, 1972.

Fairbanks, Charles H.: *Ethnohistorical report on the Florida Indians*, New York, Garland Pub. Inc., 1974.

Frykenberg, R. E.: *Land Control and Social Structure in Indian History*, Madison, Milwaukee, and London, 1969.

Gibson, Arrell Morgan: *The Chickasaws*, Norman, University of Oklahoma Press, 1971.

Hudson, Charles: *The Southeastern Indians*, Knoxville, The University of Tennessee Press, 1992.

Jay, Edward J.: *A Tribal Village of Middle India*, Calcutta, 1970.

Lawson, Edith R. : *Florida Indians : noble redmen of the South*, St. Petersburg, Valkyrie Press, 1977.

Sharma, B. D.: *Tribal Development: The Concept and the Frame*, New Delhi, 1978.

Thurston, Edgar: *Castes and Tribes of Southern India*, Madras, 1909.

Weisman, Brent R.: *Unconquered people : Florida's Seminole and Miccosukee Indians*, Gainesville, University Press of Florida, 1999.

Wright, J. L. : *Creeks & Seminoles : the Destruction and Regeneration of the Muscogulge People*, Lincoln, University of Nebraska Press, 1986.

Index